HIGHER EDUCATION, STATE REPRESSION, AND NEOLIBERAL REFORM IN NICARAGUA

This innovative volume makes a key contribution to debates around the role of the university as a space of resistance by highlighting the liberatory practices undertaken to oppose dual pressures of state repression and neoliberal reform at the Universidad Centroamericana (UCA) in Nicaragua.

Using a critical ethnographic approach to frame the experiences of faculty and students through vignettes, chapters present contextualized, analytical contributions from students, scholars, and university leaders to draw attention to the activism present within teaching, research, and administration while simultaneously calling attention to critical higher education and international solidarity as crucial means of maintaining academic freedom, university autonomy, oppositional knowledge production, and social outreach in higher education globally.

This text will benefit researchers, students, and academics in the fields of higher education, educational policy and politics, and international and comparative education. Those interested in equality and human rights, Central America, and the themes of revolution and protest more broadly will also benefit from this volume.

Wendi Bellanger is Provost and Academic Leader of the Universidad Centroamericana (UCA), Nicaragua.

Serena Cosgrove is Faculty Coordinator of Seattle University's Central America Initiative and Associate Professor in International Studies at Seattle University, USA.

Irina Carlota Silber is Professor of Anthropology at the City College of New York, USA.

Routledge Research in Higher Education

A Philosophical Approach to Perceptions of Academic Writing Practices in Higher Education
Through a Glass Darkly
Amanda French

Title IX and the Protection of Pregnant and Parenting College Students
Identifying Effective Communication and Support Practices
Catherine L. Riley, Alexis Hutchinson, and Carley Dix

Higher Education, State Repression, and Neoliberal Reform in Nicaragua
Reflections from a University under Fire
Edited by Wendi Bellanger, Serena Cosgrove, and Irina Carlota Silber

The Past, Present, and Future of Higher Education in the Arabian Gulf Region
Critical Comparative Perspectives in a Neoliberal Era
Edited by Awad Ibrahim and Osman Z. Barnawi

Students' Experiences of Psychosocial Problems in Higher Education
Battling and Belonging
Edited by Trine Wulf-Andersen, Lene Larsen, Annie Aarup Jensen, Lone Krogh, Aske Basselbjerg Stigemo, and Mathias Hulgård Kristiansen

Dismantling Constructs of Whiteness in Higher Education
Narratives of Resistance from the Academy
Edited by Teresa Y. Neely and Margie Montañez

For more information about this series, please visit: www.routledge.com/Routledge-Research-in-Higher-Education/book-series/RRHE

HIGHER EDUCATION, STATE REPRESSION, AND NEOLIBERAL REFORM IN NICARAGUA

Reflections from a University under Fire

Edited by Wendi Bellanger, Serena Cosgrove and Irina Carlota Silber

Routledge
Taylor & Francis Group

NEW YORK AND LONDON

First published 2023
by Routledge
605 Third Avenue, New York, NY 10158

and by Routledge
4 Park Square, Milton Park, Abingdon, Oxon, OX14 4RN

Routledge is an imprint of the Taylor & Francis Group, an informa business

© 2023 selection and editorial matter, Wendi Bellanger, Serena Cosgrove, and Irina Carlota Silber; individual chapters, the contributors

The right of Wendi Bellanger, Serena Cosgrove, and Irina Carlota Silber to be identified as the authors of the editorial material, and of the authors for their individual chapters, has been asserted in accordance with sections 77 and 78 of the Copyright, Designs and Patents Act 1988.

All rights reserved. No part of this book may be reprinted or reproduced or utilised in any form or by any electronic, mechanical, or other means, now known or hereafter invented, including photocopying and recording, or in any information storage or retrieval system, without permission in writing from the publishers.

Trademark notice: Product or corporate names may be trademarks or registered trademarks, and are used only for identification and explanation without intent to infringe.

Library of Congress Cataloging-in-Publication Data
Names: Bellanger, Wendi, editor. | Cosgrove, Serena, 1963- editor. | Silber, Irina Carlota, 1968- editor.
Title: Higher education, state repression, and neoliberal reform in Nicaragua : reflections from a university under fire / Edited by Wendi Bellanger, Serena Cosgrove, and Irina Carlota Silber.
Description: New York, NY : Routledge, 2023. | Series: Routledge research in higher education | Includes bibliographical references and index.
Identifiers: LCCN 2022006567 | ISBN 9781032057316 (hardback) | ISBN 9781032057330 (paperback) | ISBN 9781003198925 (ebook)
Subjects: LCSH: Education, Higher--Nicaragua. | Educational change--Nicaragua. | Education and state--Nicaragua. | Educational equalization--Nicaragua. | Neoliberalism--Nicaragua.
Classification: LCC LA463 .H54 2023 | DDC 378.7285--dc23/eng/20220516
LC record available at https://lccn.loc.gov/2022006567

ISBN: 978-1-032-05731-6 (hbk)
ISBN: 978-1-032-05733-0 (pbk)
ISBN: 978-1-003-19892-5 (ebk)

DOI: 10.4324/9781003198925

Typeset in Bembo
by SPi Technologies India Pvt Ltd (Straive)

We dedicate this book to Nicaraguan students and their families and their belief in the power of a transformative education. All royalties from sales of this book will support scholarships for low-income, Indigenous, and Afro-descendant Nicaraguan college students.

MAP OF THE REPUBLIC OF NICARAGUA

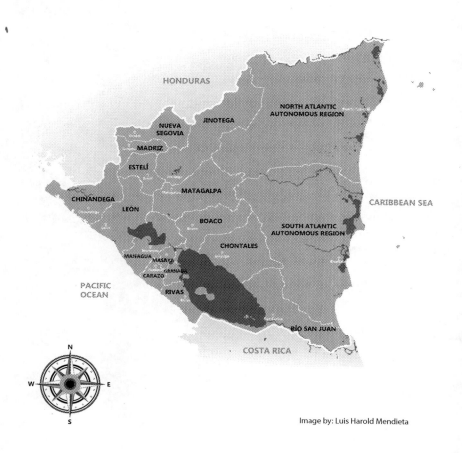

Image by: Luis Harold Mendieta

CONTENTS

Acknowledgments ix
Foreword by Florence E. Babb x
About the Editors and Contributors xvi
*A Timeline for University Autonomy in Nicaragua by
Hallie S. Evans* xviii

Introduction 1
Wendi Bellanger, Serena Cosgrove and Irina Carlota Silber

PART 1
The Repressive and Neoliberal Context of Critical Higher Education in Nicaragua 19

1 The Manifesto of the Universidad Centroamericana
   in Managua, Nicaragua 21
   José (Chepe) Idiáquez, S.J.

2 The Impact of Neoliberal Reform and Repression on Higher
   Education in Nicaragua 38
   Wendi Bellanger

PART 2
Professors and Students under Fire   61

3 Professors and the Accompaniment of University Student Struggles in Nicaragua   63
Karla Lara

4 An Ethnography of the Classroom and the Daily Effects of Repression   80
Arquímedes González

5 Rhizomatic Solidarity for (Re)flourishing: UCA Graduate Perspectives on Education, Social Change, and Persistence Amid Repression   93
Fiore Bran Aragón

PART 3
Solidarity and Implications beyond Nicaragua   117

6 Cyborg Solidarity with Nicaragua and Digital/Analogue Entanglements   119
Andrew Gorvetzian

7 University Partnerships and Solidarity 3.0 with Nicaragua   137
Serena Cosgrove

8 Lessons from Nicaragua for a Critical Higher Education   158
Irina Carlota Silber

PART 4
Coda   169

9 A Brief History of Violence in Nicaragua   171
James Quesada

Index   *189*

ACKNOWLEDGMENTS

We are grateful to the organizations who have supported this research, including the Wenner-Gren Foundation and Seattle University's Central America Initiative, as well as our universities: the Universidad Centroamericana, Seattle University, the City College of New York, the University of New Mexico, and San Francisco State University.

We extend deep gratitude to the anonymous external reviewers whose support and feedback provided important signposts for the project. Ultimately, however, we authors are responsible for the content of this book and any errors that it may contain. We are aware that our scholarship rides on the shoulders of other scholars throughout the Americas and beyond whose research questions, data, and analysis have encouraged us to ask our questions and contribute to our ethnographic exploration of a university under fire.

Each author extends gratitude to their colleagues, friends, and families who have supported this intergenerational, intercultural, and international project.

FOREWORD

by Florence E. Babb

At its core, this volume highlights two related urgencies: higher education under crushing neoliberal constraints, and one embattled Central American university—the Universidad Centroamericana (UCA) in Managua, Nicaragua—that is caught up in national political conflict and state repression that threatens its long-established autonomy and academic freedom. The editors and contributors take up questions of abiding concern, and in so doing, they show us why we need to become aware of and respond to the struggles of these educators and students in the face of an increasingly authoritarian government. Nicaragua, the nation that is at the center of this work of scholarship and solidarity, once waged a revolutionary struggle and represented a beacon of hope for many on the planet; now it provides a cautionary tale for all those who may have clung to the romance of past revolutionary figures, but are now deeply concerned to support sustainable social justice and human rights in that nation and at a global level. More than that, it also offers a contemporary and inspiring example of activism that breaks away from earlier models, led by youth and many others who are unwilling to accept the old terms of engagement and instead are struggling for a life-affirming politics, looking toward a more inclusive and just future in which gender, class, sexuality, and racial difference couple with feminist, environmental, and cultural rights, and with durable democratic practices.

I first traveled to Nicaragua in 1989, ten years after the triumph of the Sandinista revolution, when most Nicaraguans and international observers were still confident of a Sandinista electoral victory the following year. When the party of the Sandinistas, the FSLN,[1] lost to a coalition of opposition groups largely as a result of Nicaraguans' exhaustion from the U.S.-backed Contra War, the 1990s saw the sharp transfer of power from Daniel Ortega to the neoliberal government of Violeta Chamorro. That, in turn, led to a host of reversals of transformational reforms that had been brought about in such areas as landholding and agrarian reform, health care, social services, and education, as the rollback of the state meant increasing privatization and higher costs to ordinary Nicaraguans.[2] Students had in fact been central to the broad base of supporters of the Sandinista revolution, with a notable presence at the Jesuit Universidad Centroamericana (UCA) in Managua and the state-supported Universidad Nacional Autónoma de Nicaragua (UNAN), with campuses in Managua and León, respectively. These universities, among others, remained strong centers of Sandinismo until the party fractured in the mid-1990s, and thereafter they remained part of a more critical left presence in the country.

During my brief first visit, I visited the UCA to make use of its documentary resources, and I began collaborating with several faculty members who facilitated my affiliation there as a Fulbright researcher in 1990–1991. The UCA's progressive politics and scholarship were what attracted me, but I was urged by my U.S. funders to accept a second affiliation with the INCAE,[3] known as the "Harvard Business School" of Nicaragua, a better-endowed university that reflected the neoliberal orientation of that time. While the UCA was centrally located in the sprawling city of Managua and suffered the tropical heat during much of the year in sweltering pavillions, alleviated only with fans and the open air, the INCAE's campus was located outside the city at a higher, cooler elevation and with the added benefit of abundant air conditioning. The contrast, both materially and ideologically, was striking. This turned out, in fact, to be a useful double affiliation for me, as I was focusing my research on the paradoxes of Nicaragua at a moment of transition, of a largely struggling population experiencing the body blows of neoliberal measures designed to cut back the state sector and social services and give free rein to capitalist development. While most of my time was out in the city's neighborhoods interviewing women and men concentrated in the informal sector of the economy,[4] the UCA remained the university where I found the vibrancy of students and faculty engaged not only in knowledge production but in critical reflection on the past, present, and future of the nation. Around the size of my home state of New York, Nicaragua had captured my imagination, just as it had the world's, in the last quarter of the twentieth century.

However, the "verticalism" and power plays of Daniel Ortega and his supporters had divided the Sandinista party by 1995; several years later, in 1998, public allegations of two decades of sexual abuse of Zoilamérica Narváez Murillo, his adoptive stepdaughter, outraged feminists and others concerned about Nicaragua's troubled history of widespread gender-based violence. Despite the disillusionment and opposition of his many critics, Ortega's repeated efforts to return to power were finally successful in 2007, as he melded a populist rhetoric and "caudillo" (strongman) style, attracting the votes of his loyalists. While ostensibly an anti-imperialist champion of the poor, he increasingly revealed his neoliberal and authoritarian bent as he sought to build his legacy and his personal wealth around projects like a proposed transoceanic canal, showing a woeful disregard for the environment and the Indigenous Nicaraguans who would be most affected.

Thus it was not surprising that by 2018, a decade after Ortega's return to power, the political landscape had changed course to the degree that Ortega was often compared to the despised Somoza dynasty that ruled for the 43 years leading up to the 1979 revolution.[5] Nearly four decades later, the government's proposed austerity legislation to reduce the pensions of working-class Nicaraguans was the final straw that led to an uprising, once again involving university students along with others who opposed the draconian, antidemocratic politics of the regime of Ortega and his wife, Vice President Rosario Murillo. The repression that followed was ruthless and resulted in the deaths of hundreds, mostly young Nicaraguans, while thousands more, who feared retaliation, left the country and remained in exile. Public intellectuals, media figures, and feminists were among those targeted, and the climate was one of rising fear, even as some continued to express their opposition and resistance to the autocratic regime. While the Ortega-Murillo regime took a fiercely repressive stance, it also attempted to present a public face of normalcy and business as usual, including the implementation of "quality assurance" regulatory mechanisms at the UCA even while classes were suspended and the campus was under siege.[6] Since the uprising in April 2018, the Nicaraguan government has continued to repress any overt signs of protest, jailed most of the political opposition, and put a stranglehold on organizations—including the UCA, using laws and regulations to coerce those who haven't already been silenced. On November 7, 2021, the presidential election in Nicaragua awarded the presidency to Daniel Ortega with very high levels of abstention and many of his political opponents in jail or exiled out of the country.

Despite its status as a private Jesuit institution, the UCA had long counted on its portion of the guaranteed six percent of the national budget going to the support of scholarships for students from underprivileged backgrounds, and the UCA's criticism of government and paramilitary repression in response to the recent uprising was met by punitive cuts in that government support, threatening the viability of the university.[7] As Wendi Bellanger, UCA's Provost, makes clear in her contribution to this volume, Nicaragua's neoliberal turn in the 1990s was followed by a rising audit culture in the 2000s, institutionalized during the new Sandinista government and diminishing self-governance and academic freedom at the UCA. The university's foundational commitments to faith and social justice, critical inquiry, solidarity with the poor and socially disenfranchised, and indeed its autonomy were all challenged by the new, corporatist, more restrictive terms of engagement in the sphere of education, as elsewhere in the society.

With students prominent among the protesters who rose up beginning in April 2018, Nicaraguan youth were targeted both as individuals and as a collectivity. This is powerfully related in contributions by former UCA student activist Fiore Bran Aragón and UCA faculty allies Karla Lara and Arquímedes González, as well as former UCA lecturer Andrew Gorvetzian in this volume. Students' lives, as well as their right to an education free from government censure, have been very much on the line as they have fought for social justice and an affirmative politics of care and inclusion, drawing on social media and digital platforms to build solidarity. The fear of violence, economic hardship for students' families, and the state cuts to the UCA budget have meant the severe reduction in student enrollment and in financial support available at the UCA. The solidarity of other Jesuit colleges and universities in the Americas has enabled some UCA students to continue their educations elsewhere throughout the crisis. As Serena Cosgrove's chapter in this volume reveals so well, the commitment of universities like hers in Seattle, which has hosted students and faculty, has made them strongly allied in an international effort to lend a hand and stand up to the power of Nicaragua's powerful state apparatus. In the process, it is not only the UCA that benefits; its sister universities learn important lessons about the strength in collectivity and the necessity of vigilance to protect our democratic institutions domestically and internationally.

José Idiáquez, S.J., President of the UCA in Managua and a contributor to this volume, offers a passionate manifesto calling for wide condemnation of the state's violent response to the protests that began in April 2018, which led to the deepest crisis the university has experienced since its founding in 1960. He likens the repression in Managua to what unfolded in the 1980s when he was a student himself on another UCA campus, in San Salvador, El Salvador. The world looked on in horror when Archbishop Oscar Romero was killed by a sniper during a Mass in 1980 and when six Jesuits at the UCA in San Salvador, along with their housekeeper and her daughter, were brutally assassinated in 1989, targeted because of their opposition to the Salvadoran Armed Forces in El Salvador's civil war. Idiáquez makes it clear that the Managua campus and the Nicaraguan nation are facing a similar crisis of authoritarian rule and state repression, meriting global concern. In confronting the situation at the university he heads as President, he takes inspiration from the intellectual leadership of the Jesuits whose lives were tragically taken on the neighboring UCA campus in El Salvador. Idiáquez agrees with those martyred colleagues that taking up the pen can be more powerful than taking up arms, though authoritarian states may attempt to silence their critics by claiming the lives of students, faculty, staff, and university administrators. In spite of the personal threat, he avers, universities must persevere in struggling for a more just and inclusive society.

In her concluding chapter, Irina Carlota Silber traces the global relevance of the challenges facing the UCA today. She shows how public universities in the Global North—like her institution, the City University of New York—are struggling with neoliberal constraints during politically challenging times. I have seen this myself at the three state universities where I have taught over the course of four decades. A growing number of contingent (non-tenure track) faculty are paid a pittance, often on a course-by-course basis as a cost-cutting strategy. A capitalist-driven emergence of "Responsibility Centered Management" pits department against department in competition to fill classroom seats and fundraise in hopes of being granted new faculty lines. And a rising audit culture requires nearly-constant self-reporting on a host of measures that are then used by higher-ups to determine pay scales and promotions (or sometimes, the elimination of entire programs). Most chilling are the cases of faculty who are dismissed for taking public stances on sensitive political issues, particularly when they offend wealthy donors or administrators in seats of power. Frequently, those who are "let go" are women, faculty of color, and others in the most vulnerable positions at the university.

This volume should help ensure that Nicaragua and its lessons will not soon be forgotten. We come away from reading these contributors' work with still greater respect for those who insist that the nation adhere to the principles that many fought for over the course of the last century—the Nicaraguans of diverse generations and social backgrounds who have sought transformational change leading to a durable, democratic society. For their part, youth, including college students, have been critical to efforts to confront the authoritarian politics that have sedimented in the country, and they possess the hope and imagination to envision a more just, far-reaching Nicaragua.[8] Working in solidarity with partners in the region and internationally, including some of this book's contributors, the UCA academic community in Managua, Nicaragua has demonstrated the breadth of vision to bravely work toward such a future.

Notes

1 Frente Sandinista de Liberación Nacional.
2 To be sure, there were structural adjustments to education in 1988 under the Sandinista government as well, and the six percent of the national government guaranteed to university education was actually formalized in 1990; the rollback of state support was uneven after the 1990 elections, and here I am referring to the growing cost of education for families with schoolchildren. See Wendi Bellanger's chapter in this volume for more detailed discussion of neoliberal reform and the impact on the UCA in Managua.
3 Instituto Centroamericano de Administración de Empresas.
4 My research in Nicaragua extended from 1989 through 2012, focusing on the neoliberal turn since the 1990s, the gendered impact on work in the informal economy, and the social movements that emerged during that period (Babb 2001, 2019).
5 See the *New York Times* Guest Opinion by writer and poet Gioconda Belli (2021) for an account by a former Sandinista militant and now long-time critic of Daniel Ortega, written as the deeply fraudulent November 2021 election was approaching.
6 See Bellanger (this volume) for discussion of the government's strategy of normalization as it controlled dissent at the universities during this time. Relatedly, in my own research on tourism, a leading industry in Nicaragua, I found it striking that even after April 2018, the national tourism website (www.intur.gob.ni) suggested travel-as-usual, at a time when any knowledgable traveler would steer clear of Nicaragua (Babb 2020).
7 See Cosgrove (this volume) for discussion of these budget cuts and their impact at the UCA.

8 For more on the activism of youth, and especially women, see the work of Bran Aragón in this volume, Bran Aragón and Goett (2021), and Chamorro and Yang (2018). These works emphasize the younger generation's attention to issues that go beyond traditional party politics (including feminism, the environment, and LGBTQ rights) and their use of alternative strategies such as occupying universities, challenging many Nicaraguans' view that youth in their country today are apolitical or apathetic. This volume makes abundantly clear that youth are in the forefront of progressive change in Nicaragua.

References

Babb, Florence E. 2001. *After Revolution: Mapping Gender and Cultural Politics in Neoliberal Nicaragua*. Austin: University of Texas Press.

——— 2019. "Nicaraguan Legacies: Advances and Setbacks in Feminist and LGBTQ Activism." In *A Nicaraguan Exceptionalism? Debating the Legacy of the Sandinista Revolution*. Edited by Hilary Francis. Pp. 171–184. London: Institute of Latin American Studies (ILAS), University of London.

——— 2020. "Peru and Nicaragua: Tourism Development in Postconflict Eras." In *Tourism Planning and Development in Central and South America*. Edited by Carlos Monterrubio, Konstantinos Andriotis, and Dimitrios Stylidis. Pp. 156–172. UK: CABI.

Belli, Gioconda. 2021. "Daniel Ortega and the Crushing of the Nicaraguan Dream," Guest Opinion, *New York Times* 7/4/21.

Bran Aragón, Fiore Stella and Jennifer Goett. 2021. "¡*Matria libre y vivir!*: Youth Activism and Nicaragua's 2018 Insurrection." *Journal of Latin American and Caribbean Anthropology* 25(4):532–551.

Chamorro, Luciana and Emilia Yang. 2018. "Movilización social y tácticas de control en el neosandinismo. El caso de #OcupaINSS." *Cahiers des Amériques Latines* 87(1):91–115.

ABOUT THE EDITORS AND CONTRIBUTORS

Florence E. Babb, author of the foreword, is the Anthony Harrington Distinguished Professor in Anthropology at the University of North Carolina at Chapel Hill.

Wendi Bellanger, co-editor and contributor, serves as the Provost of the Universidad Centroamericana in Managua, Nicaragua.

Fiore Bran Aragón, contributor, is a former UCA student and graduate student in Latin American Studies at the University of New Mexico.

Serena Cosgrove, co-editor and contributor, is the faculty coordinator of Seattle University's Central America Initiative and Associate Professor in International Studies at Seattle University.

Hallie S. Evans, contributor, is the program assistant for Seattle University's Central America Initiative and a double major in International Studies and Spanish at Seattle University.

Arquímedes González, contributor, is a UCA Professor in the Communications Department.

Andrew Gorvetzian, contributor, is a former Lecturer at the UCA and graduate student in Social Anthropology at the University of New Mexico.

José (Chepe) Idiáquez, S.J., contributor, is the President of the Universidad Centroamericana in Managua, Nicaragua.

About the Editors and Contributors xvii

Karla Lara, contributor, is a UCA Professor in the Communications Department.

James Quesada, contributor, is Professor of Anthropology at San Francisco State University.

Irina Carlota Silber, co-editor and contributor, is Professor of Anthropology at the City College of New York.

A TIMELINE FOR UNIVERSITY AUTONOMY IN NICARAGUA

by Hallie S. Evans

Entries specific to the UCA are displayed in bold

1946	Somoza closed the Central University *(Universidad Central)* in Managua. This followed student mobilizations in 1944 against the re-election of Somoza. The mobilizations were repressed by the National Guard and students were forced to take refuge in the Guatemalan Embassy.[1]
1948	The Central American University Confederation *(Confederación Universitaria Centroamericana)* and its Central American Superior Council on Universities *(Consejo Superior Universitario Centroamericano, CSUCA)* were established. At their first forum, they published the Declaration of Principles on the Purposes and Functions of the Contemporary University and especially the Universities of Central America *(Declaración de Principios sobre los fines y funciones de la Universidad contemporánea y en especial de las Universidades de Centroamérica)* which included the importance of collaboration between universities and the state without sacrificing university autonomy and freedom in research. It championed university autonomy as an essential condition of the functions of universities.[2]
1951	Somoza closed the University of Granada *(Universidad de Granada)*. The closure was part of a move by Somoza to isolate the National University of Nicaragua *(Universidad Nacional de Nicaragua, UNN)* in León, where it was confined in a province and away from the capital.[3]
1953	Students from the Circle of Legal and Social Studies *(el Círculo de Estudios Jurídicos y Sociales, CEJIS)* wrote the "Draft Organic Law of the National University" *(Proyecto de Ley Orgánica de la Universidad Nacional)*. The purpose of the project was to work toward achieving university autonomy in Nicaragua. One of the ways CEJIS raised awareness about the state of university autonomy in Nicaragua was through a series of conferences that compared the state of university autonomy throughout Latin America.[4]

A Timeline for University Autonomy in Nicaragua   xix

1955	CEJIS motivated the creation of the Permanent Action Committee for University Autonomy *(Comité de Acción Permanente Pro-Autonomía Universitaria)*, a committee geared toward achieving university autonomy. The committee and a large group of students, collaborating with a member of the Chamber of Deputies, presented the "Draft Organic Law of the National University" *(Proyecto de Ley Orgánica de la Universidad Nacional)* to the Chamber of Deputies.[5]
1957	Mariano Fiallos Gil accepted the role of president at the UNN with the condition that all influence of party politics is expelled from the university.[6]
1958	The government approved Executive Order No. 38, the National University Law *(Ley Orgánica de la Universidad Nacional)*, which granted autonomy to the National University: the UNN becomes the Universidad Nacional Autónoma de Nicaragua (UNAN).[7]
1959	Joaquín Solís Piura, president of the students' organization at UNAN led the student struggle for university autonomy. The students demanded changes in the structure of the university administration and the way education was imparted. The student struggle was met with a massacre ordered by Somoza on July 23rd by the National Guard.[8]
1960	**The Universidad Centroamericana (UCA) was founded. It was the first private university in Nicaragua and Central America. The founding of a private Catholic university was contentious as some from the Central American Council for Higher Education Consejo** *(Centroamericano de Educación Superior, CESUCA)* **considered it to challenge university autonomy**.
1960	The Technical Commission of the Higher University Council *(Comisión Técnica del Consejo Superior Universitaria)* met in San José, Costa Rica and issued a series of recommendations to regulate the operation of private universities in Central America.
1966	University autonomy was guaranteed in Article 115 of the Nicaraguan Constitution. It allocated 2% of the general budget to the National University. Prior to this legislation, funding was exclusively dealt with by the executive branch. The establishment of a fixed budget seemed to free universities from the whims of party politics and guarantee autonomy.[9]
1972	As president of the UNAN, Dr. Carlos Tünnermann began to promote the campaign for 6% allocation of the general budget to universities.[10]
1979	**The FSLN overthrew the Somoza government. The FSLN's rise to power questioned the UCA's autonomy as the new government challenged the legitimacy of a private religious school and promoted nationalization.**
1980	The National Council of Higher Education *(Consejo Nacional de la Educación Superior, CNES)* was created under the Sandinista government in order to approve study plans and intervene in the budgets and in the appointment of university presidents. This effectively restricted university autonomy.[11]

1980	The Sandinista government took several actions to restrict the autonomy of the UCA. They integrated an FSLN representative into the UCA's board of directors, transferred the engineering majors to create a new university—the **National University for Engineering** *(la Universidad Nacional de Ingeniería)*, and made the UCA dependent on state funding by curtailing the collection of tuition fees.
1990	Law 89, the Law of the Autonomy of Institutions of Higher Education *(la Ley de Autonomía de las Instituciones de Educación Superior)*, was approved following the election of Violeta Barrios de Chamorro of the National Opposition Union *(Unión Nacional Opositora, UNO)* party. The law dictated that the government's contribution to the universities must be no less than 6% of the income of the General Revenue Budget. This restored university autonomy that was lost under the administration of CNES. Students led mass demonstrations as a result to demand adherence to Law 89 and full allocation of the 6%. Article 8 in Law 89 declared that universities have teaching or academic, organic, administrative, and financial or economic autonomy.[12]
1990	**The National Council of Universities** *(Consejo Nacional de Universidades, CNU)* **was created under Law 89. As a non-profit civil association, the UCA was included as a member of the CNU and therefore a beneficiary of the 6%. During this period, the CNU authorized the creation of new universities, often referred to as "garage universities" given their small size. Since they were not incorporated in the CNU, they were not beneficiaries of the state budget.**
1992	The 6% of the total budget was confirmed, signifying a win by student mobilizations.[13]
1995	The 6% allocation was subsequently incorporated into the 1995 constitutional reform.[14]
1996	The country's elections were won by the Liberal Constitutional Party *(Partido Liberal Constitucionalista, PLC)*, which later began to cede quotas of power to the FSLN. This complicated the ability of universities to garner independence from partisan politics. The end of the 1990s consequently saw an increase in university faculty who were hired or fired based on their association to the FSLN.[15]
2003	The ALFA Tuning Latin America Project, an extension of the EU's 2001 tuning project, introduced and reinforced corporatized education systems in Latin America. This effort championed tenets of managerialism such as audit culture. The entrenchment of the corporatized university popularized a server-client relationship between faculty and students which hindered inter-university collaboration and academic freedom and autonomy.[16]

A Timeline for University Autonomy in Nicaragua **xxi**

2006	Law 582, the General Education Law *(la Ley General de Educación)*, was approved. The law instituted the General Guidelines for Education *(Lineamientos Generales para la Educación)* and the National Educational System *(el Sistema Educativo Nacional)*, dictated the powers of the Nicaraguan state in education, and diminished the rights of educators.[17]
2007	The FSLN again rose to power in Nicaragua with Daniel Ortega occupying the presidency. This intensified limitations on academic freedom and freedom of thought as professors resorted to self-censorship to ensure their institutions could receive the 6% stipulated in Law 89. The CNU has been subsumed into Sandinista clientelism, allowing the party to influence faculty appointments and scholarship decisions. Furthermore, the students' union (UNEN) became subject to political control by the FSLN.[18]
2007	Law 621, the Law of Access to Public Information *(la Ley de Acceso a la Información Pública)* was approved. Although it was meant to improve access to public information, an important resource for researchers in universities, it is neither taught nor enforced in many universities.[19]
2011	The government passed Law 704, the Law Creating the National System for Quality Assurance of Education and Regulator of the National Council for Evaluation and Accreditation *(la Ley Creadora del Sistema Nacional para el Aseguramiento de la Calidad de la Educación y Reguladora del Consejo Nacional de Evaluación y Acreditación)*, which managed the National Council on Evaluation and Accreditation *(el Consejo Nacional de Evaluación y Acreditación, CNEA)*. While the CNEA was posited as a neutral evaluatory body, its president, vice president, and 5 of its members were elected by the National Assembly. The law required all higher education institutions to establish an accreditation process as well as an internal system of quality assurance. It also undermined the CNU's role in higher education.[20]
2018	Students across Nicaragua took to the streets en masse on April 18th to protest reforms in Nicaragua's social security system mandated by Daniel Ortega. Student mobilizations in public universities were met with massacres, persecutions, jailings, torture, and mass expulsions. Government repression was aided by university authorities and UNEN. The atmosphere in universities was changed after the mobilizations with increased police presence on campus, prohibitions of group gatherings, and increased surveillance.[21]
2018	**Diverse sectors of the Nicaraguan citizenry again took to the streets of Managua on Mother's Day to demand justice for the families of those killed in demonstrations earlier that year. The Nicaraguan police attacked protestors near the UCA, killing at least 15 people. People took refuge inside the UCA campus.**
2018	Professor Ricardo Baltodano of the Polytechnic University of Nicaragua *(la Universidad Politécnica de Nicaragua, UPOLI)* was imprisoned by the Sandinista Government.[22]

2019	The CNU decreased the UCA's state funding by 60% as an act of political retaliation to the UCA's refusal to implicate student and faculty protestors. Annual enrollment at the UCA reduced by 40% and the number of students receiving scholarships declined drastically. The continual presence of police and paramilitary groups at the UCA created a hostile academic environment, making the continuation of classes incredibly difficult
2022	The CNU decreased the UCA's state funding by 100% and then expelled the UCA from the CNU as an act of retaliation for the UCA's perceived critical position.

Notes

1 Laguna (2021).
2 Tünnermann Bernheim (2016).
3 Laguna (2021).
4 Tünnermann Bernheim (2016).
5 Tünnermann Bernheim (2016).
6 Tünnermann Bernheim (2016).
7 Tünnermann Bernheim (2016).
8 Laguna (2021).
9 Tünnermann Bernheim (2016).
10 Laguna (2021).
11 Laguna (2021).
12 Laguna (2021).
13 Bellanger (2021).
14 Tünnermann Bernheim (2016).
15 Laguna (2021).
16 Beneitone et al. (2007); Bellanger (2021).
17 Asamblea Nacional (2006).
18 Bow (2019).
19 Laguna (2021).
20 Asamblea Nacional (2011).
21 Rocha (2019).
22 Laguna (2021).

References

Bellanger, W. (2021). Chapter 3. The Impact of Neoliberal Reform and Repression on Higher Education in Nicaragua. In S. Cosgrove, W. Bellanger, & I. C. Silber (Eds.), *University under Fire: Critical Higher Education, Repression, and the Neoliberal Era in Nicaragua*. Essay, Routledge.

Beneitone, P., Esquetini, C., Gónzalez, J., Maletá, M.M., Suifi, G., & Wagenaar, R. (Eds.). (2007). (rep.). *Tuning America Latina. Deusto and Groningen* (pp. 1–420). Bilbao: Publicaciones de la Universidad de Duesto.

Bow, J.C. (2019, May 15). Alejandra Centeno: Universidades viven su propia "dictadura". *Confidencial*. Retrieved August 22, 2021, from https://www.confidencial.com.ni/nacion/alejandra-centeno-universidades-viven-su-propia-dictadura/

La Gaceta, LEY GENERAL DE EDUCACIÓN1–150 (2006). Managua.

Lara, K. (2021). Chapter 5. Educational Accompaniment and the University Students' Struggle. In S. Cosgrove, W. Bellanger, & I. C. Silber (Eds.), *University under Fire: Critical Higher Education, Repression, and the Neoliberal Era in Nicaragua*. Essay, Routledge.
Mairena, Y. (2019, May 12). Unen es el brazo de una dictadura sangrienta. *Confidencial*. Retrieved August 27, 2021, from https://www.confidencial.com.ni/opinion/unen-es-el-brazo-de-una-dictadura-sangrienta/
Martínez, E.A. (2010). *La UCA: Una historia a través de la historia*. UCA.
Rocha, José Luis. (2019). *Autoconvocados y Conectados: Los Universitarios en la Revuelta de Abril en Nicaragua*. UCA Editores.
Tünnermann Bernheim, C. (2016). *Memorias de un Ciudadano*. HISPAMER.

INTRODUCTION

Wendi Bellanger, Serena Cosgrove and Irina Carlota Silber

Welcome

Welcome to these pages, reader, here you'll learn about the Universidad Centroamericana or UCA in Managua, Nicaragua, a university under fire. There are many reasons why you might have been drawn to this book: it could be that you're concerned about the repressive turn in Nicaragua and want to know more about the stranglehold the Nicaraguan government is putting on a small but valiant university. It could be that you're interested in how neoliberal policies meld with a corporativist trend in global higher education and lead to policies that get used to police universities rather than strengthen them. Maybe you yourself are a policy maker and troubled by how global logics can become local constraints. Perhaps you work in higher education and want to understand how critical ethnography can uncover systemic violence and signal possible routes for universities to better serve their societies. Maybe you're a student, and your professor has assigned this book. It could also be that you're a former Sandinista supporter, and you want to understand how revolutionary heroes from the 1970s have become today's tyrants. Whatever your motivation, we're glad you're here. One of our goals is to open space for debate, reflection, and action. If you find this book or a part of it compelling, please share it widely: the eBook version is open access and free to all. You may know folks who might find it useful or relevant for their interests, commitments, and struggles. Furthermore, all royalties for this book will be donated for scholarships for underserved Nicaraguans to attend university. Not only do we the editors of this book believe in the book's global relevance, but every contributor has endeavored to include accessible stories—ethnographic vignettes—to frame their contributions as they chart how the real-life experiences they're sharing draw us to one important conclusion:

global policies and local politics can intersect to endorse the actions of authoritarian leaders and weaken the very institutions that are necessary for a democratic society, such as universities.

This book tells the compelling story of the UCA in Managua, Nicaragua where academic leaders have been caught in the crossfire of government repression and neoliberal constraints. It offers their experiences on the impact of these policies for the mission and pedagogies that define their university's struggle to carve out real spaces for transformative pedagogies and knowledge production in the service of inclusive world-making. In doing so, the book charts key themes at the intersection of public scholarship and debates on the future of higher education that have implications well beyond this particular case study and the Central American region. This book is an urgent call that asks us to think differently about academic paths and lives and about the role of the university, taking seriously the interlocking work of decolonial and horizontal research, radical pedagogies, and ethical institution building.

This book grows out of international, activist, and collaborative research by putting an ethnographic approach at the center of our methods, analysis, and activism. Throughout, a range of differently positioned authors from the UCA itself and other Central Americanist scholars offer an ethnographically grounded and interdisciplinary perspective on the impacts of neoliberal policies and state terror on higher education in Nicaragua in very real human terms. In this book, you'll meet administrative leaders and professors from the UCA. You'll hear the student voices of the UCA in Managua, Nicaragua as well as the perspectives of other students and professors from outside the country who are standing in solidarity with them. We believe this story is important because it's a case with implications for other universities at the juncture of state repression and neoliberal policies both in under-resourced regions of the world and beyond. It is a story steeped in history and hopes for a just and inclusive future. Because as anticolonial history makes clear, Nicaraguan university students, along with their regional neighbors, have been at the forefront of social movements since at least the 1920s (Vrana, 2017, p. 2).

Why Nicaragua?

The repression of the Nicaraguan government under the leadership of former revolutionaries Daniel Ortega and Rosario Murillo has been an unfolding process that challenges the utopian views of many who nostalgically remember the embattled Sandinista revolution of the 1980s. Though many factors have contributed to this current situation—including decades if not centuries of disastrous U.S. foreign policy and the neoliberal turn itself—the Nicaraguan government and its leadership are the ones closing political and civic space with repressive tactics and anti-democratic laws while simultaneously encouraging settler colonialism and extractivism on the Caribbean coast with its natural resource endowments and cultural diversity. Exacerbated by the Nicaraguan government's pressure and silencing of dissent, this edited volume leverages ethnographic stories and analytical contributions from a range of university protagonists at the UCA along with Central Americanist scholars standing with them in solidarity as they confront outright repression and global and local neoliberal educational reforms.

Today, in Nicaragua, the Sandinista governing party and its leaders, President Daniel Ortega and his wife, Vice President Rosario Murillo, have created a dynasty and are implementing strong-arm, authoritarian tactics to remain in power (see Goett, 2019; Hooker, 2019; and Simmons, 2019). However, there is a beleaguered group of visionaries—many of whom are young college students—calling for rule of law, freedom for political prisoners, and free elections, and they are literally being treated as traitors for their activism. Today's underdogs are college students, parish members, farmers, Indigenous and Afro-descendant communities, feminists, and the organizations—and institutions like the UCA in Managua, Nicaragua—that represent them.

A common theme throughout the book is the uprising of April of 2018, in which student protests against the Nicaraguan government's inaction regarding the Indio Maíz Natural Reserve forest fire started by mestizo settlers grew when the government proposed cuts to the social security system of the country. Environmental crisis and societal neglect lit a metaphorical match among the younger generation who had supposedly eschewed everyday politics. State police and paramilitary youth,[1] aligned with the Ortega-Murillo government, responded repressively toward the protesters. For the next six months, the repression continued, targeting youth activists, environmental defenders, feminists, farming families, Indigenous peoples, and Catholic clergy and lay people. It is estimated that between 75,000 and 85,000 Nicaraguans fled the country between 2018 and 2019 (Servicio Jesuita de Migrantes, Costa Rica 2019); as of 2019, at least 325 people had been killed and more than 2,000 injured (CIDH, 2019, p. 165); and in this same period, more than 700 people were imprisoned and prosecuted (CIDH, 2019, p. 165). Government actions led to the expulsion of activist students from public universities as well as severe penalties for healthcare workers who attend injured protesters (CIDH, 2019, p. 165; see also Goett, 2019, p. 25).

By the end of 2018, the repression had sown so much fear that an eerie quiet fell over the country like a weighted blanket. In 2019, this involved the "criminalization of demonstrators" in which representatives of the Nicaraguan judicial system prosecuted protesters for exercising their civil rights of free speech and association and incarcerated them, punishing them as traitors or *"golpistas"* for attempting to overthrow the government (Goett, 2019, p. 30). Many youth activists were killed, jailed, or left for Costa Rica predominantly. Others went to study at universities in Central America and beyond or went into hiding in safe houses across the country. Until early 2021, this was "the new normal" of Nicaragua: scaring people into silence or exile using selective violence and sustained harassment of institutions like the UCA, that are seen as critical, and activists, including many of the college students involved in the April 2018 protests. This national repressive context operated through the strategic use of new laws that seek to punish dissent and political activism. Moreover, it aimed to block international solidarity and networking with human rights activists. For example, we call attention to how the regime strong-armed four new laws through the National Assembly in 2020: Law 1040 "Law for the Regulation of Foreign Agents," Law 1042 "Special Law on Cybercrimes," Law 1055 "Law for the Defense of the People's Rights to Independence, Sovereignty, and Self-Determination for Peace," and the amendment of Art. 27 of the Constitution to establish life sentences for people who commit "hate crimes." All these laws make it legal for the government to target any political opposition or government protests or organizations who are critical. We want to note that with these laws, this book, our international collaborations, and possibly yours, áre also under fire. In 2021, overt repression resumed with the wholesale detention of leaders of the political opposition and private sector leaders deemed critical of the government. In a lead up to the November 7, 2021 presidential elections, the government of Nicaragua systematically eliminated any opposition. This election has been condemned by Nicaraguan civil society organizations and the international community as fraudulent. Not only did the Ortega-Murillo regime detain and imprison most of the political opposition leading up to the elections, but many voters stayed home in spite of intimidation from local Sandinista leaders. According to "Urnas Abiertas," the abstention in the elections was 81.5%. More than 36 countries immediately denounced the elections as fraudulent. However, the regime claimed to have won with 75% of the votes.[2]

The threats and repressive actions of the Nicaraguan state toward the UCA is a profound topic for several reasons, one of them being that there is a sobering precedent of state-sponsored violence waged against higher education in the region of Central America. On November 16, 1989 in San Salvador, El Salvador, elite-battalion soldiers, under direct orders from the High Command of the Salvadoran Armed Forces, entered the campus of the UCA "José Simeón Cañas" in San Salvador (Universidad Centroamericana-Managua's sister university) and assassinated two women collaborators and six Jesuit priests—all professors, administrators, or campus ministers affiliated with the university, including the university president, Ignacio Ellacuría, S.J., whose prolific scholarship about the role of the university in society informs how the contributors to this book conceptualize the role of the university in society. In a 1989 lecture about how universities need to be on the side of those who are pushed to the margins of their societies by systemic injustice, Ellacuría said,

> It is said that the university should not be partial or biased. We believe differently. The university should be free and objective, but objectivity

and liberty should be partial. And we are freely partial towards the poor majority because they are unjustly oppressed and in them ... lies the truth of reality.[3]

(1999, p. 304)

With this statement, Ellacuría is not discrediting critical education or objective research; rather, the contrary. He is saying that these forces need to be in active service to inclusion and justice for the poor and marginalized, not to political and economic elites. A university should use education, research, and social outreach to serve those who are most marginalized. Knowledge serves inclusion. The 1989 murder of Ellacuría and the others compels us into engaged, scholarly action and situates our project within current and connected debates on solidarity, the arc of postwar, Central American outbound migration, and the dual pressure of the threats and actions of a repressive state and neoliberal educational reforms.

Key themes and keywords

This is a book that is more than just storytelling around a crisis. Theoretically it offers us an expansive way to think about topics and practices that are often parsed out and placed in a hierarchy of value that delegitimizes the very best of our everyday university labor from research, teaching, and institution building. This book blurs these boundaries through the very way that we have juxtaposed multiple perspectives throughout—from President and Provost to student scholar-activists in exile. There are multiple terms that we'll be using throughout the book that we want to explain or will always appear in Spanish.

The reader will see that the UCA is a Jesuit university; this means that the Society of Jesus, and those who form part of the Society of Jesus are called Jesuits, imbue the institution with their ethos, pedagogy, and oversight. The Jesuits are a religious order founded in 1534 committed to providing a critical education to its students. You'll know we're citing a Jesuit when you see a name followed by S.J., which means Society of Jesus.

Proyección social is an important element to Jesuit pedagogy; it appears in Ellacuría's writing as well as in all the chapters authored by Nicaraguans given its importance to the UCA's pedagogy and engagement. When the term gets translated into English, it can appear as social outreach, community engagement, and even service learning; the term in Spanish includes all these synonyms and more. Proyección social is how a university projects itself onto the society where it's located; proyección social is how the university contributes to society through its teaching, research, and community engagement.

The reader will notice that when we refer to the nature of the April uprising or even other student-led movements in the past, we call them "autoconvocados"; on one hand, this means that they are independent movements—not connected to formal political parties or interests; it also means that they are "self-convening," "self-governing," and led from within. This type of organizing is often more spontaneous and widespread.

Relatedly, a reader will come across references to the colors blue and white that are associated with the April 2018 movement, and since then, have become the colors of the opposition, to such a dramatic extent that someone with a blue and white flag is considered a traitor and at risk of being detained. It's ironic that the national flag—two blue stripes around a white stripe—has become a sign of subversion while the revolutionary flag of the Sandinistas—half red and half black—is used to celebrate the repressive status quo.

Also, we draw our reader's attention to the words we use for the April 2018 protests in Nicaragua. This was an uprising; we'll sometimes call it a rebellion; it was not an insurrection. In Nicaragua, insurrection has particular significance. The 1979 insurrection was an armed guerrilla movement that led to the overthrow of the Somoza dynasty. In 2018, the uprising was spontaneous and generally non-violent. It was not an attempt to overthrow the state; neither was it a coup d'etat.

Finally, the reader will see multiple words we use for referring to the political party and former revolutionary movement, the Sandinistas. Named after Augusto César Sandino, who led Nicaraguan guerilla efforts against the U.S. marines in the 1920s and 1930s, the Sandinistas are also referred to as the Sandinista Front for National Liberation (FSLN). The current government of Nicaragua—led by the couple, President Daniel Ortega and Vice President Rosario Murillo—is a Sandinista government.

In this book, we offer a novel way to think through three related areas of research. First, the book tethers social movement literature to research on the violence of neoliberal educational reforms by exploring sites of hegemonic struggle (Hyatt et al., 2015) through an ethnographic critique of the neoliberal university (Bellanger, 2016; Gusterson, 2017). Second, it situates our project within debates on the arc of postwar (Babb, 2001; Cosgrove, 2010; Quesada, 1998; Silber, 2011), the attendant Central American emigration (Coutin, 2007; Heidbrink, 2020; Terrio, 2015), and the most recent threats and actions of a repressive state (Goett, 2019; Hooker, 2019; Simmons, 2019). Third, it builds upon models of engaged, public, and fugitive anthropology (Berry et al., 2017; Borofsky & De Lauri, 2019; Sanford & Angel-Ajani, 2006, respectively). These themes inform this book's contributions and are applied in the individual chapters. In the following paragraphs, we explain in greater detail the most important of these concepts for understanding the dangerous crossroads of repression and the neoliberal turn in Nicaragua: (1) neoliberalism and its impact on higher education, (2) Central American postwar studies and its attendant violences, and (3) the opportunities that ethnography and engaged research generate to draw readers closer to the realities of a university under fire.

Neoliberalism and how these policies affect higher education

Central American universities have adopted the same neoliberal reforms found at the global level. Vital to our analysis is the theory of academic capitalism (Slaughter & Leslie, 1997; Slaughter & Rhoades, 2004) because it explains how universities transform themselves to become more closely connected to the economy and integrated into the "knowledge society." Groups of internal actors in the university "[use] a variety of state resources to create new circuits of knowledge that link higher education institutions to the new economy" (Slaughter & Rhoades, 2004, p. 1). The result is a "shift from a public good knowledge/learning regime to an academic capitalist knowledge/learning regime" (p. 8). The latter has not completely replaced the former, as the two regimes coexist (p. 29), but the boundaries between the public and the private sector are increasingly blurred. In this view, universities are not defenselessly affected by external market forces; rather they actively seek those connections with the economy.

Through the theory of "academic capitalism" (Slaughter & Leslie, 1997; Slaughter & Rhoades, 2004), we can understand how neoliberal trends have taken root in Central American universities notwithstanding the significant differences between them and their counterparts in the global north. Neoliberalism thrives and connects with the ways in which academic quality is described and managed through the "audit culture" (Power, 1997). A new global discourse, the "talk of quality" (Bellanger, 2016), replaced the discourse on academic freedom and university autonomy which flourished in Central America during the 1950s and 1960s, was alive in the 1980s, and fizzled out in the 1990s. This discourse on autonomy included reflections on the university's role in society and its complex relation to powerful groups.

Neoliberal reforms go hand in hand with the implementation of quality assurance policies, discourses, and practices that claim to measure and assess quality in higher education institutions. In the Nicaraguan case, it is evident that the "audit culture" does not strengthen academic communities, instead it isolates higher education institutions from their political contexts and constructs academic quality as something that is observed in a vacuum. The analysis of neoliberal reforms and quality assurance processes in the Nicaraguan higher education system produces critical questions that should be explored in a similar way in universities in other countries given the potentially harmful effects of these policies for university autonomy and inclusive governance for higher education worldwide.

Throughout the book, we present ethnographical data that highlight the importance of building contextualized and grounded knowledge on universities and their internal actors to develop policies that can strengthen quality in education, institutional autonomy, and the mission of the university. The UCA and all Central American universities are embedded in a history and a context that shape their roles in society. They exist in extremely unequal societies and often describe their work as a contribution to solving the region's persistent economic, social, and political struggles. Neoliberal reforms do not consider the role higher education has in countries like Nicaragua; rather, they focus on higher education institutions to make them more efficient, innovative, pertinent, and productive for the economy. Likewise, our data show that quality assurance practices are blind to the issues that define and limit quality in under-resourced countries.

Central America, violence, and the postwar era

A vast interdisciplinary literature exists on Central America that takes as one of its key concerns the legacies of the Cold War and violent counterinsurgency policies that impacted the region's political, economic, and socio-cultural formation.[4] Scholars, including a growing and intergenerational cohort from Central America, have studied the region's colonial history (Dym, 2006; Grandin, 2000) and also explored the extraordinary array of social movements and political protests that marked the twentieth century (Almeida, 2008), from labor organizing in Nicaragua (Gould, 1990) to peasant collective action in El Salvador during the nation's armed conflict (Wood, 2003).[5] Much of this scholarship erupted to address the rampant human rights abuses in Central America that were bolstered by U.S. foreign policy and militarization and involved the murder of Catholic lay catechists throughout the region, the genocide of Indigenous Guatemalans, the violence on Nicaragua's Caribbean coast, to mention a few. Since the 1990s, with the signing of United Nation's brokered peace processes in countries such as El Salvador (1992) and Guatemala (1996), and with the end of the counter-revolutionary war in Nicaragua with the election of Violeta Chamorro (1990), scholars have built what has become a powerful area of focus, the study of aftermaths of violence, insurgency, and war (Babb, 2001; Montoya, 2018; Nelson, 2009; Sprenkels, 2018).

A field of transitional justice has explored the making of peace and transitions to democracy at all levels of society from rural women-single heads of households to politicians at the negotiating table.[6] Much of this research is framed by a commitment to human rights, leveraging knowledge in the pursuit of justice, accountability, transformation, repair, and healing. From analyses of Truth Commission Reports to calling attention to the persistent impunity of state-led wartime crimes against civilians, scholarship is often entwined with what we will discuss below as public, activist, or engaged research. It is also invested in the sequelae of trauma (Fassin & Rechtman, 2009), and the role of historical memory, in the long-unfolding arc of what has arguably become an established field of "postwar" studies. This framing looks specifically at topics such as the transformation of insurgent groups into political parties; electoral politics and democratization; rule of law, governance, and corruption; environmental racism and extractivism; Indigenous rights and persistence as well as Afro-descendant rights and inclusion; gendered social movements and transnational labor organizing; "epidemic" (gang) violence; and of course, migration—that dramatic expulsion of Central Americans seeking a dignified life to places such as the United States, Mexico, and Europe.[7] The postwar is necessarily linked to diasporas, to transnational processes, to the making of multiple belongings now several generations deep.

For this book, it is important to note that since around 2014, the Central American countries of El Salvador, Guatemala, and Honduras have been categorized in much policy and academic writing as the "Northern Triangle," again always in the context of postwar "surges" of gang violence and endemic poverty that propels migrants, including "unaccompanied" minors to make the profoundly precarious journey through Mexico to primarily the United States.[8] This literature that attends to affective economies, to remittances, to what is lost and what is gained, to the struggles for citizenship rights across borders, has only recently turned to the Nicaraguan diaspora—because migration as a survival strategy hasn't had the same recent history as its neighbors (e.g. Bran Aragón & Goett, 2020; Yarris, 2017). Recently, with changes in the national context, scholars must now take seriously not only the aftermaths of the Sandinista revolution but also the unfolding violence of the Ortega-Murillo repressive regime and the resulting new migrations of Nicaraguan citizens. This book asks us to hold space for expanding our global imaginary of postwar Central America and specifically what the case of the UCA in Nicaragua can tell us about that long struggle for truth, justice, and accountability.

Engaged social science research and ethnography

In times when researchers must acknowledge how their research practices serve local struggles given centuries of colonial agendas being replicated sometimes (un)knowingly by academics, we've made a special commitment to include the scholarship of those who are the most impacted by the policies and practices described in this book. Not only are the contributors to this volume a diverse cadre of administrators, professors, and students from Nicaragua and beyond, but we've also all spent time learning and practicing the art of ethnography, a research method that is rooted in the practices of participant observation, privileges situated knowledge, and being present with deep respect to the communities in which we work. It also involves a careful attention to how we write and how we share the stories of the folks most affected by the processes we're describing. The "thick description" (Geertz, 1973) of the ethnographic method allows us to share stories that make the reader feel like they're living the complexities and challenges facing our Nicaraguan colleagues at the UCA. This oppositional knowledge production builds upon activist anthropology, which is collaborative and positioned through each of our particular perspectives. It is both method and theory building aimed at unmasking structural and systemic violence and contributing to transformative change through a granular attention to the quotidian. Here too there is a powerful literature that moves us beyond facile ideas of witnessing and pushes us to think through our public scholarship—how we develop, pursue, and present our research, with whom, to whom, and for what purpose. For example, a new generation of feminist theorists of color have coined the term "fugitive anthropology," an activist approach that works within complicated and entangled liberatory projects in the always "contested space of the academy" (Berry et al., 2017, p. 556) that is rooted in the "legacy of white heteropatriarchy" (p. 558). We understand this as a solidarity that must do better than past projects. We are beholden to each other in this commitment to academic persistence and meaning making in the twenty-first century. This is the "thick possibility" of an engaged research practice.

Methods

This book emerges from interinstitutional collaborations with UCA leadership, faculty, and students and the global initiatives on the part of the City College of New York and Seattle University. International and intergenerational scholarship across institutions has been facilitated through multiple Latin American Studies Association conference panels between CCNY, UCA, and SU as well as multiple years of collaborative research and faculty exchanges. And thanks to a Wenner-Gren Foundation workshop grant, we were able to spend a week in January of 2021 together virtually sharing important theoretical and methodological frames for the book and workshopping early drafts of all the chapters. From the pursuit of engaged ethnographic writing emerges an analysis of the UCA's everyday and its implications for global higher education and the need to act in solidarity to preserve university autonomy. These topics are all brought together through an ethnographically predicated call for academic solidarity. As a result, the book offers a transgressive vision of the future that seems both improbable given the challenges and possible given the strength of contributors' commitments: a university at the service of its country's youth, a university that speaks truth to power, a university that includes representation of its country's diversity.

Book overview

In brief, this edited volume documents the entwined impact of repressive state policies and neoliberal constraints on the academic autonomy of the UCA in Managua, Nicaragua—an autonomy that we argue is vital for critical higher education, academic freedom, and the formation of the next generation. The lessons learned and strategies for survival that the UCA is implementing are not only groundbreaking but useful for other embattled institutions of higher learning across Latin America, the global south, and even in the global north. Chapters give ethnographic voice to the lived experiences of administrators, professors, and students committed to critical education and the commitments that their learning brings. In addition to chapters by the UCA upper administration, professors, and former students, we also have contributions from internationally recognized Central Americanist scholars for the foreword and final chapters. In this volume, we pursue an ethnographically grounded analysis that articulates critical social science interventions in the field of higher education research with a *university manifesto* that contests paralyzing neoliberal educational policies and violent militarization. This book is divided into four sections: Part 1, which includes the first two chapters, provides the reader with the necessary context to understand the repressive and neoliberal context of critical higher education in Nicaragua from the perspective of two administrative leaders at the UCA and what solidarity the UCA needs at this time. Part 2 focuses on the experiences of UCA professors and students during these hard times and comprises three chapters from faculty and student perspectives. Part 3 describes the politics of solidarity and the implications of what's happening to the UCA from global perspective through the lens of different forms of solidarity and a global reflection on the importance of university autonomy. Part 4, the book's coda or final chapter, provides the interested reader with the historical context to understand the deep roots of paramilitary and state violence in Nicaragua, a legacy that the Ortega-Murillo regime uses to its own benefit.

One of the most important chapters in this book, Chapter 1, includes José (Chepe) Idiáquez, S.J.'s manifesto of the UCA, in which we get to see the complicated terrain he has had to navigate as the president of the UCA. Building upon Idiáquez's LASA/Oxfam America 2019 Martin Diskin Memorial Lecture, this chapter opens with the powerful phrase, "La juventud universitaria fue la primera que despertó en abril"—university youth led an awakening in April of 2018 that led to widespread protest, which Idiáquez explains was rooted in a series of failed state responses to diverse issues across generations and landscapes. This chapter locates the genesis of the current political crisis in an active, critical student body of high school and college students across the country. From this important context, he develops a liberatory politics of education that calls for a response. Simultaneously grounded in rich ethnographic detail and framed by the scholarship of martyred university president, Ignacio Ellacuría, S.J., Idiáquez puts the university at the service of inclusion and the marginalized sectors of society.

Chapter 2 is the product of over a decade of research by Wendi Bellanger, the Provost of the UCA, and focuses on the effects of neoliberal reform on a university under fire. This chapter discusses how neoliberal reform in higher education and its associated quality assurance practices have intersected with the Nicaraguan state's attack on university autonomy and its repression of students and academics. It also offers a critique of the ways in which a focus on access and funding in higher education has been complicit in sidelining a critical discussion on institutional autonomy and academic freedom. In this elision, universities have been absorbed into networks of clientelism put in place by the FSLN party and its government. The chapter highlights how the technocratic focus on accreditation has not strengthened quality in the services provided by higher education institutions. Instead, it has contributed to weaken universities as social institutions that can and should contribute to society by offering a permanent critique of injustice and proposing creative responses to the country's enduring social challenges, a model described and championed by Ignacio Ellacuría, S.J. in El Salvador.

Part 2 opens with the challenges to teach in these circumstances. Chapter 3 is written by Karla Lara, a professor of Communications at the UCA. This chapter highlights the role of faculty members in Nicaragua as they teach their classes and accompany student activism. Lara examines historical data on student movements and contemporary Nicaraguan student activism for both formally constituted and *auto-convocado* movements. She describes Nicaraguan professors' roles as allies during the three most significant periods of student protests in the country's history: the struggle for university autonomy in 1958; the movement to gain 6% of the state budget for universities, which started in 1972; and the uprising that began in April 2018. This accompaniment has led to dismissals and reprisals against professors seen as taking the side of protesting students. Lara proffers a *"pedagogy of accompaniment"* from the classroom and on the frontlines of struggle, one which translates as the accompaniment of youth in the pursuit of a better future amid repression and cuts in state funding for higher education.

Renowned Nicaraguan writer and a professor at the UCA, Arquímedes González, weaves poignant stories throughout Chapter 4 as he describes what it's like to be a UCA professor in times of violence and fear. With attention to detail and the style of a storyteller, Professor González uses ethnographic stories to describe what is happening in the classroom in Nicaragua today as college students navigate learning during an ongoing crisis. Autoethnographic analysis reveals that polarization and fear encounter altruism and learning on a quotidian basis in UCA classrooms. This description of what is happening in the classroom helps us to understand how the violence has affected the learning process. Continuing to teach and to learn requires adjusting to the "rhythm" marked by repression, taking advantage of the rare moments of tranquility, adapting to difficult circumstances, and refusing to surrender to fear. He highlights the strategies students are using to continue studying and learning while they face the challenges of sustained repression and violence in the streets. He focuses on the undergraduate students of the Department of Communications, who describe the country's complicated reality through different writing assignments focused on the daily reality of Nicaragua.

Following these two chapters from the perspective of professors, we have Chapter 5 by Fiore Bran Aragón who has interviewed multiple UCA students to complement her own story of studying at the UCA even as the 2018 crisis exploded. This chapter explores the role of the UCA as an educational institution promoting social change and solidarity in Nicaragua in the context of the April 2018 uprising. To this end, the author shares her own experiences as a former UCA student in dialogue with other 2019 graduates of the UCA Humanities College, all of whom have been involved in the struggle for social justice in Nicaragua. Against the socio-political context of Nicaragua and its impact on higher education, these reflections are analyzed using Ignacio Ellacuría, S.J.'s theorizing about the mission of the Jesuit university in Central America and the concept of rhizome as a metaphor for resistance. Using these interwoven elements, the author describes the role of the university as an agent for social change in the context of the April 2018 uprising, with special emphasis on the ethico-political questioning of the younger generation. She subsequently presents the perspectives of other graduates regarding the achievements and challenges of the university as an agent for social change in the face of state repression. In conclusion, the author calls for intergenerational and multisectoral dialogue and presents a proposal for rhizomatic solidarity, both within the university community and between the international community and Nicaragua, that will allow the university to flourish even under repression.

Part 3 of the book comprises three chapters about solidarity and other global implications. Chapter 6 tells the story of solidarity from an international perspective. Andrew Gorvetzian's chapter complements Bran's focus on a new generation of Nicaraguan activists through Gorvetzian's own U.S. story of what he calls "cyborg solidarity." The 2018 uprising and ensuing political crisis in Nicaragua has had devastating ramifications for those experiencing its effects first-hand; the impacts have also extended far beyond the country's borders. Connecting the crisis in Nicaragua to global patterns of climate change, digital media, the erosion of democratic practices, and general precarity, this chapter uses auto-ethnographic vignettes to explore how the wide dissemination of videos, photos, WhatsApp messages, and other digital media sources brought the terror of the crisis to people who were far away from the crisis, but whose preoccupation for loved ones was intimately experienced on phone and computer screens. This digital intimacy with a faraway crisis calls for cyborg solidarity, a way of theorizing the disorienting experience of witnessing crisis through a screen and mobilizing digital intimacy for ongoing solidarity. Understanding how the digital world expands our notions of shared space forms the ground for practicing solidarity across differences and is vital for a world characterized by persistent precarity that confronts us all: authoritarianism that threatens democratic values, global pandemics, and the far-reaching consequences of climate change.

Chapter 7 is written by Serena Cosgrove, a professor at Seattle University, and grounds the book's arc in a call for a new politics of solidarity in which she summarizes the history and phases of transnational solidarity with Nicaragua and Central America, more broadly. Cosgrove explores different phases of solidarity between the United States and Central America from the early twentieth century, to the civil wars of the 1980s and 1990s, to the need for renewed solidarity today. Using an ethnographic framing of Seattle University's institutional solidarity with their partner university, the UCA in Managua, Nicaragua, Cosgrove critically reflects on the strengths of solidarity and weaknesses of solidarity efforts in the past, including the lack of critical analysis about the neoliberal turn back in the 1980s and 1990s. She argues that affective, academic solidarity with Nicaraguan counterparts, what the author calls Solidarity 3.0, is necessary to address the entwined impacts of repression and neoliberal constraints and support the UCA and the challenges it is facing.

Chapter 8 picks up important examples and points from all the contributors. Irina Carlota Silber, a professor at City College of New York, explains how the case of the UCA holds important lessons for universities around the world by theorizing the transformative role of universities in Central America, in particular, and Latin America, more broadly, many marked by both homegrown repression and international pressures. To make this larger comparative argument, Silber brings an ethnographic lens to bear upon the very making of this book by weaving together key themes that cut across this university manifesto—from a liberatory politics of education to the need for solidarity—that propels critique and collaboration. In so doing, Silber offers applicable lessons about the hazards of critical education, the importance of university autonomy, and strategies for resisting the harsh consequences of both neoliberalism and repression. Thus, this chapter presents the vital role of a critical university—be it in Nicaragua or New York City—during times of conflict, repression, migrations, postwar contradictions, and the neoliberal turn.

The Coda comprises Chapter 9, the book's last chapter, which tells the history of Nicaragua. Written by James Quesada, a professor at San Francisco State University, this chapter is for those who wonder how the current Nicaraguan government with its revolutionary roots became an authoritarian state, similar in many ways to the Somoza dynasty it overthrew in 1979. In this chapter, Quesada presents the historical and political context of state and paramilitary violence and how these forces affect Nicaragua today. Citing extensive historical scholarship, Quesada argues that a history of weak governance and paramilitary violence simultaneously facilitates state and paramilitary repression against protestors and other institutions. This chapter focuses on the uses of violent means to secure power beginning with Spanish colonialism, and from there, the immediate postcolonial independence period that saw the intense rivalry between the *caudillo* leaders of Liberal and Conservative forces that impeded consolidation into a nation-state, leading to U.S. intervention that ironically led to the nation-state finally becoming unified. This is the legacy that the Ortega-Murillo regime—even as they claim Christian values and Socialist policies—uses today to stay in power. Disrupting the single story that state violence in Nicaragua ended with the overthrow of the Somoza dynasty in 1979, Quesada presents a more nuanced history that describes how *caudillista* or strong-arm violence has been used to advance political and economic interests which in turn has had particularly deadly consequences for university autonomy from the twentieth century forward and made universities pivotal sites of contestation in Nicaragua.

Call to action

In his manifesto, José (Chepe) Idiáquez, S.J. describes the Central American legacy regarding the risks of critical higher education in Central America and calls us to bear witness and act in solidarity to preserve the important role that the UCA plays in Nicaraguan society. This is also called on behalf of universities in general that are committed to *proyección social* in their own respective societies, particularly in societies where democracy is limited and civil, political, and community rights are at risk. May the UCA's courageous stand inspire people to consider actions of solidarity. This is our version of academic solidarity with Nicaragua. How might you and your institution follow Ignacio Ellacuría, S.J.'s call—which he shared ten days before he was killed in 1989: "… to keep your eyes on what is happening in Nicaragua and El Salvador and to help us"[9]?

Notes

1 The historically pro-Sandinista, mass youth organization, the Juventud Sandinista or Sandinista Youth, is being utilized by the Ortega-Murillo regime to impose heavy-handed treatment on the opposition, particularly youth. See Chris Jillson's 2020 *NACLA* article, "The Anti-Sandinista Youth of Nicaragua," which explains the repressive role that the Sandinista Youth are playing now.
2 The November 7, 2021 election has received national and international press coverage. On abstention in voting, see reporting by *Confidencial* (https://www.confidencial.com.ni/english/urnas-abiertas-estimates-81-5-abstention-rate-in-voting/) and mainstream media coverage by the *New York Times* (https://www.nytimes.com/2021/11/07/world/americas/nicaragua-election-ortega.html) including the statement made by U.S. President Joe Biden (https://www.whitehouse.gov/briefing-room/statements-releases/2021/11/07/statement-by-president-joseph-r-biden-jr-on-nicaraguas-sham-elections/).
3 "Suele decirse que la Universidad debe de ser imparcial. Nosotros creemos que no. La universidad debe pretender ser libre y objetiva pero la objetividad y la libertad pueden exigir ser parciales. Y nosotros somos libremente parciales a favor de las mayorías populares, porque son injustamente oprimidas y porque en ellas, negativa y positivamente, esta la verdad de la realidad." (Excerpt from Ellacuría's November 6, 1989 essay, "El Desafio de las Mayorías Populares" or "The Challenge of the Poor Majority," published in 1999: 304).
4 See for example, Edelberto Torres-Rivas (1993), Leigh Binford (2016), Victoria Sanford (2003), and Charles Hale (1994).
5 See for example volume 153 (2019) of the journal *Realidad* and volume 25 (2020) of the *Journal of Latin American and Caribbean Anthropology*.
6 See Priscilla Hayner (2011) for an overview of transitional justice and peace processes.
7 Examples of this literature include Alvarado et al. (2017); Burell and Moodie (2015); Cosgrove et al. (2021); Green (1999); Kampwirth (2004); Loperena (2020); Marroquín (2014); Montoya (2012); Popkin (2000); Quesada (1998); Rivas (2014); Wade (2016); Weld (2014); Wolf (2017); Yarris (2017); Zilberg (2011).
8 See for example Dominguez Villegas and Victoria Rietig (2015); Lorenzen (2017).
9 "… y yo les pido a ustedes aquí presentes como personas y tal vez como estamentos oficiales que pongan a sus ojos en Nicaragua y en El Salvador y nos ayuden" (Excerpt from Ellacuría's November 6, 1989 essay, "El Desafio de las Mayorías Populares" or "The Challenge of the Poor Majority," published in 1999, page 306).

Bibliography

Almeida, Paul. (2008). *Waves of Protest: Popular Struggle in El Salvador, 1925–2005.* Minneapolis, MD and London: University of Minnesota Press.
Alvarado, Karina D., Alicia Ivonne Estrada, and Ester E. Hernández, eds. (2017). *U.S. Central Americans: Reconstructing Memories, Struggles, and Communities of Resistance.* Tucson, AZ: The University of Arizona Press.
Babb, Florence. (2001). *After Revolution: Mapping Gender and Cultural Politics in Neoliberal Nicaragua.* Austin, TX: University of Texas Press.
Bellanger, Wendi. (2016). "Teaching to Clients: Quality Assurance in Higher Education and the Construction of the Invisible Student at Philipps-Universität Marburg and Universidad Centroamericana in Managua." PhD dissertation, Philipps-Universität Marburg.
Berry, Maya J., Claudia Chávez Argüelles, Shanya Cordis, Sarah Ihmoud, and Elizabeth Velásquez Estrada. (2017). "Toward a Fugitive Anthropology: Gender, Race, and Violence in the Field." *Cultural Anthropology* 32(4): 537–565.
Binford, Leigh. (1996). *The El Mozote Massacre: Anthropology and Human Rights.* Tucson, AZ: University of Arizona Press.
Binford, Leigh. 2016. *The El Mozote Massacre: Human Rights and Global Implications,* rev. and exp. ed. Tucson: Arizona University Press.
Borofsky, Robert and Antonio De Lauri. (2019). "Public Anthropology in Changing Times." *Public Anthropologist* 1(1): 3–19.
Bran Aragón, Fiore Stella, and Jennifer Goett. (2020). "Matria Libre Y Vivir!: Youth Activism and Nicaragua's 2018 Insurrection." *The Journal of Latin American and Caribbean Anthropology* 25(4): 532–551.
Burell, Jennifer L. and Ellen Moodie. (2015). "The Post-Cold War Anthropology of Central America." *Annual Review of Anthropology* 44:381–400.
Cosgrove, Serena. (2010). *Leadership from the Margins: Women and Civil Society Organizations in Argentina, Chile, and El Salvador.* Piscataway, NJ: Rutgers University Press.
Cosgrove, Serena, José Idiáquez, Leonard Joseph Bent, and Andrew Gorvetzian. (2021). *Surviving the Americas: Garifuna Persistence from Nicaragua to New York City.* Cincinnati: University of Cincinnati Press.
Comisión Interamericana de Derechos Humanos. (2019). *Migración Forzada de Personas Nicaragüenses a Costa Rica,* Septiembre.
Coutin, Susan Bibler. (2007). *Nations of Emigrants: Shifting Boundaries of Citizenship in El Salvador and the United States.* Ithaca, NY: Cornell University Press.
Dominguez Villegas, Rodrigo and Victoria Rietig. (2015). *Migrants Deported from the United States and Mexico to the Northern Triangle: A Statistical and Socioeconomic Profile.* Washington, DC: Migration Policy Institute.
Dym, Jordana. (2006). *From Sovereign Villages to National StatesCity, State, and Federation in Central America, 1759–1839.* Albuquerque, NM: University of New Mexico Press.
Ellacuría, Ignacio. (1999). *Escritos Universitarios.* San Salvador, El Salvador: UCA Editores.
Fassin, Didier, ed. (2017). *If Truth Be Told: The Politics of Public Ethnography.* Durham, NC: Duke University Press.
Fassin, Didier and Richard Rechtman. (2009). *The Empire of Trauma: An Inquiry into the Condition of Victimhood.* Princeton, NJ: Princeton University Press.
Geertz, Clifford. (1973). *The Interpretation of Cultures: SELECTED ESSAYS.* New York: Basic Books.

Goett, Jennifer. (2019). "Beyond Left and Right: Grassroots Social Movements and Nicaragua's Civic Insurrection." *LASA FORUM* 49(4): 25–31.
Gould, Jeffrey. 1990. *To Lead as Equals: Rural Protest and Political Consciousness in Chinandega, Nicaragua, 1912–1979.* Chapel Hill, NC: University of North Carolina Press.
Green, Linda. (1999). *Fear as a Way of Life: Mayan Widows in Rural Guatemala.* New York: Columbia University Press.
Grandin, Greg. (2000). *The Blood of Guatemala: A History of Race and Nation.* Durham, NC: Duke University Press.
Gusterson, Hugh. (2017). "Homework: Toward a Critical Ethnography of the University AES Presidential Address." *American Ethnologist* 44(3): 435–450.
Hale, Charles. (1994). *Resistance and Contradiction: Miskitu Indians and the Nicaraguan State, 1894–1987.* Stanford, CA: Stanford University Press.
Heidbrink, Lauren. (2020). *Migranthood: Youth in a New Era of Deportation.* Stanford, CA: Stanford University Press.
Hooker, Juliet. (2019). "Civil Society in Revolt against the Leftist Authoritarianism of the Ortega/Murillo Regime." *LASA FORUM* 49(4): 23–24.
Hayner, Priscilla. (2011). *Unspeakable Truths: Transitional Justice and the Challenge of Truth Commissions*, 2nd Edition. New York: Routledge.
Hyatt, Susan Brin, Boone W. Shear, and Susan Wright, eds. (2015). *Learning under Neoliberalism: Ethnographies of Governance in Higher Education.* New York and London: Berghahn Books.
Idiáquez, José. (2019). LASA/Oxfam America Martin Diskin Memorial Lecture. https://forum.lasaweb.org/files/vol50-issue3/Awards-4.pdf.
Jillson, Chris. (2020). "The Anti-Sandinista Youth of Nicaragua." NACLA: February 5, 2020. Accessed June 6, 2021: https://nacla.org/news/2020/02/05/anti-sandinista-youth-nicaragua.
Kampwirth, Karen. (2004). *Feminism and the Legacy of Revolution: Nicaragua, El Salvador, Chiapas.* Athens, OH: Ohio University Press.
Loperena, Christopher A. (2020). "Adjudicating Indigeneity: Anthropological Testimony in the Inter-American Court of Human Rights." *American Anthropologist* 122(3): 595–605.
Lorenzen, Matthew. (2017). "The Mixed Motives of Unaccompanied Child Migrants from Central America's Northern Triangle." *Journal on Migration and Human Security* 4: 744–767.
Marroquín, Amparo Parducci. (2014). "La Migración Centroamericana: Apuntes para un mapa provisional." *ECA* 69(736): 91–103.
Montoya, Ainhoa. (2018). *The Violence of Democracy: Political Life in Postwar El Salvador.* New York: Palgrave Macmillan.
Montoya, Rosario. (2012). *Gendered Scenarios of Revolution: Making New Men and New Women in Nicaragua, 1975–2000.* Tucson, AZ: The University of Arizona Press.
Nelson, Diane. (2009). *Reckoning: The Ends of War in Guatemala.* Durham, NC: Duke University Press.
Popkin, Margaret. (2000). *Peace without Justice: Obstacles to Building the Rule of Law in El Salvador.* University Park, PA: Pennsylvania State University Press.
Power, Michael. (1997). *The Audit Society. Rituals of Verification.* New York: Oxford University Press.
Quesada, James. (1998). "Suffering Child: An Embodiment of War and Its Aftermath in Post-Sandinista Nicaragua." *Medical Anthropology Quarterly* 12(1): 51–73.

Rivas, Cecilia M. (2014). *Salvadoran Imaginaries: Mediated Identities and Cultures of Consumption*. New Brunswick, NJ: Rutgers University Press.
Sanford, Victoria. (2003). *Buried Secrets: Truth and Human Rights in Guatemala*. New York: Palgrave Macmillan.
Sanford, Victoria and Asale Angel-Ajani. (2006). *Engaged Observer: Anthropology, Advocacy, and Activism*. New Brunswick, NJ: Rutgers University Press.
Servicio Jesuita de Migrantes-Costa Rica. (2019). personal communication, November 10.
Silber, Irina Carlota. (2011). *Everyday Revolutionaries: Gender, Violence, and Disillusionment in Postwar El Salvador*. Piscataway, NJ: Rutgers University Press.
Simmons, Shakira. (2019). "Grito por Nicaragua, un grito desde la Costa Caribe." *LASA FORUM* 49(4): 32–36.
Slaughter, S. and L. Leslie. (1997). *Academic Capitalism: Politics, Policies and the Entrepreneurial University*. Baltimore, MD: The Johns Hopkins University Press.
Slaughter, S. and G. Rhoades. (2004). *Academic Capitalism and the New Economy: Markets, State, and Higher Education*. Baltimore, MD and London: The Johns Hopkins University Press.
Sprenkels, Ralph. (2018). *After Insurgency: Revolution and Electoral Politics in El Salvador*. Notre Dame, IN: University of Notre Dame Press.
Terrio, Susan J. (2015). *Whose Child Am I?: Unaccompanied, Undocumented Children in U.S. Immigration Custody*. Oakland, CA: University of California Press.
Torres-Rivas, Edelberto. (1993). *Historia General de Centroamérica*. San José de Costa Rica: FLACSO.
Tsing, Anna Lowenhaupt, Andrew S. Mathews, and Nils Bubandt. (2019). "Patchy Anthropocene: Landscape Structure, Multispecies History, and the Retooling of Anthropology: An Introduction to Supplement 20." *Current Anthropology* 60(20): 186–197.
Vrana, Heather A. (2017). *Anti-Colonial Texts from Central American Student Movements 1929–1983*. Edinburgh: Edinburgh UP.
Wade, Christine J. (2016). *Captured Peace: Elites and Peacebuilding in El Salvador*. Athens, OH: Ohio University Press.
Weld, Kirsten. (2014). *Paper Cadavers: The Archives of Dictatorship in Guatemala*. Durham, NC: Duke University Press.
Wolf, Sonja. (2017). *Mano Dura: The Politics of Gang Control in El Salvador*. Austin, TX: University of Texas Press.
Wood, Elisabeth Jean. (2003). *Insurgent Collective Action and Civil War in El Salvador*. Cambridge: Cambridge University Press.
Yarris, Kristin. (2017). *Care across Generations: Solidarity and Sacrifice in Transnational Families*. Stanford, CA: Stanford University Press.
Zilberg, Elana. (2011). *Space of Detention: The Making of Transnational Gang Crisis between Los Angeles and San Salvador*. Durham, NC: Duke University Press.

PART 1

The Repressive and Neoliberal Context of Critical Higher Education in Nicaragua

1
THE MANIFESTO OF THE UNIVERSIDAD CENTROAMERICANA IN MANAGUA, NICARAGUA

José (Chepe) Idiáquez, S.J.

> "What is the role of a university in society?" is a question about what constitutes the orientation and purpose of what a university seeks to accomplish …The dominant classes cannot set its orientation; rather, it must be the actual interests, rigorously analyzed, of the oppressed majorities.
>
> *Ignacio Ellacuría, S.J., 1999: 47–48*

Introduction

La juventud universitaria fue la primera que despertó en abril … university students were the first ones to wake up in April 2018 to what had been going on. I had gotten used to the bifurcation of telling international colleagues that Nicaragua seemed safer than many other Central American countries, on the one hand, while friends across the country told stories of fear and reprisals for actions deemed critical of the Sandinista government, on the other. The repression wasn't equal for all; for example, a university president could still criticize a bill presented in the National Assembly, but isolated communities, grassroots leaders, and people without international contacts were often afraid to voice their criticisms. They would do it in a lowered voice, leaving me wondering if they were confessing something to me as a priest or afraid someone would hear and turn them in. Indigenous leaders were being targeted on the Caribbean Coast. Farmers protesting the Interoceanic Canal were being followed by police. Feminist marches were being stopped by riot police. And yet, it wasn't until April 2018, when government inaction regarding the forest fire in the Indio Maiz Natural Reserve catalyzed youth indignation and an "autoconvocado" movement emerged. This younger generation had tended to avoid politics: the contradictions between revolutionary rhetoric and neoliberal inequalities had spoiled any appetite for party politics. And yet, the more the forest fire burned, their own slow burn burst into flame and the first protests in April 2018 were impassioned, spontaneous, peaceful, massive …

DOI: 10.4324/9781003198925-3

and police and paramilitary youth responded harshly, first throwing rocks and then shooting into protest marches. For the first time in many years, the repression was evident to all: it was covered by journalists; it was witnessed by the country; and it even made international news. As the weeks unfolded after the April uprising, there was new breath, there was new hope. Change could happen and it could be autoconvocado or self-led; Nicaragua didn't need caudillo or strong-arm leaders to inspire the masses.

I knew days in advance that the Mother's Day march on Sunday, May 30, 2018, was going to be big. It was the combination of mothers upset at the violence and a young generation alive with hope about achieving change. There were going to be thousands at the march. That morning, I glanced at Ignacio Ellacuría, S.J.'s book, University Essays, as I drank my first cup of coffee. Dog eared and underlined throughout, it fell open to the excerpt that opens this chapter. A university—particularly a Jesuit university in Central America—must serve the poor majorities, especially when they are not allowed to express themselves freely. As the opening quote indicates, it is important to consider critically the role of the university in society. I remember discussions we had in the 1980s when Ellacuría himself was our professor in El Salvador; he told us theology students that university action wasn't joining the fight, rather it was using the proyeccion social—everything that the university has to offer society—and putting it at the service of those who are excluded and suffer. I knew I needed to join the Mother's Day march; I wasn't fighting; rather, I was joining a pacific protest for inclusion and participation.

The march started from a well-known roundabout, la Retonda Paul Jenie, and would end at the front gate of the UCA, where some of the mothers who had lost children to the repression were going to speak to the crowd. The foreign press reported that at least 500,000 people were marching; it was a river of people singing, chanting, and carrying Nicaraguan flags and signs that said "Eran estudiantes, no delicuentes" (They were students, not criminals); "Libertad y democracia para Nicaragua" (Liberty and democracy for Nicaragua), and "Las madres exigimos justicia" (We mothers demand justice). I was exhilarated, proud to be part of this autoconvocado movement for justice, inclusion, and democracy. As we got close to the UCA, I got a ride back to campus so that I could meet the march when it arrived. I wanted the mothers who had lost children protesting the government to have a chance to talk: their voices needed to be heard. I had only been back on campus for a couple of minutes and was walking across campus to the main gate when I heard shots. Again and again and again. I heard screaming. As I ran to the campus gate, I asked a member of the university public safety team what was happening. He told me that police were shooting from rooftops into the crowds and protesters were falling onto the ground wounded. I could see through the fence that people were being pushed up against the wall of the university. More shots and more screaming. I said, "For god's sake, open the gates; let people get away from the violence." Thousands of people poured onto campus and made their way to exits on the other side of the campus so they could escape the brutality. And then I heard my name being called. "Father Chepe, we have an injured protester." Just outside of the building of the UCA's College of Business, a young man who was bleeding from his head had been laid on the steps. I called for towels to stop the bleeding. I called for an ambulance. The pandemonium was at its climax: people were still running and screaming, I could still hear shots, and I looked down at the young man on the building steps, his blood now covering me. I felt so powerless as I held him. Ambulances couldn't make it in because the police were shooting at their tires. Finally, a car arrived, loaded him in, and raced away. Two hours later I learned that he had died on the way to the hospital. I returned to my office after making sure remaining mothers and protesters got safely home. We had used university vehicles to help move people off campus and away from the violence once it was safe to drive. An eery silence ensued. I put my head in my hands. No government should target its own people in this way. What does it mean to be a president of a university when young people are being shot at the university gates? It means that you must bear witness, you must accompany them; you can't back away from injustice. You must open the gates and put the university at the service of those who have been targeted.

I write this chapter three years after that fateful Mother's Day in 2018. Nicaragua continues to face a crisis due to lack of governance, democratic spaces, and repression. As the president of the Universidad Centroamericana (UCA) in Managua, Nicaragua, I am at the helm of the UCA as it confronts the worst crisis since its founding 60 years ago. The government has targeted the UCA for its critical stance and commitment to freedom of thought, and in retaliation, our budget has been slashed. There's frequently a police cordon around the university, and the new laws that the government has passed to punish organizations seen as traitors mean that we're functioning without accreditation and permissions. In the chapters that follow, you'll read about how this national context and a whole set of institutional challenges are affecting administrators, professors, and students. You'll also hear from colleagues in the United States trying to stand in solidarity with us. Amid this reality, I return to the scholarship and example of Ignacio Ellacuría, S.J., the former president of the Universidad Centroamericana "José Simeón Cañas" (UCA) in San Salvador, El Salvador, whose words open this chapter and who was assassinated in November of 1989. It's his advice I'm following, a prophecy about solidarity and accompaniment in the hardest of times. A university must serve people on the margins even if this stance generates reprisals. In this chapter, I discuss Ellacuría's legacy and how his scholarship informs what the UCA in Managua, Nicaragua is doing today to survive. Then, I explain what is happening in Nicaragua and why the world should be concerned about a repressive regime targeting a small liberal arts university in Managua, Nicaragua.

How did I learn to lead a university?

Unfortunately, the current situation in Nicaragua is not new by Central American standards. My experience as a theology student for four years in the 1980s at the UCA in San Salvador allowed me to see how critical thinking in a university can challenge the interests of the oppressors and how that reality gains strength when you are committed to accompanying people who are suffering oppression. El Salvador was in the middle of a civil war (1980–1992), and I did not want to leave the people of my parish, but Amando López, S.J., my spiritual director, told me that it would be a big mistake to stay in El Salvador and not keep preparing myself academically. He said that staying was a short-term vision, and the struggle for oppressed people demanded both academic preparation *and* social commitment. At that time, we knew that Colonel Zepeda had made clear his hatred for the Jesuits of the UCA, and he was the ranking member of the Salvadoran military command who would give the order to carry out the assassination at the UCA. On that fateful night of November 16, 1989, six of my Jesuit companions and professors and two dear friends were murdered by elite soldiers from the Atlacatl Battalion of the Salvadoran army right there on the UCA campus. They were Amando López, S.J., my spiritual director; Ignacio Ellacuría, S.J., president of the university; Segundo Montes, S.J., a sociologist; Ignacio Martín-Baró, S.J., a social psychologist; Juan Ramón Moreno, S.J., a parish priest; and Elba Ramos, who worked with the Jesuits, and her daughter, Celina Ramos.[1] At the UCA of El Salvador, the Jesuits had succeeded in building an interdisciplinary leadership team whose critical thinking and social analysis applied the disciplines of sociology, social psychology, philosophy, theology, spirituality, and educational theory to understand the Salvadoran reality. This *proyeccion social* or application of the university to reality was particularly important to Ignacio Ellacuría, S.J. Indeed, he was viewed by the wealthy elites and their military enforcers as troublesome and dangerous. As a university president, Ellacuría left an immense legacy that continues to inspire me and many others who work for inclusion and justice across Central America and beyond.

Even with the differences between Nicaragua today and the El Salvador of 40 years ago, what Nicaragua is experiencing now under the Ortega-Murillo regime is similar to the persecution of that time. At the UCA of Nicaragua, we are convinced that Ellacuría's scholarship about the role of the university continues to be relevant for El Salvador and all of Central America, and above all for Nicaragua. The task before us now, if we want to live up to our academic responsibility, is to take this vision and apply it to the twenty-first century. As president of the UCA of El Salvador, Ignacio Ellacuría, S.J., always urged others to think with theoretical rigor and commitment to those on the margins. Writing and speaking in a context of civil war, he had an expansive vision of a university that was committed to transforming the social reality of El Salvador. He considered the task of the university to be unmasking the oppression of the poor majorities:

> The reality of the nation and the Salvadoran people should not be understood only in terms of entrenched injustice and structural violence, or even in terms of international dependence. It must be understood in terms of a divided society in which both sides are in conflict because the interests of the dominant minority are irreconcilable with those of the oppressed majorities.
>
> *(Ellacuría 1999: 43)*

I recall his words often because it is important to understand that the primary objective of education is not to prepare students for success, prestige, or competition; rather, education must prepare students to seek the most effective ways to create a more just and more inclusive society.

As I reflect on the murder of my colleagues and friends in El Salvador, I remember also how strongly they were criticized by various sectors of Salvadoran society. They said what they had to say, and they based it on their scholarly work about what was unfolding in El Salvador, knowing that it was impossible to please everyone in a context of such extreme violence, impoverishment, and political polarization. They were aware of what could happen to them. Now, more than three decades after that appalling slaughter on the campus of the UCA in San Salvador, something very similar is happening in Nicaragua: every day we experience attempts to terrorize and paralyze critical thinking at the UCA of Nicaragua, and the violence has increased greatly since 2018. About such a situation, Ellacuría said:

> The pressure can present itself in very different forms, ranging from systematic campaigns against the institution and certain persons in the institution to taking more directly coercive and alarming measures. There are many ways in which university autonomy can be attacked, both at the institutional and the individual level. With the pretext of curbing the excesses of university autonomy, other excesses are enacted, such as curtailing university autonomy for the sake of class or party interests.
>
> *(Ellacuría 1999: 63–64)*

This passage urges us to reflect on what it means to teach in the classroom, to carry out research, and to cultivate critical thinking. Ellacuría challenges us to assess where we stand as scholars, administrators, and students and to ask ourselves whether we are supporting a system that oppresses the poor majorities—and whether we are willing, as he and his companions were, to suffer the same fate as the excluded.

What are the antecedents of April 2018?

In April 2018, Nicaragua experienced a spontaneous citizen rebellion that was unexpected by the government. The uprising was *autoconvocado*; it was mostly peaceful and civic-minded, and it had few visible leaders. Those protesting the government were mainly the young people in the principal cities of the country. To many outside observers, things had seemed to be going well in Nicaragua. The economy was growing, albeit within neoliberal constraints, and the country knew nothing of the deadly gang violence that existed in neighbors to the north, such as El Salvador, Honduras, and Guatemala. Many of us living in Nicaragua, however, knew that the situation was not as rosy as it appeared, and we had a feeling that things were going to end badly. Our apprehension was based on the direction the country had been taking since Daniel Ortega, his wife, Rosario Murillo, and their allies had returned to power in 2006. At that time, Ortega began applying methods of social and political control that tended steadily toward a populist dictatorship. The new government began to close space for citizen participation, limit state accountability, and reduce the autonomy of municipalities and universities. The power that Ortega amassed between 2008 and 2016 can be explained by three key factors: first, corruption, especially as regards the more than $4.5 billion that Nicaragua received from Venezuela, most of which went into the pockets of the Ortega-Murillo family. Journalists who investigated this misuse of funds have called it one of the greatest acts of corruption in the Nicaragua's history (Chamorro 2020: 23). Second, the Ortega-Murillo family's controls the Supreme Court of Justice, the Supreme Electoral Council, the National Assembly, the Attorney General's office, the Comptroller of the Republic, the army, the paramilitary or Sandinista youth, and the public universities. The control extends also to the student movement called UNEN and the Sandinista Youth, both of which, with the support of the National Police, serve as shock troops for attacking protestors and organizations seen to support them. Third, repression by means of threats and selective murders terrorizes and paralyzes the population. Students, small farmers, and members of Indigenous groups are the ones who have borne the brunt of these crimes. Between 2011 and 2020, according to the Center for Justice and Human Rights of the Atlantic Coast of Nicaragua (CEJUDHCAN), at least 49 Miskito were killed, 49 were injured, 46 were kidnapped, 4 were disappeared, and 1,000 were forced to flee to Honduras. These crimes were carried out with the help of soldiers and paramilitaries known as "colonos" or settlers, persons hired by the government or by landowners to dispossess the Indigenous people of their lands (2021).

In 2013, Ortega gained legislative approval, without consultation and in record time, for the law granting the concession for the interoceanic canal. This law placed the nation's sovereignty and the most important source of water for the region in the hands of Wang Jing, a Chinese businessman who was supposed to build the interoceanic canal through Nicaragua. The reckless decision to proceed with such a megaproject without doing the required preliminary feasibility studies shows that Ortega has little interest in protecting the country's environment. Had the project been carried out, it would have caused significant environmental catastrophes, including the destruction of Lake Nicaragua and the San Juan River. As one scientist stated, the project leaves in the hands of "a mysterious company what is the responsibility of the state, and it presents the country with a colossal threat that could have an irreversible impact on the tropical forests and the main water reserve in the region" (Huete 2015: 22). The controversial project of the interoceanic canal gave rise to a vigorous protest movement prior to the rebellion of April 2018. It was a citizens' movement of the small farmers and Indigenous communities living along the proposed route of the canal whose land would be expropriated. Calling their organizing efforts, "the Movement in Defense of our Land, the Lake, and National Sovereignty," they carried out more than a hundred demonstrations in the zone and attracted international attention.

The Nicaraguan Academy of Sciences held several forums on the UCA campus for the purpose of discussing the viability of the proposed canal; they were attended by international scientists at the invitation of Dr. Jorge Huete, molecular biologist, member of the Nicaraguan Academy of Sciences, and senior vice president of the UCA. The Ortega government immediately objected to the forums, and a functionary came to ask me "to suspend the activities that Dr. Huete is sponsoring." I responded:

> These debates are supported by the office of the president of the UCA. It is our responsibility as a university to discuss these crucial issues that will determine the future of Nicaragua. The UCA is in favor of development, but not just any kind of development.

By 2016, the year of new presidential and legislative elections, Ortega had gained absolute control of the state, but he was also faced with limitations that had not existed previously. Petroleum aid from Venezuela had diminished because of the crisis in that country, and discontent in Nicaragua was increasing because of the government's control of economic opportunities and politics. Obtaining a job, a scholarship, a permit, a fair judicial ruling, or any benefit deriving from a state agency became increasingly dependent on having the backing of the governing party's political secretaries in municipalities and neighborhoods. Ordinary citizens began to feel frustrated and increasingly defenseless in dealing with government institutions. The intimate fusion of state-party-family became ever more evident in the country's political and economic life.

Despite apparent resignation by most of the population and the firm hold that Ortega had on state power, he was worried in mid-2016 about the possibility of losing the absolute majority his party enjoyed in the National Assembly. He therefore made three decisions that contributed to the crisis of April 2018: first, making use of his control over the Supreme Court, he expelled all the opposition deputies from the Assembly. Second, he prohibited the political alliance between the center-right and the center-left that was threatening his power and was expecting to gain many seats in the elections. Third, he chose his wife, Rosario Murillo, as the candidate for the vice presidency. Ortega, in this way, demonstrated that his project was not only to establish an authoritarian, institutional dictatorship but to set up a dynasty. Rosario Murillo became the first person in the line of succession. The "ghost" of Somoza's dynastic dictatorship, which had lasted half a century, was revived again in the national imagination. The 2016 elections saw the largest abstention in Nicaraguan electoral history. As corruption increased, democratic culture was weakened, and a culture of suppliance was reinforced. In the space of just ten years, the Nicaraguan people had experienced the defeat of a dictatorship (that of Somoza in 1979) by the force of arms and the electoral defeat of a revolutionary government (that of the FSLN in 1990) by the power of the ballot box, but now both those paths were closed to them. They did not want to return to armed conflict, and they were being denied the ability to choose their government with their votes.

What happened in April 2018?

The year 2018 began in relative calm, but there were two protests that catalyzed the uprising, both arising from the discontent of millennial youth. At the beginning of April, a vast expanse of the Indio Maíz Biological Reserve was being consumed by an intense wildfire. Environmentally minded young people demonstrated at the UCA, demanding from the government decisive and urgent responses that never came. The Indio Maíz Biological Reserve is an ancestral territory located in southeastern Nicaragua, on the border with Costa Rica. The owners of 80% of the reserve are the Rama and Kriol Indigenous peoples, who have an autonomous government called the Rama and Kriol Territorial Government. Their autonomy and their lands are now at risk, however, because of extractive mining and monoculture projects that benefit settlers, the Ortega-Murillo family, and its allies. The logging and livestock companies enjoy the protection of the army and the police even as they indiscriminately destroy the reserve. In 2017, a conference of diverse stakeholders was held at the UCA to discuss the defense of the reserve and other environmental struggles. This event, organized by the UCA and publicized by the university radio station, did much to strengthen collaboration among academics, students, scientists, journalists, and environmentalists. At the same time, it was an opportunity to provide the country with an account based on research, science, and facts about what was happening in Indio Maíz (Ruíz 2020: 26). The conference upset the government, which sent a functionary to the UCA with the warning that we had better keep quiet and not "misinform" the public because they were "trying to put out the fire in the reserve." I told the government representative that, as president of the UCA, I was convinced that it was part of our academic responsibility to denounce the destruction of a biological reserve that was of vital importance for the future of the country and Central America. In the end, what extinguished the fire was the arrival of heavy rains.

The second protest occurred on April 16, 2018, when Ortega gave the green light to reform the social security system, which was bankrupt due to government mismanagement. Among other measures, the reform reduced pensions for the elderly. On April 18, another protest against the reform was repressed by government police "shock forces," members of the Sandinista Youth, and armed paramilitaries who attacked the protesters on motorcycles. Despite the repression, more protests broke out the very next day in León, Managua, Masaya, and other parts of the country. The demonstrators were mostly young people defending their grandparents and other elderly folk who were at risk of having their pensions drastically reduced. As students from various universities took to the streets, other sectors of the population began to join them. The protests that day made absolutely clear the breadth and depth of the Nicaraguan people's rejection of the injustices and abuses committed by the regime. The anger that had been accumulating for over a decade finally erupted. It was an abrupt awakening, a "rebellion of consciousness."

The protests kept growing in the following days in the principal cities and in many rural areas as well, and the government's response was fierce repression. "Let loose with everything" was the order given by Murillo on April 19, 2018 to Sandinista political secretaries across the country. "Everything" meant using any means, no matter how violent, to quell the uprising. From the very first, anti-riot police and snipers used weapons of war. "Shoot to Kill" was the title of Amnesty International's first report describing the regime's lethal response during April and May 2018. The repression was like gas poured on a fire. During the month of April, people's solidarity and indignation turned the youth uprising into a movement that reached across the country. "They were students, not criminals!" was the first refrain the people chanted in the streets. In Nicaragua, killing university students means killing the great hope of poor families, for whom having a son or daughter enrolled at a university is a cherished dream. Grasping this reality is essential for understanding the repudiation provoked by the regime's armed attack on university students. "We let you get away with everything else, but you should never have touched our youngsters" read a placard that an elderly woman carried in her hands during the first march that took place in Managua. With that piece of cardboard, she was directly addressing Daniel Ortega. She would let him get away with everything else—the political control of institutions, the electoral fraud, the generalized corruption—but she would not let him kill university students.

Experiencing a new awakening, hope was palpable, intense, and expansive. The movement was autoconvocado or self-organized: nobody directed it, and nobody organized it. During April and May 2018, Managua was the scene of many mass protests, the likes of which hadn't been seen since the overthrow of Somoza. The same was true of León, Masaya, and other parts of the country. Soon the small farmers fighting against the canal contributed to the protest by building barricades on the highways. The city residents did likewise, and by mid-May, the circulation of vehicles was largely paralyzed across the country. As I described in the opening of this chapter, the largest mobilization that took place was the Mother's Day march in Managua on May 30: in peaceful solemnity, half a million people of all ages marched ten kilometers through the capital. That same day a dozen young people were shot down near the UCA. We knew then that, if the regime could commit such a crime on a day so special to Nicaraguans, it would stop at nothing to suppress the uprising.

Even with the repression, the government did appear to be considering concessions. By April 22, 2018, Ortega had already canceled the social security reform, and he called for a national dialogue, asking the bishops to act as mediators. The dialogue began on May 16 and lasted until June 23, 2018, but it was little more than a futile televised exercise given the lack of commitment to negotiate by the government. The dialogue revealed that the regime was not interested in seeking a solution that would bring about democratic change. Soon thereafter, the government began to describe what had happened in April and May 2018 as an attempted "coup d'état," and it has maintained this misrepresentation of events ever since. Even while the dialogue was still in process, the regime began its so-called "operation clean-up," whose purpose was to forcibly remove the hundreds of roadblocks and barricades that protesters had erected across the country. Uniformed police, armed with heavy weapons and accompanied by hooded paramilitaries in civilian dress, carried out military operations typical of an occupation army. The "clean-up" swept through Masaya, Jinotepe, Diriamba, Jinotega, and other cities, culminating in mid-July 2018. Dozens of people were summarily executed, and hundreds more were arrested for bringing food and water to the roadblocks, treating the wounded, or having participated in some way in the protests. Many people had to flee Nicaragua and seek refuge in Costa Rica and other countries. It is now estimated that "more than one hundred thousand persons and more than ninety journalists" have left the country out of fear or because of threats of violence from the police and the paramilitaries (Amnesty International 2021: 23).

Despite many efforts, the dialogue reached no agreement that would put a stop to the repression or respond to citizens' demands for democracy, but it did result in the arrival in Nicaragua of several important international delegations. The Inter-American Commission on Human Rights (IACHR), an autonomous body of the Organization of American States (OAS), arrived in May. In June, Nicaragua received delegations from the Follow-up Mechanism for Nicaragua (MESENI) and the Interdisciplinary Group of Independent Experts (GIEI), both of which are also organisms of the OAS. Arriving also in June was the Office of the U.N. High Commissioner for Human Rights (OACNUDH). After investigating and documenting the events in the country, these organizations prepared reports that corroborated what I've written above. In return, the OACNUDH was expelled from the country in August, and the MESENI and the GIEI were expelled in December 2018.

Due to the Global Magnitsky Act, Roberto Rivas, the president of the Supreme Electoral Council, had already been sanctioned by the U.S. government in December 2017. In July 2018, after the carnage of "operation clean-up," the "Magnitsky Nica Act"[2] applied sanctions against three more individuals: Francisco Díaz, the Chief of Police and Ortega's father-in-law; Fidel Moreno, political secretary of the governing party in Managua; and Francisco López, president of Albanisa (the counterpart of the Venezuelan oil company PDVSA) and treasurer of the governing party. All four were sanctioned for acts of corruption, and the last three for human-rights violations. In November 2018, by U.S.

executive order, a rather unusual sanction for similar crimes was levied against Rosario Murillo and Néstor Moncada Lau, the presidential couple's agent; the sanction had consequences like those of the Global Magnitsky Act. International sanctions, especially individualized ones such as these, have been extremely important for undermining the regime. Despite the international condemnation, the regime's arbitrary acts continued, and in December 2018 the repression intensified. On Christmas Eve, several non-governmental organizations (human rights groups, public policy research centers, women's organizations) were outlawed; their facilities were raided, and their bank accounts confiscated. Two highly influential media sources were also closed: the news source, "Confidencial," directed by Carlos Fernando Chamorro, and that of "100% Noticias," directed by Miguel Mora and Lucía Pineda Ubau, both graduates of the UCA's Department of Communication. Mora and Pineda Ubau were kept in solitary confinement in prison and accused of inciting hatred and "exercising critical journalism." Many exiled journalists continued to report from Costa Rica and the United States about what was happening in Nicaragua, and they have a large following on the Internet.

What is happening today?

At the start of 2021, Nicaragua was still being silenced. Ortega has issued a series of laws intended to frighten and punish the population and, at the same time, to "legalize" repression. The principal laws are the following: Law No. 1042, the "Special Cybercrimes Act"; the "Life Sentence Law" (affecting Article 37 of the Political Constitution), to be applied to persons whom the government considers to have committed "hate crimes"; Law No. 1040, the "Regulation of Foreign Agents Act," which hinders any projects of civil society that depend on international cooperation, and which also prevents the UCA from receiving international funds for its academic activities and other work; Law No. 1055, the "Defense of the Rights of the People to Independence, Sovereignty, and Self-determination for Peace Act," which inhibits persons seeking to participate as candidates in the elections of November 7, 2021; and a slightly ridiculous law that seeks to create a "National Secretariat for Matters of Outer Space, the Moon, and Other Celestial Bodies" (*Envío* 2020: 6).

Clinging to power at all costs, the Ortega-Murillo government denies the reality of the uprising of April 2018 and stubbornly continues to call it a "failed coup." According to the IACHR, some 325 people lost their lives in the uprising; the number of wounded is estimated at about 4,000 but maybe many more. Many of them will be disabled for life. It is impossible to know the number of disappeared persons. An estimated 100,000 persons have been forced into exile to escape the repression. Most have fled to Costa Rica, which has demonstrated an admirable spirit of solidarity. More than 600 people remain in the country's prisons, suffering torture and inhumane conditions. On May 16, 2019, one year after the start of the first National Dialogue, Eddy Antonio Gómez Praslin, who held both U.S. and Nicaraguan citizenship, was shot in the back in the Modelo Prison in Tipitapa. He had been imprisoned for more than five months, accused of "terrorism," but his real crime was joining the youth protests in Matagalpa. "I'm fighting for you because my time has passed," the 57-year-old told the young people. Seventeen other political prisoners were wounded in the same attack.

What happened in 2018 was not a coup attempt. No plans for a coup were ever presented, nor was any planning group ever identified. International human rights organizations have affirmed this repeatedly: there is no evidence to corroborate what the government is claiming, namely, that there was a U.S.-funded coup attempt against Nicaragua's left-wing government. Ortega's relations with Washington were quite cordial for a full decade. The Ortega government was clearly neoliberal in orientation, albeit with some anti-imperialist rhetoric. Nicaragua was open to transnational corporations, and extractive mining was unfolding rapidly. Control of the government by the Ortega-Murillo family guaranteed stability, in sharp contrast to the political volatility in the countries of the northern triangle. What happened in April 2018 was completely unforeseeable, including for the United States. Although for years we had feared that things would "end badly," we never suspected the degree of criminality, cruelty, and viciousness of which Ortega, Murillo, and their followers were capable.

Those months of political and social upheaval produced an acute economic crisis in Nicaragua, which plunged into a recession in October 2018. The economy has continued to slow: half a million people have lost their jobs, investment has dropped significantly, tourism has collapsed, and 30% of the dollar deposits kept by the national bank have been sent to foreign banks. During this recession, a desperate budget reform was imposed by Ortega in February 2019 to increase tax revenues to cover the budget deficit, but it only deepened the economic stagnation. And sadly, Nicaragua's claim to be "the safest country in Central America" is no longer applicable, rather the opposite.

The fortitude of the Nicaraguan people, made manifest for many months on the streets throughout the country, has been reduced to hushed resistance or, as Amnesty International said in its latest report, "silence at any cost" (Amnesty International 2021: 1). Any mobilization is declared illegal by the police. The rights to assembly, organization, demonstration, and free speech have been de facto annulled. Nicaragua is now experiencing a state of undeclared emergency. Terror reigns through sheer power, and the population is fearful. Or as one political prisoner said: "Nicaragua is today a country of the buried, the imprisoned, the exiled, and the terrified, … but not the defeated."[3] The greatest quality of the blue-and-whites is their power of resistance, which has been strengthened through the pressure of international actors. The human rights agencies of the OAS and the UN, as well as organizations such as Amnesty International and Human Rights Watch, issue regular reports on what is happening in Nicaragua, denouncing the serious human rights violations that have occurred and continue to occur. In addition, the European Union and the United States government have sanctioned key Nicaraguan government officials.

How has the repression affected the UCA?

The people of Nicaragua have been facing repression for more than four years. Despite the pressure that the UCA has endured in retaliation for the role it has played, we have been able to persist. Up to this day, the UCA is the only institution of higher education in the country in which students are free to express their opinions and beliefs. It is the only university where professors can discuss the crisis and share their views openly. The reason why we have become an island surrounded by universities that have collapsed into silence is that we have strengthened our commitment to our mission of working for justice in our society. Our small leadership team of university administrators has faced many challenges during the crisis. The National Council of Universities has decreased state funding by 100%. There is no customs clearance for the UCA, and other ministries and state entities have created obstacles for the university's functioning, like the ones faced by NGOs and the independent media. The government wants the UCA to be complicit with the repression, like the other universities, or else to disappear. Because of the drastic budget reduction, many students have been unable to receive scholarships. We have lost more than 3,000 undergraduate students (about 40% of the pre-crisis enrollment). Many students have left the country or are afraid to return to campus. There are also 80% fewer graduate students, perhaps as a direct result of the economic crisis. The students who have been able to persevere have lost valuable time. In 2018, we could offer only the first semester, but later in the year, from October to December, some of our students enrolled in a virtual term. Meanwhile, the campus remained in a state of siege, and we had to adapt our working hours to the daily rhythms of violence. For months, the streets surrounding the university were patrolled by police. Approaching or leaving the campus can still be daunting. Sometimes our staff members are afraid to walk out in the street wearing UCA T-shirts or other articles with the UCA name and logo on it.

Our academic community has differing perspectives about what the UCA should be doing. Some (especially our younger professors and some students) wish for a more confrontational attitude toward the government, while others are more fearful and would prefer the university to be cautious, discreet, and even silent. Some students want the university to close indefinitely in protest, while others want us to act as if nothing is happening; they want to return to the normality that existed before the crisis. Some students are thriving with virtual learning because it represents the only chance to continue studying while they cannot come to campus, but others loathe the virtual courses and say they don't compare with the student-centered classroom. Some parents are proud of the university and the student demonstrations organized on the campus, but others are concerned and ask us to stop them. In short, once simple decisions about day-to-day activities are now very complex. The psychological impact of the crisis on our community is also evident. Cases of depression, addiction, and anxiety have increased as a result of the crisis. We have increased our team of psychologists and our counseling services for students, and we have trained professors in how to provide psychological first aid. In these unfortunate times, we have grown as a team and learned what is important. Our experience has shown us that by strengthening institutional autonomy, developing academic partnerships, and promoting the commitment of our staff and teachers to the university and to society, a university can withstand many threats to its financial stability.

Since I became president in 2014, the UCA's priorities have become sources of strength in the current crisis. One of them, developing international academic relations, has become an important source of solidarity across the region, the hemisphere, and the world. Even though our exchange programs were affected because we could no longer receive foreign students, most of our partner universities continued receiving our students, extending the time they could stay, and opening new opportunities for them. These networks of solidarity not only included fundraising activities but also produced a legion of 40 volunteer teachers from other Jesuit universities of Latin America, who became part of our faculty and taught virtual courses from October to December 2018. That experience filled us with hope, and it was also academically enriching.

Currently in Nicaragua, as in other countries, universities are expected to fulfill many kinds of demands. For us, the most important challenge is educating students not just to "succeed" but to be committed professionals and responsible citizens who are conscious of their society's problems and willing to help solve them. That is what Ellacuría calls us to do:

> The university can provide the best objective analyses of reality, it can facilitate the discovery and the implementation of practices for confronting the different problems of reality, it can prepare the analytical frameworks, and it can help to find and apply solutions.
>
> *(Ellacuría 1999: 71)*

Ellacuría's vision of the university is what informs the efforts of our team of teachers and staff at the UCA. It is what has kept us grounded and focused. Despite the chaos, we are still providing an education to our students; we are still an academic community; and we have plans for the near future, for which our international networks will provide much support. While we are working under siege at all levels, we realize that we must leave aside all personal protagonism and promote collective leadership. As a result, even if we are fearful, anxious, or confused about what lies ahead, we know what we must do as a university. We must defend academic freedom and the right of young people to receive a critical higher education.

What can be done?

One of the most positive features of the 2018 uprising is that it was for the most part pacific and mass-based. During Nicaragua's almost 200 years of independence, our country has gone from civil war to civil war and from one period of repression and violence to another. In a country that has grown used to resolving its conflicts by force of arms, it is an enormous achievement when most of the population is convinced that the solution to their problems must be non-violent. This conviction represents a major change in the national political reality, a change that must be preserved and promoted. Whether out of conviction or out of necessity, an important characteristic of the citizens' resistance, both organized and unorganized, is that it has brought together young people with older folk, students with business owners, farmers with city dwellers. Out of that extraordinary unity, a new project for Nicaragua can be born. As a university, we must support this movement and encourage it. Nonviolence is the only way to build a better Nicaragua.

A commitment to nonviolence and staying critical as a university requires international support. A key aspect of solidarity is our joint work with other universities around the globe that are also using critical education in the fight for justice and social transformation in their own communities. This solidarity among sister universities is something that flows both ways. When other universities support our persistence, they learn a lesson and are inspired by us. At the same time, their accompaniment helps keep the world's eyes on our struggle so that more tragedy is averted. This type of horizontal accompaniment is the sign of a new political culture, and is summed up in the following quote from Serena Cosgrove's chapter at the end of this volume:

> This new political culture inspires a radical commitment, making it easier to commit to academic solidarity, in which we and our institutions realize that when Ellacuría calls us towards a preferential option for the poor, we choose to center the margins, not the elites. This choice means being at the service of the people who face systemic violence every day.

For us to escape from the material and moral rubble of this stage of our history, both the country and the UCA need solidarity. As regards our country, the paramilitary groups, which for months have been committing crimes with impunity, must be disarmed with international support, and the National Police must be completely reorganized. International cooperation will be needed to ensure a genuine process of transitional justice, one based on the investigations and findings of the GIEI. Such a process will ensure that the truth of what has happened here becomes known, that the people gain access to justice and reparation, and that tragedies such as those experienced since April 2018 will never happen again. As we were pointedly told by Claudia Paz y Paz, Guatemalan jurist and member of the GIEI, "The world cannot take its eyes off Nicaragua."

As regards the UCA, it is important that other universities spread the word about what is happening to us, that they invite our students for an exchange of experiences, and that their professors teach virtual classes that our students can take. Within the university, we still have a lot to do. The university must seek the power that only the truth possesses to make our contribution to the transformations that Nicaragua needs; that is an integral part of our academic task. Since the UCA and many other universities worldwide provide space where diverse creeds and ideas can coexist and flourish, we believe that embracing and respecting such diversity will enhance our teaching, our research, and all our tasks of *proyección social*. I want to point out that a humanistic formation should prepare our students to face failure without renouncing their goals and to live with their own weaknesses without being disheartened. A university cannot be neutral; it cannot remain impassive in the face of painful realities. We want to build a community that engages in fruitful dialogue, but that means always asking ourselves honestly: What are we working for? Whom do our labors serve? Ignacio Ellacuría, S.J., knew the answers to these questions. In his last speech, delivered ten days before he was assassinated on the campus of the UCA of El Salvador, he stated:

> It is sometimes said that the university must be impartial. We believe not. The university must try to be free and objective, but objectivity and freedom may require partiality. And we are freely partial in favor of the popular majorities because they are unjustly oppressed and because in them, negatively and positively, is the truth of reality.

Emblematic of this struggle is what happened to Álvaro Conrado, a 15-year-old boy who was a student at the Jesuit high school, Instituto Loyola, in Managua. On April 20, 2018, while he was bringing water to the university students protesting near the cathedral, he was fatally shot in the neck by a sniper. When I talked afterwards with his mother, she was supposed to be the one receiving consolation from me, but I was the one who ended up being consoled. I have seen her speak more and more forcefully about what is happening in Nicaragua. Once a shy, quiet woman, she is now a spokesperson for the Association of the Mothers of April (AMA), which has its offices at the UCA. "It hurts me to breathe" were the last words of Alvarito Conrado as he lay wounded by a police bullet. That phrase moved an entire nation. "Today all Nicaragua breathes for you," we proclaimed in the marches of May 2018, the moment of our greatest enthusiasm and hope. And today, as we think about the future, we need to remain committed to a Nicaragua in which no one struggles to breathe. This is my manifesto; this is my request to you: as you read the rest of this book, think about how you might be able to help us breathe.

Notes

1 Elba Ramos worked as a housekeeper at the Jesuit residence; she was a low-income woman who as a child had labored in the coffee plantations. Celina, her daughter, was

a bright 15-year-old who dreamed of getting a scholarship to study business administration at the UCA.
2 The Magnitsky Global Act authorizes the President of the United States to impose economic sanctions on citizens around the world who have committed human rights abuses or acts of corruption in their own countries. This law, first passed in 2012, was initially directed against Russian citizens. In December 2018 the U.S. government enacted the Magnitsky Nica Act, which sanctions Nicaraguan officials for these same crimes and also puts strict conditions on loans from international organizations to Nicaragua, except those destined for health and education. Some 27 officials of the regime have been sanctioned by the Magnistky Nica Act (*Envío* 2018: 7).
3 The Spanish statement rhymes: "... *un país de enterrados, encerrados, desterrados y aterrados ... pero no de derrotados.*"

References

Amnistía Internacional. (2021) *Silencio a cualquier Costo–Tácticas del Estado para Profundizar la Represión en Nicaragua*. London, Reino Unido: Amnesty International Ltd.

Bejarano, Manuel. (2014) Las carreras del canal. *El Nuevo Diario*, 23 de julio: https://www.elnuevodiario.com.ni/economia/325503-carreras-canal/

CEJUDHCAN. (2021) Nicaragua: Briefing conjunto: Un año de violencia sistemática contra quienes defienden los derechos indígenas. *OMCT, CENIDH, CALPI; CEJUDHCAN*, enero. Disponible en: https://www.omct.org/es/recursos/llamamientos-urgentes/nicaragua-briefing-conjunto-un-a%C3%B1o-de-violencia-sistem%C3%A1tica-contra-quienes-defienden-los-derechos-ind%C3%ADgenas

Chamorro Barrios, Carlos Fernando. (2020) Nicaragua antes y después de la rebelión de abril. En: *Anhelos de un nuevo horizonte-Aportes para una Nicaragua democrática*. Cortés Ramos, Alberto; López Baltodano, Umanzor; Moncada Bellorin, Ludwing, editores. San José Costa Rica: FLACSO.

Ellacuría, Ignacio. (1999) *Escritos Universitarios*. San Salvador: UCA Editores.

———. 1999 El Concepto Filosófico de Tecnología Apropiada. En: *Escritos Filosóficos, Tomo III*. San Salvador: UCA Editores.

Equipo de trabajo. (2018) *Revista Envío*, Año 37, No 430–431, enero-febrero: p. 7.

———. (2020) *Revista Envío*, Año 39, 464, noviembre: pp. 5–8.

———. (2021) *Revista Envoi*, 466–467, Enero-Febrero: pp. 5–6.

Huete-Pérez, Jorge A., Rafael Lucio, yManuel Ortega-Hegg. (2015) *El Canal Interoceánico por Nicaragua-Aportes al debate*. 2ª Edición. *Academia de Ciencias de Nicaragua*. Serie: Ciencia, Técnica y Sociedad.

Marina, José Antonio. (2010) *Las culturas fracasadas. El talento y la estupidez de las sociedades*. Barcelona: Editorial Anagrama.

Ruíz, Amaro. (2020) La reserva Indio Maíz. *Revista Envío*, 465, diciembre 2020. pp. 25–31.

2
THE IMPACT OF NEOLIBERAL REFORM AND REPRESSION ON HIGHER EDUCATION IN NICARAGUA

Wendi Bellanger

Introduction

After a year into the crisis which had started in 2018, I got used to the explosions and screams that became a permanent soundtrack to the hours working in my office at the Universidad Centroamericana (UCA) in Managua, Nicaragua. I got used to seeing colleagues burst into tears in the middle of meetings. I crossed my fingers with every WhatsApp message I received, hoping it wasn't about another student kidnapped by the police or paramilitaries. Our discussions about curriculum development, teacher recruitment, or university policies were interspersed with remarks about dangerous incidents, tortures, disappearances, jail, risks we were exposed to every day. We came to campus hoping not to encounter a Toyota Hilux in the street, the vehicles used by armed men to track down and kidnap anyone they considered suspicious of opposing the government. The first one to leave campus at night would inform the others—via a call or WhatsApp message—if they saw police patrolling a nearby street so we could avoid that route. Sometimes we closed the campus at short notice and canceled classes because of the danger. Some colleagues believed we should confront the government, protest, and go on strike. They coached students, helped them to organize their movement, dedicated hours to the resistance efforts; one of them completely abandoned his responsibilities to assist the main opposition group while his colleagues shielded his absence from the upper administration. In contrast, other colleagues wanted us to follow a diplomatic, accommodative stance; they feared for their jobs and their lives. While the former demanded we organize demonstrations on campus, the latter accused us of allowing them to occur. Some parents called to blame the campus protests as the cause for a son or daughter failing a course. Many people wanted the UCA to admit the students who had been expelled from the public universities without academic records,[1] grant them scholarships, and graduate them quickly, if possible in a year—even if we didn't offer their major. Teachers, students, and the public criticized the university in many

DOI: 10.4324/9781003198925-4

contradictory ways, all the time. They wanted the UCA to shield them from human rights violations; they wanted it to be a political force helping to topple the government; or they expected it to be a savvy player in the world of corrupt politics. People wanted many things from an institution that didn't know how long it would resist simply being a university.

I often think about university administrators who suffered similar experiences in the past. Central American universities have a history of resistance, of survival in the midst of conflict, and of active involvement in national political affairs. Politics, nation-building, development, social justice, inequality, and poverty have always been central issues in these academic communities during decisive moments in history. The three Jesuit universities of Central America, *Universidad Rafael Landívar* (Guatemala), *Universidad Centroamericana "José Simeón Cañas"* (El Salvador), and *Universidad Centroamericana* (Nicaragua) form a trio of universities that have all paid the price for "speaking truth to power". As mentioned by President Idiáquez, S.J. in his chapter, the unthinkable happened in 1989, on El Salvador's UCA campus, when six Jesuit priests and two women were killed. Their martyrdom is the result of a struggle we understand. Their fate remains valid in today's Central America.

While our universities persist in their commitments, they also survive in a context of state repression and relentless neoliberal reforms. Using the example of the UCA in Nicaragua, this chapter highlights the ways state violence is sometimes specifically directed toward universities, their students and staff, and it illustrates the way in which an authoritarian government can dismantle university autonomy through political clientelism directed toward academic communities. The chapter will also describe how, following global neoliberal reforms, universities have become increasingly similar to corporations, imbricated with a particular managerial strategy.

In the corporatized university, professors become managed workers, and administrators in leadership positions are expected to act as CEOs (Tuchman, 2009). Universities are turned into competing institutions that sell their "services" at the highest possible price to a captive market of students, and to other clients such as corporations, governments, the military industrial complex (Giroux, 2007), and varied organizations, through research, innovations, and patents. In this context, science is described as a commodity (Salomon, 1985), and universities as institutions that produce and commercialize it for the sake of their country's economic growth (Gibbons, 1985). These expectations are encased in narratives about the "knowledge economy" or "knowledge society" in which academics are encouraged to constantly assess their contribution and position. Concomitantly, universities compete for their place in ranking systems that leverage science and "best value" in what has been described as a "corporate takeover" (Giroux, 2009) of the university.

Quality assurance regimes—an essential element of the corporatization of higher education—emerge as key contributors to the weakening of academic communities' capacity to defend university autonomy in Central America, leaving them vulnerable to authoritarian control. They entail the use of terms such as quality, client satisfaction, and continuous improvement, which sidestep relevant social and political discussions. The recent violent repression by the Ortega-Murillo regime in Nicaragua has exposed how Central American universities still suffer under the tyranny of national governments and other powers.[2] They struggle with their role in traditional and hierarchical Central American societies, torn between promoting social change and reproducing the status quo. Developing quality assurance schemes, as universities around the world are expected to do, does not help these institutions face the real threats to academic quality endemic to these societies. These schemes are in fact quite compatible with the strategies of populist and repressive regimes that target academia, and similarly focus on the control of professors and students.

To show how quality assurance and state repression intertwine and generate a taxing environment for university autonomy, I begin with a brief account of the struggle of Central American universities for autonomy and academic freedom, focusing on the Nicaraguan case, from the 1960s to the Ortega-Murillo government. That is, from the flourishing of the discourse and struggle for university autonomy—as displayed by the founders of the Central American Superior Council on Universities (CSUCA)[3] and later in the work of Ellacuría, S.J., martyred President of the UCA in El Salvador—to its deterioration and dismantling as it was reduced to the defense of "the 6%," the percentage of the national budget allocated to universities in Nicaragua. Then I will describe quality assurance and corporatization's discourse on quality, which does not take into account substantive elements of the student-teacher relationship and other social and cultural factors that deeply affect the teaching/learning experience. In the fourth section, I present in detail the Nicaraguan quality assurance regime as a case study describing how it became embedded within an authoritarian regime's strategy to control universities and promote their corporatization and political subjugation. Finally, this chapter concludes by underscoring the urgency to re-focus discussions in academia in order to strengthen university autonomy and academic freedom.

Vital to my analysis is the theory of academic capitalism (Slaughter & Leslie, 1997; Slaughter & Rhoades, 2004) because it explains how universities transform themselves to become more closely connected to the economy and integrated into the "knowledge society." Groups of internal actors in the university "[use] a variety of state resources to create new circuits of knowledge that link higher education institutions to the new economy" (Slaughter & Rhoades, 2004, p. 1). The result is a "shift from a public good knowledge/learning regime to an academic capitalist knowledge/learning regime" (p. 8). The latter has not completely replaced the former, as the two regimes coexist (p. 29), but the boundaries between the public and the private sector are increasingly blurred. In this view, universities are not defenselessly affected by external market forces; rather they actively seek those connections with the economy. This theory helps us understand how neoliberal trends have taken root in Central American universities notwithstanding the differences between them and their counterparts in the global North. Neoliberalism rests comfortably on the ways in which academic quality is described and managed through the "audit culture" (Power, 1997). A global discourse, which I call the "talk of quality," replaced the discourse on academic freedom and university autonomy which had flourished in Central America during the 1950s and 1960s, was alive in the 1980s, and included reflections on the university's role in society and its complex relation to powerful groups. As a result, Central American universities' capacity to defend their autonomy from authoritative regimes has progressively weakened. During Ortega-Murillo's repressive government, this new discourse and management practices contribute to distract academics from the actions that have steadily eroded university autonomy.

The Struggle for University Autonomy in Nicaragua and the Devastating Effects of the Ortega-Murillo Government

After the April 2018 rebellion, there was a massacre, persecution, jail, torture, and mass expulsion of students from public universities. Then there was a return to classes and "a new normal" with militarized campuses, prohibitions of group gatherings, and increased vigilance. Many young people were demanding justice. In disregard of all of this, in her welcome speech to the 114th session of the CSUCA, the President of the National Autonomous University of Nicaragua (UNAN),[4] the biggest public university in Nicaragua, and also the President of the National Council of Universities (CNU), talked about peace and reconciliation. She didn't acknowledge the massacre, didn't talk about the suffering of the academic community or the violation of the campuses by the Police. She claimed the university was flourishing in its mission to bring development and peace to Nicaraguan society.

University autonomy has an important history in Central America, which matured in connection with global developments on the matter. In 1950, a statement from the International Conference convened by UNESCO had stipulated as one of university autonomy's three basic principles: "the tolerance of divergent opinion and freedom from political interference" in universities. Later, in 1965, university autonomy was defined by the International Association of Universities (IAU) as the authority to decide who will teach what to whom, who will graduate, and what will be researched. The importance of university autonomy was underscored again by the IAU in 1998.[5] However, in spite of its recognition, this basic condition for the proper functioning of universities has always suffered from pressures from different sources, not always clearly identified. Significantly, the interest in discussing university autonomy, very poignant 70 years ago, has decreased in the recent decades.

In 1959, there were only 12,327 university students in Central America (Tünnermann Bernheim, 2016, p. 123), but important developments in academia were already occurring in the region. The Central American University Confederation[6] and its Central American Superior Council on Universities

(CSUCA) were created in 1948. In this first regional forum, Central American universities went beyond the *Cordoba Reform* (1918)[7] in their *Declaration of Principles on the Purposes and Functions of the Contemporary University and especially the Universities of Central America*,[8] a document that presented their educational philosophy and inspired the developments that followed, including plans for integration of higher education in the region (Tünnermann Bernheim, 2016, pp. 113–114).

The General Secretariat of the CSUCA released a statement in 1948 declaring the importance of the collaboration between the university and the state to solve national problems without sacrificing the former's autonomy and independence in research (Waggoner, Wagonner & Wolfe, 1964, p. 449). This was a significant position as the history of universities in Central America had been marked by frequent interventions of the state to control administrative and teaching appointments (p. 450). The statement "proclaimed university autonomy as an indispensable condition for the exercise of the practice of academia" (Tünnermann Bernheim, 2016, p. 114, my translation). Seventy years after this "Golden age" (p. 127), the CSUCA is no longer a champion for the defense of university autonomy. It is, however, a promoter of regional quality assurance regimes.

In the 1950s, the protection of the university from political manipulation was a priority. When Mariano Fiallos Gil was asked to serve as President of the University of Nicaragua in León, he accepted under the condition of expelling all party politics from the university (Tünnermann Bernheim, 2016, p. 100). This was also important for the students. The *National University Law*[9] and the first projects discussing university autonomy were thought out and initially drafted by students who later became professors (pp. 100–102). Finally, on March 25, 1958, Executive Order No. 38 granted autonomy to the National University. In 1966, university autonomy became part of the Constitution in Nicaragua (Article 115), and it was established that 2% of the general budget should be assigned to the National University (Tünnermann Bernheim, 2016, p. 146). Before that, funding came from the Executive Branch and was considered the main reason for the fragility of university autonomy. For Fiallos Gil, it kept the university "subjected to the humors of militant politics" (Tünnermann Bernheim, 2016, p. 107, my translation). For this reason, the establishment of a fixed budget, independent of the Executive Branch's control and party politics, was considered the key to guarantee university autonomy. The jubilation caused by obtaining the 2% of the national budget faded with the rise in enrollment experienced between 1965 and 1970.[10] The pressure prompted UNAN university president Tünnermann to promote the 6% campaign in 1972. In 1990, with the passing of Law No. 89 (Law for the Autonomy of Higher Education Institutions), the 6% contribution to the universities of the state budget was approved,[11] and later, in 1992, it was confirmed as 6% of the total budget.[12] The technicalities about the calculation of the 6%, as well as the distribution of the budget between the ten universities that comprise the CNU (also created in 1990 by Law 89),[13] has monopolized the discussion about university autonomy from the 1990s to the present.

While Art. 8 of Law 89 declares universities have "teaching or academic," "organic," "administrative," and "financial or economic" autonomy, public debate and demands have focused on the compliance of Art. 55, which declares that a minimum guarantee for university autonomy is that universities shall receive 6% of the government's national budget.[14] Underlying this view is the conviction that as long as the government guarantees "the 6%", autonomy is a resolved issue. However, financial resources and academic freedom are definitely not the same thing. During the 1990s and first half of 2000s, there were yearly student protests demanding "the 6%" actively encouraged by the FSLN. These protests disappeared with the arrival of Ortega to power in 2007. Since then, university autonomy has been progressively dismantled even as funding was guaranteed—"the 6%" has been provided every year—and access promoted—some admission requirements have been removed; the Nicaraguan Open Online University (UALN)[15] was created to provide online majors to any high school graduate; new campuses were opened; and also in a certain way contributing to access, many private universities (known as "garage universities") have been legally approved by the CNU.

Since 2007, university autonomy has been ostensibly guaranteed by the FSLN government's willingness to provide the budget. Simultaneously public universities were absorbed into a network of political clientelism (Stokes et al., 2012) set up by the party. The unions—comprising academic and administrative staff—as well as the student union (UNEN), were intertwined with the FSLN. The CNU, a collegiate body, was subsumed into the network of Sandinista clientelism, including university presidents. These networks decided who was fired or hired, who got a scholarship or who would lose it, and which topics should and shouldn't be taught[16] according to the party's interests (Acción Universitaria et al., 2021). Therefore, by controlling funding and access to higher education through a network of political clientelism, the FSLN's government dismantled university autonomy while giving the impression of safeguarding it.

Funding of universities became the door through which the FSLN took complete control of public higher education in Nicaragua. Staff appointments and purges conformed to political decisions, and the allocation of scholarships became an effective clientelist strategy. Academic authorities were appointed through elections, according to the law; however, as Ernesto Medina, a former UNAN León President says: "elections were brutally manipulated by the force of the party through all the common antics used by political parties to put pressure on some people and offer benefits to others" (Acción Universitaria et al., 2021, p. 49, my translation). Student leaders worked as "brokers" and "party leaders" in a system in which "parties distribute benefits to individuals and attempt to hold them accountable for their votes" (Stokes et al., 2012, p. 18). In Medina's words:

> The admissions system was also manipulated so that many of the students who accessed universities developed the idea that they were there thanks to the favor of a political authority from UNEN or the FSLN who worked in the university.
>
> *(Acción Universitaria et al., 2021, p. 50, my translation)*

In this case, more than votes in national elections (which the FSLN guaranteed through other means, mainly the control of the electoral system), they sought the students' allegiance and support in the streets and in public events, filling up plazas during political celebrations. Through these mechanisms, university autonomy was sacrificed on the altar of populist politics and authoritarian control.

Thus, the transformative role student organizations had in the 1950s and 1960s in Nicaragua was neutralized in the ensuing decades. A simultaneous process in which non-Sandinista students tended to voluntarily relinquish the space, while the FSLN maintained its interests, resulted in the party's control of the UNEN. Public university students were forced to become political clients of the Ortega-Murillo regime. They were expected to satisfy brokers (student leaders and university authorities) with apparent loyalty and obedience to the FSLN. Their access to higher education and their opportunities in the university depended on their standing with the brokers (Bow, 2019; Mairena, 2019; Acción Universitaria et al., 2021). Unsurprisingly, during the uprising of April 2018, the Nicaraguan government repressed protesting students with the collaboration of UNEN and university authorities (Rocha, 2019; Acción Universitaria, et al., 2021).[17] The students' role in the struggle for university autonomy and their influence on national politics have been relevant in Nicaraguan history but seldom studied (Baltodano Marcenaro, 2007; Rocha, 2019). They helped achieve or preserve university autonomy at different points in history but have also been vulnerable to cooptation by political parties since the 1950s (Waggoner et al., 1964, p. 459) to the present. UNEN was notorious for its violent clashes demanding the 6% in the 1990s. Since April 2018, it has been identified as a repressive arm of the regime within universities.

Given that Central American universities remain vulnerable to political clientelism, Ignacio Ellacuría, S.J.'s perspective is relevant today. Analyzing the Law of the University of El Salvador,[18] he suggested there should be "legal protection of the university from anyone who aimed, from a position of power, to obstruct [its] work" (1999, p. 31, my translation). Ellacuría invites us to get involved in a discussion to prevent "the disfiguration of the mission of the university by the activism of political parties or by its submissiveness to those who maintain the status quo" (p. 33, my translation). Furthermore, for Ellacuría, universities should not only serve their students but the whole country and all citizens, by critiquing injustice and proposing creative responses (pp. 22–23). We should be discussing how to deepen our universities' capacities to foster a much-needed democratization of knowledge that could promote inclusive development (Arocena, Göransson & Sutz, 2018). This is precisely the conversation that has been missing in Nicaraguan academia for the last couple of decades. It has deteriorated and lost political force by focusing on "the 6%" instead of highlighting the responsibility of the state to protect the university as a self-governing institution. At the same time, it has been eviscerated by quality assessment discourses that define quality without a connection to a political reality.

The Corporatization of Higher Education, Audit Culture, and the Weakening of University Autonomy

Suits, ties, blazers, high heels, the auditorium was full with UCA staff witnessing a formal ceremony on occasion of the accreditation of the Master in Business Law. The agency presented a diploma stating that, having confirmed the quality of the program, it granted its accreditation for three years. There was celebration and satisfaction for the culmination of a process that had begun six years before and finally achieved what everyone called "a public recognition of quality for the program" and "a guarantee for students that the program is committed to quality and continuous improvement." A year passed and we realized that the program had become the most expensive in the University. Keeping up with the costs of the improvement plan approved by the agency and maintaining the secretarial staff needed to keep the collection and systematization of information demanded by the agency meant that funds from other programs had to be diverted to sustain it or that the cost had to be transferred to the students through an increase in tuition fees. The accreditation process automatically increased the cost of the program without changing anything substantial for professors or students.

The UCA was founded in 1960. It was the first private university in Central America, when higher education enrollment in the region oscillated merely between 0.6 and 2.2% (Brunner, 1990). With the decade came a steady rise in demand, unfulfilled by the public universities. As a result, during the 1980s and 1990s, private universities emerged and absorbed two student groups: those who aspired to a place in public universities but were not admitted and those who preferred to attend private, costlier, more exclusive universities but couldn't travel abroad. A market logic developed, and throughout Central America, 70% of university students ended up attending private universities (Walter, 2000). In Nicaragua, there are now 60 universities, 56 of which are private. Most of these are pejoratively called "garage universities" because they are small, often functioning in a house, have almost no full-time staff, no research agenda, no basic facilities such as libraries or laboratories, their lecturers don't have graduate degrees, and their monthly tuition fees are adjusted to what low-income families can pay. In 2018, only 28.79% of higher education students were enrolled in public universities (CNU, 2018, p. 11). Moreover, some public universities created private schools or programs that charge tuition fees like private universities with corresponding differences in infrastructure and conditions for these paying students.

In this context of great educational and institutional disparities, the discourse on quality management gained support as it reinforced the notion that a corporatized higher education system can connect to the market for everybody's benefit, while proper managerial practices can guarantee quality for students across the system or at least, secure their trust.[19] While issues of quality haven't been regulated in Central America as a result of this discourse, the "audit culture" (Power, 1997) has been solidly established, steering universities on the path of corporate models with the acquiescence of internal actors. Through the lens of the theory of academic capitalism, these quality assurance practices appear as "narratives, discourses and social technologies that justify and normalize these changes."[20] Concepts like quality, client satisfaction, and continuous improvement are part of a "one size fits all" managerial approach designed for competition in the student market.

Furthermore, promoting reforms in universities is perceived as tantamount to building efficient routes to development in poor countries. For example, the Organization for Economic Co-Operation and Development (OECD), the European Union (EU), the World Trade Organization (WTO), and the World Bank started playing important roles in shaping educational policy in Latin America, through lending policies and the promotion of quality assurance regimes.[21] In 2002, the WTO included higher education as a commercial service regulated by the General Agreement on Trade in Services (GATS).[22] Many of the conditions that international corporatized universities rely on, such as corporations buying their research, students accessing loans to pay hefty sums of money for tuition and services such as room and board, tuition dollars from international students, or having a large full-time teaching and research staff with PhDs, are nonexistent in Central America. However, Central American universities have established the same managerial discourse (quality assessment, rankings, continuous improvement) as their European and American counterparts, and developed ways in which to access a market for their research (international cooperation) and attract more paying students (increased privatization). Indeed, the "audit culture" provides the basis for the corporatization of universities in the Central American context.

Most significant for the subject of university autonomy, the "audit culture" has a direct influence on university politics and policies, on the members of the university, and on their interactions. Quality assurance has become the main social technology that normalizes the portrayal of higher education as an inexorably private investment, an exercise in personal satisfaction, extraneous to the collective struggles that stem from the real-life experiences of students and their professors in the region. As a result, Central American universities have chosen a path far removed from Ellacuría's vision of a "political" university that is aware of the historical reality of society and "trying positively to make a difference in the restructuring and conformation of society … and permanently asking itself which powers it is actually serving or should be serving" (1999, p. 95, my translation).

The discourse on quality does not include conceptualizations or reflections on university autonomy and academic freedom. As a governing technology (Foucault,

1988), quality audit puts in place "rituals of verification" (Power, 1997), such as teacher evaluations, through which a customer service relationship is constructed to replace the traditional pedagogical student-teacher relationship. A focus on teachers' performance is based on notions of commodity economies, blind to the students' views, which seem more compatible to those of gift economies (Mauss, 1990; Cooper, 2004). In the "audit culture," the administration requires the collaboration of students entering the exercise via a client identity. Their answers become data, registered evidence that feeds the quality assurance system.

The construction of students as clients has permeated policies and analyses of higher education, which accept as "a truth universally acknowledged" that students have a consumer consciousness. The lack of grounded research on students has reinforced these assumptions about them. Fieldwork in academia, as Gusterson (2017) calls for, is urgently needed. Aiming to contribute to this matter, I conducted a comparative empirical study (Bellanger, 2016)[23] based on two cases: the UCA and Philipps-Universität Marburg in Germany, two very different institutions in contrasting contexts that, nevertheless, are actively immersed in academic capitalism and quality assurance, and have developed similar managerial structures and "talk of quality." The comparison revealed important elements of classroom interactions, the learning process, and the "student culture"[24] that are concealed by a "tyranny of transparency" (Strathern, 2000) based on questionnaires and indicators used to manage students' opinions, concealing more than what they reveal.

Professors focus on developing a performance style that is recorded in evaluation questionnaires. As a Business professor from UCA said:

> I follow up the variables that are part of the evaluation questionnaire and bring them up during the whole term so that students remember things they usually forget when they fill out the evaluation form. That's how I get good results.

A corporatized university needs professors who follow directions instead of their own experience. As another professor mentioned:

> Evaluation totally changes the routine of what you do. You have to plan everything all over again. Someone who says 'I do things in this way and I will keep on like this' does not fit. We need people who are flexible because some indicators are tremendous. To achieve quality, just like corporations have ISO, European system or whatever it is called, you marry a system that helps you improve quality.

This shows that in the "talk of quality" a willingness to constantly change and blindly adapt to the evaluation system's directions is perceived as a fundamental characteristic of a university professor.

Observed from the university administration's viewpoint, quality assurance is a practical way of monitoring quality in the classroom, a simplification that allows for quick decision making, and a way of managing students' opinions about the institution, in other words risk management or "uni-directional forms of disclosure and transparency over dialogue" (Power, 2010, p. 17). Observed from the classroom level, the questionnaire fails to contain reality. Evaluation promotes an individualized view of the problem of quality in higher education, one that depends on the teacher's compliance with a set of indicators, and that can be reflected in student satisfaction. Problems and solutions are thus sought at the individual level. Students are encouraged to judge their teachers individually, not to openly discuss their views, which could produce more pondered opinions or at least collective, nuanced, contextualized, and debatable student feedback, an environment more akin to academic freedom.

The corporatized university requires the development of new identities in teachers and students, also the establishment of a culture of "competitive accountability" (Watermeyer, 2019) that may be uncomfortable[25] but cannot be resisted. In the words of a quality manager from the UCA:

> The university that does not join the process runs the risk of being displaced from its status in the academy and the market because, at the end of the day, the production of knowledge is linked to the market and to a position in the rankings.

Although there is an awareness of a disconnection between quality assurance and reality, it isn't pointed out as a threat to academic freedom or autonomy. In the words of a professor:

> We do have to be careful when wanting to fulfil indicators that are not helpful in our own context. Some agencies ask for indicators that have nothing to do with the national reality and sometimes you get stuck on those indicators and neglect others that are more necessary in the national context.

However inadequate or taxing these practices are perceived, there is a widespread sense of resignation to them.

Accreditation processes are considered by UCA professors as grueling feats, more absorbing than any research project or teaching endeavor. During the accreditation of the Major in Architecture, four professors stayed overnight on campus for several days in a row to finish a report, leaving in the mornings only to shower and return to teach. A Psychology professor lamented that the evaluation process drove a colleague to a nervous breakdown and early retirement.

Four years after a failed attempt in the accreditation of the Industrial Engineering program, a former Dean told me:

> What happened to us was terrible, traumatic, wearing. We regretted having entered the process without needing to. What for? Why did we start chasing an accreditation if we were alright, we were doing things properly? [...] It was a boom, everybody talked about accreditation, that if a program was accredited it was better recognized by society and the students feel motivated because you are giving them quality.

University autonomy flourished in Central America through the encouragement of permanent open dialogue between members of academic communities, with collaboration instead of competition between universities. It also involved a discussion on the pressing issues that generate social inequality, not the measurement of student satisfaction. The capacity to defend university autonomy is denied through the practices of quality assurance. Furthermore, its managerial strategies debilitate the political agency and organizational capacity of actors in universities. Thus, the corporatization of higher education undermines the single most important condition for quality in higher education. The corporatized university is focused on sustaining the "value" of its degrees in the job market because it believes in a "liquid" education (Bauman, 2009), one that offers knowledge as a product designed to be consumed and then discarded in order to acquire a new one. Accordingly, the concept of quality is constantly redefined by accreditation agencies, punctiliously predicated on notions of comparability and standards, of usefulness in the market. In practice, this is confusing to follow, especially for a Central American university in a politically, economically, and socially unstable context. However, processes continue apace because agencies do not deal with the political context of a university they are accrediting. They approach it as an institution devoid of political interactions.

Simultaneously, the student-as-client discourse generates a manager-centered practice that stays within a pre-established framework. Universities can avoid mission-critical issues and still obtain more and "better" accreditations, and advance in the rankings by keeping the flow of the right kind of information. The corporatized university "improves" quality while it rejects the notion that precariousness and instability in the academic workplace can have a relation to academic quality. Reputation boosts are achieved through specific managerial decisions and strategically placed spending, even when serious problems remain. At the UCA, the scarce access to updated scholarship, insufficient number of full-time professors, classism and racism, gender discrimination, lack of basic competencies in first-year students, and the country's chronic financial and political instability, are problems that remain unaddressed by quality assurance. Society's problems are reflected in the classroom and determine who deserves respect, credibility, and attention. Rather than strengthening universities' capacity to defend an inclusive classroom, autonomy, and academic freedom, quality assurance sets these issues completely aside. As a result, faced with an authoritarian regime, the corporatized academic community has few resources to counteract populist and repressive strategies of control.

Evaluation and Accreditation in Nicaragua

After enduring a very difficult 2018, our sense of fragility heightened in 2019 when the National Council of Universities (CNU) drastically cut our funding in retaliation for our critical stance. The UCA became the black sheep of Nicaraguan universities, and we felt it in every meeting. The CNU increased our stress and workload with sudden special requests to systematize and turn in large amounts of information. Meanwhile, the National Council for Evaluation and Accreditation (CNEA), following the government's wishes for a pretense of normalcy in the country, expected us to keep our "improvement plan" on track and prepare for the peer evaluators' visits. Also blind to the crisis was the Central American Graduate Studies Accreditation Agency (ACAP)[26] of the Central American Council for Higher Education Accreditation (CCA),[27] which had granted accreditation to our Master in Business Law. After the pomp and circumstance of the accreditation ceremony came the harsh reality of an accreditation we couldn't sustain economically. We had decided to discontinue the process before the crisis upon a cost-benefit evaluation. In July 2018, our campus was closed but the ACAP kept insisting we continue the process and accept the follow-up visit of the peer evaluators. With our president under death threats, our campus under siege, severe budget cuts, and a permanent state of emergency and chaos, national and regional evaluation and accreditation processes continued in what seemed to be a parallel reality.

The quality assurance regime established in Nicaragua has proven to be very compatible with the government's control over and repression of universities, displaying the standard discourse on quality and avoiding altogether the discussion on university autonomy. This section briefly describes the regime, its functioning, and compatibility with neoliberal reforms and government repression.

Two laws introduced evaluation and accreditation in Nicaragua: Law No. 582, General Education Law (2006),[28] and Law No. 704, Law for the Creation of the National System for Quality Assurance in Education and Regulator of the National Council for Evaluation and Accreditation (2011).[29] They also introduced a new balance of power which undermined the traditional control of the CNU over higher education institutions (Tünnermann Bernheim, 2008, p. 237), granted by Law No. 89, Law for the Autonomy of Higher Education Institutions (1990).[30] As the organism in charge of coordinating and advising universities, distributing the budget, authorizing the creation of new universities, and approving or canceling academic programs (Asamblea Nacional, 1990, Arts. 55–61), not being granted the responsibility to organize the evaluation and accreditation processes was a blow to the CNU's authority.

Law 704 established that all higher education institutions, public and private,[31] had to initiate an accreditation process and establish an internal system of quality assurance. The CNEA was to define the mechanisms of the accreditation and promote a "quality culture," "evaluation culture," and "continuous improvement" throughout the system. The aim was to guarantee to the public that higher education institutions have quality, and to generate information for students, employers, parents, the State, and other education institutions (Asamblea Nacional, 2011, Art. 6). According to the Law, if a university fails to follow the process, gives false declarations in its reports, or commits bribery, the CNEA shall report it to the National Assembly, leading to the possible closure of a private university or the sanctioning of a public university. Accreditation is compulsory, and in the case of failure, it carries negative consequences. Indeed, both Laws 582 and 704 contain aspects which reveal that the accreditation process will not strengthen university autonomy nor curtail the proliferation of "garage universities." For example, the President, Vice President, and five members of the CNEA are elected by the National Assembly. This suggests an obvious control of politics in higher education accreditation processes.

Instead of being a regulator for quality in higher education, the CNEA was conceived as a political enabler and regulator for the business of higher education in Nicaragua. While its processes can burden established, formal universities, they grant the seal of approval that will keep the existing "garage universities" in business. Unsurprisingly, the law was promoted mainly by a representative in the National Assembly who owns a university. From the start, the CNEA's focus seemed precisely to be the legitimation of these "garage universities." Its first President said they only need to invest in infrastructure and teacher training in order to gain accreditation (Castillo Bermúdez, 2015). He claimed to dislike the term "garage universities" because "many universities that own big buildings and enjoy a certain prestige started out in houses, with very few staff and students" (Jarquín, 2013). He stated that, contrary to what happened in El Salvador when they created the accreditation system, in Nicaragua, no university should fear being forced to close (Jarquín, 2013). However, he added that it would be difficult for new universities to be created, as they would have to meet the CNEA's standards without the benefit of time. Clearly, the CNEA pretends to regulate higher education as a market, with an emphasis in helping the existing "garage universities" to become established. Simultaneously, university autonomy is weakened because this quality assurance regime grants the National Assembly direct control over universities. This explains why the CNEA became complicit in the government's strategy of pretending normalcy in the country and controlling dissidence in universities.

Conclusion: The Asphyxiation of University Autonomy

As the crisis continued to unfold, public universities expelled activist students and fired critical professors. At the UNAN (the country's largest public university), in a performance of loyalty to Ortega, faculty danced "El comandante se queda"—popularly misspelled "El komandante zequeda"—[The Commander Stays] in a general assembly, imitating the police and paramilitaries' viral celebration of the massacres. It dawned on us that the regime would continue imprisoning, torturing, and killing with impunity for as long as it wanted to. With this realization, trust became an issue in our small academic community. People whispered about whose husband or wife worked for the government, whose sister was a Minister, they talked about certain law professors and their direct ties with the regime, they talked about the janitor who had been seen as a paramilitary holding an AK-47 in a killing mission, they pointed at security guards who allegedly worked for the FSLN in the 1980s. A lecturer said her Communications students wrote their essays about the rebellion but didn't present them in class, fearing a classmate could denounce them. A Masters-level student decided to stop attending classes when a classmate was appointed to a very important position in the government. She feared her classmate would have her imprisoned or killed. When a lecturer appeared in the news praising the police who had killed and tortured so many students, nobody wanted her teaching in the university anymore, but nobody wanted to tell her. A group of students accused the security guards of allowing a "government spy" into one of their demonstrations and then "protecting" him by escorting him out of the campus when he was being attacked by them. In a demonstration, they accused the upper administration of turning students in to the police. A lecturer who avoided discussing the conflict in class complained that she was cornered by her students and asked to "define herself." Teaching got harder and harder; and yet, for accreditation processes, it was business as usual.

This chapter explored the dangerous intersection where academic capitalism and state repression collide: the spot where universities turn professors into managed personnel and students into clients. As managed personnel, professors learn to play according to the rules of a system, be it quality assurance or party politics, altogether avoiding important discussions about the university's mission in our society. As clients in a corporatized university, the complexity of the students' realities becomes invisible to the system that feeds decision-making processes. As clients of an authoritative and populist regime, public university students are absorbed into networks of clientelism devised to erode the autonomy of a university.

Current debates should delve into how to avoid universities' submission to "quality" as is defined in a system of academic capitalism, framed in the "talk of quality," or to the clientelist strategies of a tyrannical government that poses as a benefactor of the poor. A capacity to analyze and debate is not cultivated in either of these systems. By producing satisfied students or vassals of a ruling party, universities lose their capacity to educate proactive and critical citizens, which is the mission of the Universidad Centroamericana in Nicaragua. In the case of professors, their subjectification into "quality teachers" ignores the complex realities of teaching. Trust in their capacities is replaced with a technology of quality assessment that doesn't help them find ways to encourage academic spirit in a polarized, violent, repressive, and frightening context. The use of violence to suppress the voices of university students, professors, and staff is on the rise at a global level (Global Coalition to Protect Education from Attack, 2018). The debate about universities should be aimed at detecting all kinds of threats to academic freedom before it is too late.

In Nicaragua, from the beginning of their government in 2007, the Ortega-Murillo regime deployed a strategy against universities focused on eroding their autonomy. By 2018, it reached a point where even university presidents facilitated the repression on their students.[32] The UCA preserved its autonomy because the government's networks of clientelism couldn't effectively penetrate the institution. Political "brokers" in the university do not have power over the scholarship and tenure system. Also, the UCA belongs to a global network of universities entrusted to the Society of Jesus, commonly referred to as the Jesuits, which provides a moral compass and the possibility of global solidarity. Nevertheless, internal pressures and external aggressions generate important challenges to academic quality.

University autonomy is still a utopia in Central America, perhaps as much as it was in the 1950s. This certainly is a challenge all around the world as academic freedom suffers pressures stemming from different sources.[33] In Central America, the role of financial institutions and multilaterals should be analyzed to see how they also affect university autonomy and how "one size fits all" policies can have ruinous effects. The framework that places universities as competing corporations is promoted by the WTO, the OECD, UNESCO, the EU, the World Bank, the IADB, and other organizations that provide funding[34] and technical assistance to develop circuits of knowledge such as those described in the theory of academic capitalism (Slaughter & Leslie, 1997; Slaughter & Rhoades, 2004). They support programs and policies that promote competition and the commercialization of knowledge instead of its democratization. These organizations are perceived as experts in education; they define what is promoted in networks that support higher education systems. The World Bank presents itself as an authority on the subject even though its expertise is based on its own previous publications and pilot projects (Klees, Samoff & Stromquist, 2012). Education is described by the Bank as a service in need of technical management and governance. It proposes solutions that will fit all countries and promotes the higher education system's adequacy for the labor market and the global economy.

A discussion on university autonomy needs to be promoted with the purpose so clearly stated by Ellacuría, S.J.: "to prevent the university from becoming a servant to the powers that configure Latin American society" (1999, p. 33, my translation). When the discussion focuses on funding and is framed by the "talk of quality," it fails to strengthen university autonomy and academic freedom, it fails to produce a realistic and consciously critical observation of academics through a grounded and honest view, such as that offered by Watermeyer (2019), and it falls short of a much-needed reflection on what kind of university autonomy our society needs, such as the notion of "connected autonomy," which describes a university in constant dialogue with external actors in order to better serve society (Arocena, Göransson & Sutz, 2018, pp. 188–193).

Quality assessment has become one of the government's ways of exercising political control over universities with their consent and collaboration. By promoting the discourses that produce disciplined teachers and students, and by using "the 6%" to create networks of clientelism, the last vestiges of university autonomy have been dismantled. The deadly synergy of neoliberal reforms and the repression of the Ortega-Murillo regime is strangling the country, but it is also depriving universities of autonomy and academic freedom. In Nicaragua, university autonomy has been hijacked by a repressive regime that implements internationally promoted strategies to corporatize universities and subjugate them to an antidemocratic political order.

Notes

1 The practice of expelling students and erasing or denying them official academic records has been documented by journalists and civil society: Munguía (2020), Romero and Villavicencio (n.d.), Acción Universitaria (2021).
2 Journalists and mainstream news sources now refer to the "Ortega-Murillo regime" due to the amount of power Rosario Murillo, vice president and wife of Daniel Ortega, wields. See Kai Thaler's 2020 article about Nicaragua in *Foreign Policy*: https://foreignpolicy.com/2020/04/17/ortega-virus-murillo-nicaragua-is-stumbling-into-coronavirus-disaster/.
3 Consejo Superior Universitario Centroamericano.
4 Universidad Nacional Autónoma de Nicaragua, Managua.
5 In 1998, the IAU issued the policy statement "Academic Freedom, University Autonomy and Social Responsibility," which included as point number 1:

> The principle of Institutional Autonomy can be defined as the necessary degree of independence from external interference that the University requires in respect of its internal organization and governance, the internal distribution of financial resources and the generation of income from private sources, the recruitment of its staff, the setting of the conditions of study and, finally, the freedom to conduct teaching and research.
>
> *(1998, p. 1)*

6 Confederación Universitaria Centroamericana.
7 Reforma de Córdoba.
8 Declaración de Principios sobre los fines y funciones de la Universidad contemporánea y en especial de las Universidades de Centroamérica.
9 Ley Orgánica de la Universidad Nacional.
10 While Nicaragua and El Salvador had annual appropriations subjected to variations, Guatemala and Honduras also had 2% of the national budget as well as tax exemptions, while Costa Rica had 10% of the annual budget of the Ministry of Public Education (Waggoner, Wagonner & Wolfe, 1964, p. 453).
11 Ingresos ordinarios.
12 Ingresos ordinarios y extraordinarios.
13 Although the UCA is a private university, it became part of the CNU because during the 1980s the Sandinista government's Consejo Nacional de la Educación Superior (CNES) decided that the School of Engineering should be removed from the UCA to create a new public university (UNI). This reduced student enrollment to a great financial cost for the UCA, which requested a subsidy that was granted, along with

the relocation of the Schools of Psychology, Sociology and Journalism from the UNAN to the UCA. Through ups and downs the financial assistance from the state remained part of the university's budget (Alvarado Martínez, 2010, pp. 203–209), and when Law 89 was passed, the UCA was included as a member of the CNU along with other private institutions.

14 In addition, CNU universities have special tax exemptions.
15 Universidad Abierta en Línea de Nicaragua.
16 For example, critical discussions about the interoceanic canal project were strictly prohibited in all universities.
17 The repression was similar to the Tlatelolco massacre occurred in México in 1968 under Díaz Ordaz's government. Likewise, during this period the budget for higher education had increased (Levy, 1979, p. 143).
18 Ley Orgánica de la Universidad de El Salvador.
19 These managerial practices came to Central America when the EU's Bologna Process travelled to the Global South with the EU's support of its internationalization agenda. The ALFA Tuning Latin America Project (2003) was an extension of the original Tuning Project (2001), which shaped the European Higher Education Area (Tuning Latin America Project, 2014). It promoted Europe as central in the global scene of higher education and the knowledge society (Beneitone et al., 2007). The EU also supported the ALCUE NET Project (2013–2017), aimed at similar objectives through research collaborations, and the ALFA Program, through which European universities taught Latin-American counterparts how to adopt practices, concepts, and frameworks to attain quality.
20 The theory of academic capitalism describes how universities develop links to the economy through a series of mechanisms that involve internal as much as external initiatives:

> New circuits of knowledge that link state agencies, corporations and universities in entrepreneurial research endeavors are developed. New funding streams support these knowledge constellations and interstitial organizations emerge to facilitate the new knowledge circuits. Intermediating networks between public, non-profit and private sectors are initiated by actors from the various sectors to stabilize the new circuits of knowledge and organizations that facilitate entrepreneurial activity on the part of universities. At the same time, universities build extended managerial capacity that enables them to function as economic actors. Narratives, discourses and social technologies that justify and normalize these changes are developed, elaborated and articulated by all the players, and deployed via social technologies.
>
> *(Slaughter & Cantwell, 2012, pp. 587–588)*

21 In Nicaragua, through several projects the World Bank promoted school decentralization in the 1990s, with the result of increased inequalities, corruption and barriers for the poor (Delgado Rocha, 2022). For a list of projects see: https://projects.bancomundial.org/es/projects-operations/projects-summary?lang=es&searchTerm=&countrycode_exact=NI.
22 General Agreement for Trade Services.
23 The main subjects of the study were undergraduate students at Marburg and UCA. The strategy for data collection included observation during lectures, seminars, and teacher evaluation, individual semi-structured interviews and focus groups with undergraduate students at both universities, and a mix of semi-structured and unstructured interviews with teachers and quality experts at both universities. The interview with students had 25 open-ended questions about the following issues: quality in a university; quality in a course; quality teacher; bad teachers and what to do about them; student satisfaction (who or what does it depend on/ is it a synonym of quality?); causes of failure (who/what to blame); university rankings and competition between

universities; teacher evaluation; are students clients?; evaluation/accreditation; grade inflation and lowering standards. Three case-vignettes were written for the purpose of generating questions and discussion in the focus groups. In Marburg 29 students (16 females and 13 males) were interviewed in sessions that lasted between 30 minutes and two hours, most of them lasting one hour. Eight students were interviewed using the focus group method. In Nicaragua 27 students (11 males and 16 females) were interviewed in sessions that lasted between one and two hours. Nineteen students were interviewed using the focus group method.

24 Students focus more on aspects of their teachers' personality, relationship and emotional response to them, and less on their teaching techniques, clarity or knowledge. Different elements of the teacher's personality and practices gain or lose relevance depending on students' notions about knowledge. The study also showed evidence of "college management," the students' strategies to adapt the university to their choices (Nathan, 2005).

25 Students interviewed considered the idea of them being clients as essentially incoherent (Marburg) or uncomfortable and insulting (UCA).

26 Agencia Centroamericana de Acreditación de Posgrado.

27 Consejo Centroamericano de Acreditación de la Educación Superior.

28 Ley General de Educación (2006).

29 Ley Creadora del Sistema Nacional para el Aseguramiento de la Calidad de la Educación y Reguladora del Consejo Nacional de Evaluación y Acreditación (2011).

30 Ley de Autonomía de las Instituciones de Educación Superior (1990).

31 According to the CNEA there are 55 universities in Nicaragua, 10 members of the CNU (which receive public funds and they call "public"), and 45 private (http://www.cnea.edu.ni/miembros). On the other hand, for the CNU there are 60 universities in the country, 10 members of the CNU and 50 private universities they call "legally established" (http://www.cnu.edu.ni/universidades-miembros-del-cnu/universidades-legalmente-establecidas/). In recent meetings for the CNEA accreditation process it was stated that there are now 63 universities in the country.

32 In sharp contrast, when in July 23, 1959 there was a massacre of students in León, President Fiallos Gil publicly denounced Somoza's National Guard when he travelled days later to Buenos Aires to participate in the General Assembly of the *Unión de Universidades de América Latina* (UDUAL).

33 In the United States, for example, trustee involvement in elite universities has been explored by Barringer et al. (2020) to show how this involves risks for academic freedom and a shift in the balance of power. In Britain, pressures from University Grants Committees and local planning authorities have been analyzed as a threat to academic freedom (Moody & Eustace, 2012, pp. 46–47).

34 Training on university management and the commercialization of research in Latin America and Europe is supported by UNESCO through the Columbus association. In its website it is possible to obtain numerous examples on this perspective on universities and research. The production of experts on this subject is done through special courses for member universities, targeting administrators (http://www.columbus-web.org/en/).

References

Acción Universitaria. et al. (2021). *Libro Blanco: Las Evidencias de un Estado Totalitario: Violaciones de los Derechos Humanos en Universidades Públicas de Nicaragua. Documentación de Casos de la UNAN Managua, UNAN León, Universidad Nacional Agraria (UNA) y Universidad Nacional de Ingeniería (UNI)*. Managua: Author.

Alvarado Martínez, E. (2010). *La UCA: Una Historia a través de la Historia*. Managua: Universidad Centroamericana.

Arocena, R., Göransson, B. & Sutz, J. (2018). *Developmental Universities in Inclusive Innovation Systems: Alternatives for Knowledge Democratization in the Global South*. Cham, Switzerland: Palgrave Macmillan.
Asamblea Nacional. (1990). Ley No. 89: Ley de Autonomía de las Instituciones de Educación Superior. Managua: Asamblea Nacional. *La Gaceta, Diario Oficial*, 20 de abril de 1990, (77).
Asamblea Nacional. (2011). Ley No. 704: *Ley Creadora del Sistema Nacional para el Aseguramiento de la Calidad de la Educación y Reguladora del Consejo Nacional de Evaluación y Acreditación*. Managua: Asamblea Nacional.
Baltodano Marcenaro, R.H. (2007). *Organizaciones Juveniles de las Paralelas Históricas en Nicaragua 1950–1969*. Masters Dissertation. Managua: UNAN-Managua.
Barringer, S.N., Taylor, B.J., Riffe, K.A. & Slaughter, S. (2020). How University Leaders Shape Boundaries and Behaviors: An Empirical Examination of Trustee Involvement at Elite US Research Universities. *Higher Education Policy*. DOI:10.1057/s41307-020-00193-y.
Bauman, Z. (2009). Education in the Liquid Modern Setting. *Power and Education*, 1(2), 157–166.
Bellanger, W. (2016). *Teaching to Clients: Quality Assurance in Higher Education and the Construction of the Invisible Student at Philipps-Universität Marburg and Universidad Centroamericana in Managua*. Marburg: Philipps-Universität Marburg. Doctoral Dissertation.
Beneitone, P., Esquenti, C., González, J., Maleta, M., Siufi, G. & Wagenaar, R. (eds.). (2007). *Tuning America Latina: Reflections on and Outlook for Higher Education in Latin America*. Informe Final. Proyecto Tuning America Latina. Deusto and Groningen: University of Deusto, University of Groningen.
Bow, J.C. (2019). Alejandra Centeno: Universidades Viven supropia "dictadura". *Confidencial*. Available at: https://confidencial.com.ni/alejandra-centeno-universidades-viven-su-propia-dictadura/
Brunner, J.J. (1990). *Educación Superior en América Latina, Cambios y Desafíos*. Chile: Editorial Fondo de Cultura Económica.
Castillo Bermúdez, J. (2015). Sin Plata para Nuevos Planes. *La Prensa*. Retrieved on July 18, 2015, from http://www.laprensa.com.ni/2015/07/18/nacionales/1868688-sin-plata-para-nuevos-planes
CNU. (2018). Rendición Social de Cuentas 2018. *Consejo Nacional de Universidades*. Available at: http://www.cnu.edu.ni/Rendiciones/Rendicion-2018/RSC2018.pdf
Cooper, P. (2004). The Gift of Education: An Anthropological Perspective on the Commoditization of Learning. *Anthropology Today*, 20 (6), 5–9.
Delgado Rocha, B.A. (2022). Autonomía Escolar: Participación, Descentralización y Calidad Educativa. In Universidad Rafael Landívar, Universidad Pedagógica Nacional Francisco Morazán, UCA & UCA. *Calidad de la Educación en Centroamérica: Dinámicas y Tensiones entre el Modelo de Educación y el Modelo de Desarrollo*. (pp. 147–188). San Salvador: Publicaciones Académicas UCA.
Ellacuría, I. (1999). *Escritos Universitarios*. San Salvador: UCA Editores.
Foucault, M. (1988). Technologies of the Self. In L.H. Martin, H. Gutman & P.H. Hutton (eds.). *Technologies of the Self: A Seminar with Michel Foucault*. (pp. 16–49). Amherst & London: The University of Massachusetts Press & Tavistock Publications.
Gibbons, M. (1985). The Changing Role of the Academic Research System. In M. Gibbons & B. Wittrock (eds.). *Science as a Commodity: Threats to the Open Community of Scholars*. (pp. 2–20). Essex: Longman Group Limited.

Giroux, H.A. (2007). *The University in Chains: Confronting the Military-Industrial-Academic Complex*. New York: Paradigm Publishers.

Giroux, H. (2009). Beyond the Corporate Takeover of Higher Education: Rethinking Educational Theory, Pedagogy, and Policy. In M. Simons, M. Olssen & M.A. Peters (eds.). *Re-Reading Education Policies: A Handbook Studying the Policy Agenda of the 21st Century*. (pp. 458–477). Rotterdam, Boston and Taipei: Sense Publishers.

Global Coalition to Protect Education from Attack-GCPEA. (2018). *Education under Attack: 2018*. Education Above All; Columbia University, Mailman School of Public Health. Available at: http://www.protectingeducation.org/sites/default/files/documents/eua_2018_full.pdf

Gusterson, H. (2017). Homework: Toward a Critical Ethnography of the University. AES Presidential Address, 2017. *American Ethnologist, 44* (3), 435–450. DOI:10.1111/amet.12520.

International Association of Universities – IAU. (1998). *IAU Policy Statement: Academic Freedom, University Autonomy and Social Responsibility*. Author.

Jarquín, L. (2013). Nicaragua Acreditará sus Universidades en Diez Años: 57 Instituciones a Primera Etapa del Proceso. *El Nuevo Diario*. Retrieved on March 13, 2013, from http://www.elnuevodiario.com.ni/nacionales/280377-nicaragua-acreditara-sus-universidades-diez-anos/

Klees, S.J., Samoff, J. & Stromquist, N.P. (eds.). (2012). *The World Bank and Education: Critiques and Alternatives*. Comparative and International Education: A Diversity of Voices, 14. Rotterdam, Boston, Taipei: Sense Publishers.

Levy, D. (1979). University Autonomy in Mexico: Implications for Regime Authoritarianism. *Latin American Research Review, 14* (3), 129–152.

Mairena, Y. (2019). UNEN es el brazo de una dictadura sangrienta. *Confidencial*. Available at: https://confidencial.com.ni/unen-es-el-brazo-de-una-dictadura-sangrienta/

Mauss, M. (1990). *The Gift: The Form and Reason for Exchange in Archaic Societies*. London and New York: Routledge.

Moody, G.C. & Eustace, R. (2012/1974). *Power and Authority in British Universities*. Oxon: Routledge Library Editions: Education.

Munguía, I. (2020). Autoridades Universitarias "los Desaparecieron" y les Prohíben Ingreso. *Confidencial*. Available at: https://www.confidencial.com.ni/nacion/autoridades-universitarias-los-desaparecieron-y-les-prohiben-ingreso/

Nathan, R. (2005). *My Freshman Year: What a Professor Learned by Becoming a Student*. Ithaca and London: Cornell University Press.

Power, M. (1997). *The Audit Society. Rituals of Verification*. New York: Oxford University Press.

Power, M. (2010). *Organized Uncertainty: Designing a World of Risk Management*. New York: Oxford University Press.

Rocha, J.L. (2019). *Autoconvocados y Conectados: Los Universitarios en la Revuelta de Abril en Nicaragua*. Managua and San Salvador: UCA Publicaciones & UCA Editores.

Romero, K.T. & Villavicencio, F. (n.d.). Los Universitarios Expulsados por la Dictadura de Daniel Ortega. *Revista Niú*. Available at: https://niu.com.ni/los-universitarios-expulsados-por-la-dictadura/

Salomon, J.J. (1985). Science as a Commodity—Policy Changes, Issues and Threats. In M. Gibbons & B. Wittrock (eds.). *Science as a Commodity: Threats to the Open Community of Scholars*. (pp. 78–98). Essex: Longman Group Limited.

Slaughter, S. & Cantwell, B. (2012). Transatlantic Moves to the Market: The United States and the European Union. *Higher Education, (63)*, 583–606.

Slaughter, S. & Leslie, L. (1997). *Academic Capitalism: Politics, Policies and the Entrepreneurial University*. Baltimore: The Johns Hopkins University Press.
Slaughter, S. & Rhoades, G. (2004). *Academic Capitalism and the New Economy: Markets, State, and Higher Education*. Baltimore and London: The Johns Hopkins University Press.
Stokes, S.C., Dunning, T., Nazareno, M. & Brusco, V. (2012). *Brokers, Voters, and Clientelism: The Puzzle of Distributive Politics*. Cambridge: Cambridge University Press. DOI:10.1017/CBO9781107324909.
Strathern, M. (2000). The Tyranny of Transparency. *British Educational Research Journal*, 26(3), 309–321.
Tuchman, G. (2009). *Wannabe U: Inside the Corporate University*. Chicago: The University of Chicago Press.
Tuning Latin America Project. (2014). Tuning: América Latina. Retrieved on August 10, 2014, from http://tuning.unideusto.org/tuningal/
Tünnermann Bernheim, C. (2008). La Calidad de la Educación Superior y su Acreditación: La Experiencia Centroamericana. *Avaliação: Revista da Avaliação da Educação Superior*, 13 (2), 313–336. DOI:10.1590/S1414-40772008000200005.
Tünnermann Bernheim, C. (2016). *Memorias de un Ciudadano*. Managua: Hispamer.
Waggoner, B., Wagonner, G.R. & Wolfe, G.B. (1964). Higher Education in Contemporary Central America. *Journal of Inter-American Studies*, 6(4), 445–461.
Walter, K. (2000). La educación en Centroamérica: Reflexiones en Torno a sus Problemas y su Potencial. CA 2020: Documento de Trabajo # 10. Available at: http://ca2020.fiu.edu/Themes/Knut_Walter/Walter.pdf
Watermeyer, R. (2019). *Competitive Accountability in Academic Life: The Struggle for Social Impact and Public Legitimacy*. Cheltenham and Northampton: Edward Elgar Publishing Limited. DOI:10.4337/9781788976138.

PART 2
Professors and Students under Fire

3
PROFESSORS AND THE ACCOMPANIMENT OF UNIVERSITY STUDENT STRUGGLES IN NICARAGUA

Karla Lara

The university can provide the best objective analyses of reality, it can facilitate the discovery and the implementation of practices for confronting the different problems of reality, it can prepare the analytical frameworks, and it can help to find and apply solutions.[1]

—*Ignacio Ellacuría (1999, p. 78)*

Introduction

"*Long live the students!*" *is the song of Violeta Parra, a Chilean folk singer, that pays tribute to the courage of students throughout Latin America, and it sounded loudly between April 10 and 18, 2018, outside the Universidad Centroamericana (UCA) in Managua. Every day we could see students from various universities waving blue and white flags as they shouted slogans against the government's disastrous mishandling of the fire raging in the Indio Maíz Biological Reserve in the south of the country. Their outrage at this neglect of "our common home"*[2] *added to the anger at the government's attempt to reduce the pensions of the elderly and to raise the age of retirement. In the classrooms, many of us professors were faced with the need to decide about students' requests for permission to leave class to exercise their right to protest, a right that is set forth in Article 30 of the Political Constitution of the Republic of Nicaragua.*[3] *The dilemma arose because in our classrooms there is a constant circulation of students from 7:00 AM to 8:45 PM. Given this situation, many of us—I dare say the majority—agreed to allow students to leave several minutes before the end of class sessions. The leaders of the mobilizations were even permitted to miss some classes, but never more than the 20% allowed by university rules.*[4]

The accompaniment that university professors have provided to the struggles of university students in Nicaragua has been a key element in supporting students in their academic formation and engagement of social issues. The three historical

DOI: 10.4324/9781003198925-6

moments I describe in this chapter respond to struggles in which university students confronted political power in Nicaragua. My goal is to explain how the work of accompaniment has been a key factor in helping students carry their struggles forward. To analyze and give context to each period, I have read and analyzed existing interviews of former student leaders and interviewed 16 student leaders who were or who still are important figures in each of the selected periods. I begin with the student struggle for university autonomy in 1958, and I continue with the struggle for the allocation of 6% of the General Revenue Budget to the universities, a process that began in 1972 and finally became law in 1990. I conclude with the uprising of April 2018, which arose out of the protests of students from various universities.

I have elaborated a definition of *holistic accompaniment* on the basis of elements that have been highlighted by student leaders in their struggles. These elements are related to what Central American universities can do for their respective countries, as described by Ignacio Ellacuría, S.J. in the opening quote of this chapter. As regards accompaniment at the university level, some authors contend that an educator should provide guidance not only in teaching a subject but also in proposing a mission for life. Accordingly, the definition of accompaniment that I want to recommend as a starting point is that of Riveros (2011), which is cited by Solís-Cortez (2015). In this conception, accompaniment is a human action that involves "going with someone, keeping company, being with someone, participating, sharing another's feeling."

> Accompaniment is thus defined as an ongoing action or intervention that consists of walking alongside someone to offer whatever we are, whatever we know, and whatever we possess, and in this way to facilitate the journey of the person being accompanied so that they reach their goal.
>
> (p. 75)

This definition of accompaniment comes close to the conception held by the student leaders and the professors whose interviews I analyzed. They considered that accompaniment needs to be understood not only in situations of relative normalcy but also in situations where both students and professors are engaged in a struggle that tests their formation to the limit. According to student leaders engaged in struggle, the most important elements of accompaniment are "paying attention to the reality experienced by young people, critical thinking, empathizing with the struggles that students are going through, providing orientation for thoughtful discussion, respecting the students' struggle space, having confidence in young people's ability to face their reality," and in some cases "providing guidance with socio-emotional issues."

In this chapter, I define holistic accompaniment in the processes of student struggle as the action of accompanying them in their mission to transform reality. Such accompaniment involves closely monitoring their learning processes so that they can use a particular subject for a specific purpose, but it should not lose sight of other elements such as paying attention to the reality that young people experience, empathizing with the various problems they go through in their struggles, and helping them with socio-emotional issues. Although not all subjects lend themselves equally to such accompaniment, every educator should be given a basic orientation about how to assist in these areas during student struggles. The purpose of holistic accompaniment, therefore, is to support students both to advance in their own formation and to engage in the student struggle in a focused, active, and attentive manner so that they place their knowledge and skills at the service of their society through conscientious practice of the subjects in which they are trained. This is the making of a pedagogy of accompaniment.

The vision of Ignacio Ellacuría, S.J. (1999) regarding the role of the university and its service to society helps us to understand why holistic accompaniment in the processes of student struggle is a key function of university teaching: the universities, in his view, are called to respond to the reality of the society in which they are immersed.

> It is obvious that the university is a social reality, and for that very reason it is conditioned by the structure of the reality that is society. Any attempt to understand the university as something outside society, as something immune to the solicitations and pressures of society, is an ideologized and ultimately counterproductive attempt to exist independently of what society is at a given moment.
>
> (p. 70)

It is in the processes of student struggle that the social function of the university is put to the test. Since the students are the ones who transmit that mission in their words and actions as citizens, the university must offer them accompaniment that can help them find coherence between what they learn in the classroom and what is required of them in the streets. By drawing on the perceptions of student leaders and the professors who accompany them, this chapter offers insights into the importance of providing holistic accompaniment for university students engaged in political struggles. It proposes that professors should view this activity as fundamental in a context of repression such as that being experienced today in Nicaragua, and it seeks to give greater visibility to this labor of accompaniment, which often goes unnoticed but is a vital aspect of the educator's task. This is what I'm calling a pedagogy of accompaniment. The chapter draws on the insights of those who have participated in three historical moments: first, the student struggle for university autonomy in the 1950s; second, the student struggle for 6% of the national budget in the 1990s; and third, the student struggle of the year 2018 against the mismanagement of the nation's natural resources and the violation of human rights by the government of Daniel Ortega and Rosario Murillo.

Holistic accompaniment and university autonomy

At the beginning of the 1950s, the Universidad Nacional de Nicaragua (UNN), located in the department of León, was the country's oldest university, the flagship of higher education in Nicaragua. It had a teaching staff made up of professionals who were skilled in diverse disciplines but who lacked specific training to be university professors. Moreover, as Dr. Carlos Tünnermann recalls, "the professors were appointed by the Ministry of Education and the university president, so there was no autonomy in the university."[5]

> Ours was a generation of students that arrived at the same time, and we became aware that this situation could not continue. The university had about 800 students, and it was the only one in the country. Somoza had closed the Universidad Central (in Managua) in 1946 and the Universidad de Granada in 1951 because he thought it was better to have only one university in León, corralled off in a province and not in the capital. Remember that the students of the Universidad Central in 1944 were the ones who had led the fight against the re-election of Somoza; they were the ones assaulted by the National Guard and had to take refuge in the Guatemalan embassy.
>
> *(C. Tünnermann, personal communication, October 8, 2019)*

In this context, the struggle for university autonomy signified a hope for change in the way the university was administered and how education was imparted. It meant a dramatic shift from having instructors who devoted little time to student formation to having full-time professional professors who dedicated themselves to the formation of young people. As president of the students' organization at the UNN, Joaquin Solís Piura[6] led the student struggle for university autonomy and witnessed the now historic student massacre of July 23, 1959.[7] Recalling the educational style of the university at that time, he says that the students truly appreciated the efforts the professors made to share their knowledge, but at the same time they wanted more.

> I have fond memories of all of them, but they were doctors, lawyers, and pharmacists who had their own offices. That was their main occupation; that was their central job. They used to give an hour or two of class as a sideline, and I think they also wanted to help us students, who were a little abandoned there. The professors arrived for their class and then walked home or to work. There was not a single full-time professor; not even the deans were full-time. It was rudimentary, as I say. I am very grateful to those professors because we learned something from them. They tried to study their subject, and they taught it as well as they could, but they were not men who dedicated themselves to teaching. As a result, there was very

little accompaniment. Besides, many of them were not even paid; we students were impressed by that, seeing a man who gives up his time to give us classes. Some were doctors who were attending to patients and earning their pesos, but they put time aside to come and give us classes. They made an effort to read the textbook at night, and even if they just repeated it to us, that was better than nothing. It would have been worse if we had had no one to bring us the lights of science.

(J. Solís Piura, personal communication, October 9, 2019)

Carlos Tünnermann and Joaquín Solís represent the generation that in the 1950s was closely linked to significant transformations in universities, the most notable of which was the transition to university autonomy. Both were student leaders and later university presidents. They recall that the teaching methods were changed, from instructors who came only to lecture on their subjects to professors who dedicated considerable time to listening to students and then advising and motivating them. This transformation was especially marked by the spirit of Mariano Fiallos Gil, who is remembered as a motivational professor and university president. Fiallos successfully advocated for university autonomy in Nicaragua during his term as president[8] of the Universidad Nacional de Nicaragua, and he changed its name, calling it the Universidad Nacional Autónoma de Nicaragua (UNAN), as it is still known today. For its motto, he adopted "To Freedom through the University," a phrase evocative of the liberating mission that Ellacuría proposed for the Jesuit universities of Central America. Ellacuría was convinced that "only the university's engagement with historical socio-political reality allows us to see that reality as it truly is" (1977, p. 52). Dr. Tünnermann recalls that when he was appointed secretary general of the UNAN, the first words Dr. Fiallos spoke to him were these:

> We have to start by dusting this university off. We have to open all the windows, let fresh air in, and let the university project itself onto the national stage. We have to study the nation's problems in order to speak out about them. There will be academic freedom, and we will allow all forms of sound thought, everything that is meant by university autonomy.
>
> *(C. Tünnermann, personal communication, October 8, 2019)*

In those early years of university autonomy in Nicaragua, academic freedom was experienced in all its splendor. Holistic accompaniment was evident, both in the classroom and in the student struggles against the Somoza dictatorship, an oppositional stance shared by many students at the time.

Vilma Núñez, who then was a student leader and is now an emblematic figure in the defense of human rights in Nicaragua, had Mariano Fiallos Gil as a teacher. She recalls that both as teacher and president, he promoted educational accompaniment in those difficult years.

> Mariano Fiallos Gil was not a president who kept to his desk. He was not an absentee president. He was a president to whom many of us students (I can't say all) felt very close. I hold very present the figure of Mariano Fiallos, who was not a university administrator but a mentor who, by his new style of direction and guidance, showed us what the university should be. In a practical way he encouraged us students to reflect on and commit ourselves to the university struggle, the struggle for university autonomy. Moreover, as a teacher he encouraged thoughtful discussions.
>
> *(V. Núñez, personal communication, October 4, 2019)*

Vilma Núñez also remembers that, when she was a student, her professors did not mix their political views with the matter they were teaching.

> I met professors who were Somocistas: they defended Somocismo and were even party militants. For example, I remember three persons quite fondly. Dr. Ernesto Barrera, besides being a member of the Nationalist Liberal Party, was a magistrate of the Court of Appeals of León, but as a teacher he was calm, genial, and very open. I do not recall any instance in which he discriminated or took a negative attitude toward the majority of us students, who were already tending one way (against the Somoza dictatorship). None of the professors was negatively disposed toward the students, nor do I recall that any of us students had negative attitudes toward the professors, which is something very different. I also had other professors who were Somocistas. In labor law we studied union organization, the right to strike, and everything about workers' rights. And that teacher was coming from Somocismo (the Liberal Party). He was a civil magistrate in the Court of Appeals of León, but he freely discussed the origin of the labor struggles, a topic that was already quite ideological. We studied the history of the labor movement, and there was never any bias on his part when he presented material in class.
>
> *(V. Núñez, personal communication, October 4, 2019)*

The writer Sergio Ramírez was another member of the generation that fomented the autonomy process. Like Vilma Núñez and Joaquín Solís, he lived through the massacre of July 23, 1959, carried out by the National Guard under orders from President Luis Somoza. He recalls that Mariano Fiallos Gil was an educator who constantly motivated his students to reflect thoughtfully on the national reality.

> One afternoon in June 1957, a tall, thin man with prominent cheekbones, dressed in white linen, appeared at the Casa de los Leones, where the law faculty was located at the time. He approached some students who were waiting in the corridor for their teacher, and he told them that he was the president of the university. He sat on the bench with them and asked them

about their classes, the quality of the teaching, and the adequacy of the building. Since the professor did not arrive (they almost never did, limiting themselves to being there only on the day of the final exam), he spoke to them at length about the concept of the university, the idea of autonomy, the role of the student, and a series of topics that always pointed toward the future.

(S. Ramírez. s/f. Mariano Fiallos. Biografía *[Chapter 1])*

Thanks to the struggle for university autonomy, the educators in those days enjoyed political independence and academic freedom in teaching, but these elements have been lost today in the public universities, which have been made instruments of the ruling party's political interests.[9]

With respect to the socio-emotional component of educational accompaniment in the 1950s, the massacre on July 23, 1959, was an event that clearly marked a before and an after in the teacher/student relationship. When the four students were murdered and the whole university campus in León was mourning them, much closer bonds developed between professors and students. Student leaders of the time recall with gratitude the direct support they received from their professors in the classroom. During the massacre, the professors also came to the assistance of the injured students, and they participated together in the memorial service. Their accompaniment continued during the struggles to win funding for the universities and to make university autonomy a constitutional mandate.

Professor Ricardo Baltodano of the Polytechnic University of Nicaragua (UPOLI), who was imprisoned by the Sandinista government in 2018, recalls that the professors of the 1970s were strongly supportive of the students' struggle and helped them to develop critical thinking so that they could make wise strategic decisions.

> The professors were always very open-minded. They knew we were actively involved, but they had a horizontal relationship with us. We explained things to them, and they understood perfectly and would reschedule classes for us. We would go to classes with other groups to make up what we missed. In fact, they introduced us to Marxism, which I later rejected, but at that moment it was for me something new and interesting; it opened my mind and made me ask questions. We understood it well. Marxism gave us instruments that allowed us to divide society in a very simplistic way, but that seemed great to us at that time.
>
> *(R. Baltodano, personal communication, October 8, 2019)*

When the Sandinista National Liberation Front (FSLN) was in power during the 1980s, university autonomy began to decline. A selective mechanism was used to appoint professors, and academic freedom was eliminated. In this context, it was nearly impossible to provide holistic accompaniment and to develop critical thinking about the real problems of our nation. Tünnerman states that the National Council of Higher Education (CNES) was created in the 1980s; its function was to approve study plans and even to intervene in the budgets and in the appointment of university presidents. This council was eventually transformed into the Ministry of Higher Education, which tried to follow the Cuban model.

> Autonomy was lost. The presidents were hand-picked by the government. They wanted to imitate the Cuban model, and they neither understood what autonomy was nor wanted anything like it. The truth is that the 80's sacrificed university autonomy, which was recovered only after they lost the elections. Autonomy was restored and defined by Law 89, which not only establishes autonomy but incorporates the 6% for ten universities: the state universities plus the private ones that serve the public interest. The 6% was very helpful for defending the universities' activities during the period when the nation's presidents were not very sympathetic to the universities, which continued to be dominated by Sandinistas.
> *(C. Tünnermann, personal communication, October 8, 2019)*

As university autonomy was restricted in the 1980s, there was little consideration given to the scholarship of Mariano Fiallos Gil or Ignacio Ellacuría. Since the students were not engaged in struggles in that decade, professors' work was limited to course instruction rather than holistic accompaniment.

A lost opportunity for university autonomy

University autonomy began to be recovered in 1990, with the electoral victory of Violeta Barrios de Chamorro of the National Opposition Union (UNO) and the defeat of the Sandinista National Liberation Front (FSLN). Both students and professors began to hold demonstrations again, their main objective being the assignment of a fair budget allocation, in accord with the Law of University Autonomy (Law 89) (Asamblea Nacional, 1990). This law dictates that the government's contribution to the universities must be no less than 6% of the ordinary (recurring) and extraordinary (special or one time) expenditures of the General Revenue Budget. During this period, the students were protesting against those who interpreted the law to include only the 6% of ordinary income; they were insisting the amount allocated to the universities should also include the 6% of the extraordinary income, as contemplated by the law. That struggle was led by a student organization and by professors' unions, all of them linked to the FSLN. Demanding the full allocation of the 6%, they coordinated several demonstrations against the government of Violeta Barrios de Chamorro. Some leaders of that period state that on several occasions they sat down with

Daniel Ortega and told him that their fight "should not go that way." Given the funding and support they were receiving from that party, however, it was very difficult for them to disengage from partisan conflicts.

Ricardo Baltodano recalls that classroom debates about fair budgetary allocation to the universities helped provoke the first mobilizations for the 6%, but he acknowledges that the professors' concerns about job security and economic stability also motivated them to support the struggle.

> Those great mobilizations were supported by the student body, as well as by a belligerent UNEN leadership and a belligerent institution, so that there was full identification between the students and the institutional leadership. The struggle for the 6% was organized with the student movement at its base, but it had the full support of the university administration. All the professors in supervisory positions were generally very supportive of the struggle because they understood the cause and agreed with it. Besides, they knew that the 6% was going to benefit them. Why? Because the union insisted that every year there should be a salary increase, and that increase not only gave the teacher more political and ideological power, but it improved their lot in concrete material terms. So naturally it suited us professors that they provide more money, because later we would have greater possibilities when negotiating with the university authorities.
>
> *(R. Baltodano, personal communication, October 8, 2019)*

Lludely Aburto, who was national vice president of the UNEN between 1990 and 1992 and today is a prominent defender of the rights of women and local populations, recalls that the professors were a key force in the process of struggle, not only because they allowed the 6% allocation to be debated openly and critically in the classrooms, but also because they fully agreed with the students that this allocation would allow many young people from the interior of the country to have access to university studies. He also recalls that, before sitting at the negotiating table, the students were advised by their professors that "there were professors who were being imprisoned and beaten by the police in the streets."[10] For his part, Carlos Tünnermann confirms that the allocation of the 6% was a direct result of this struggle led by students and supported by professors.

> The professors also went to the marches, fighting for the 6%. One student was even killed at the doors of the Central Bank, Roberto González. An auditorium (at the UNAN-Managua) now bears his name. In the end, the correct interpretation was given to the law, which stipulates "6% of the ordinary and extraordinary resources of the government."
>
> *(C. Tünnermann, personal communication, October 8, 2019)*

Thus, in the 1990s, both students and professors returned to the streets and won the 6% for the universities, but at the end of that decade, the lack of autonomy again became a problem. Once more, the government and political parties directly intervened in the hiring of professors and in defining what was to be taught.

The early 1990s witnessed some recovery of university autonomy. The professors were fostering critical thinking, and they tried to maintain it, but later in the decade the limitations on autonomy became more evident. Already in the early 1990s, the FSLN had control of the public universities through the unions of professors and administrative workers; the discussion of issues to be negotiated in those sectors was therefore limited. In the academic sphere, the Sandinista influence became more apparent when the 1996 elections were won by the Liberal Constitutional Party (PLC), which later began to cede quotas of power to the FSLN. Vilma Núñez was one of the professors who suffered when the public universities were again made dependent on partisan politics. By the end of the 1990s, just as had happened in the 1980s, the public universities were subjected to the control of the FSLN.

> On July 23 every year in León, there used to be an exchange of books with flowers when a new university president entered office. In 1998, when the case of Zoilamérica was made public[11] and I assumed her defense, they did not invite me to the ceremony and didn't do so ever again, even though they had always invited me before. So that was when the partisan influence began to be evident. My husband is a dentist; he taught in the dental school for 37 years, but he retired without being recognized for his 37 years of work. They told him they had no money to pay him. When my husband filed a suit for his retirement benefits, his claim was denied by the labor judge, who was also a university professor. So we ended up badly off.
> *(V. Núñez, personal communication, October 4, 2019)*

Thus, by the end of the decade, the public universities saw an increase in the number of professors who were hired or fired depending on their relation to the FSLN. This development became progressively more pronounced, and when the FSLN returned to power in 2007, it became the standard way of proceeding. It is important to stress that this issue of hiring did not provoke much debate in the universities until after 2010; it was only then that the media began to publish denunciations of the prejudicial manner in which professors were hired in both basic and higher education.

Holistic accompaniment vs. political indoctrination

From mid-2018 through 2019, there was a significant increase in the number of professors who were expelled from public universities and then applied to teach at the UCA in the Bachelors of Arts (B.A.) in Communications. I had the opportunity to interview three such candidates, who told me how traumatic it was to be dismissed from the public universities simply for sympathizing with the struggle of their students. One teacher from the UNAN-Managua told me that the university staff were forced to carry out nocturnal surveillance at the university to prevent students from "taking over the campus." Listening to their experiences made me reflect on the evident decline in university autonomy in the classrooms, but I also felt deep admiration for these colleagues who wanted to continue in the teaching field, even though their fidelity to this mission had left them unemployed.[12]

As can be gathered from the memories of the protagonists of the student struggles, both university autonomy in general and academic freedom and thought in particular have been seriously limited in Nicaragua; even the materials to be imparted must conform to the expectations of a political party. That is why holistic accompaniment and a formation in values are extremely important in the private universities that still preserve a degree of university autonomy. Universities such as the UCA and the Universidad Católica del Trópico Seco (UCATSE) have stood out for the resistance shown by their professors and students in favor of freedom of thought and expression, basic rights that have gradually been lost in the public universities. A focus on values in education continues to be very necessary today for social transformation. The accompaniment that professors provide in a context of repression and lack of freedom, such as we now experience, demands an orientation that goes beyond learning a discipline. Our teaching must be focused on training men and women to face the nation's problems from the perspective of their various professional fields. In this section, I will highlight holistic accompaniment as it relates to the teaching of values and how it enacts a pedagogy of accompaniment. For that purpose, I will use the concept of values proposed by Orozco (1988) and cited by Tünnermann (2012), and considering that, I will analyze the relationship between students and professors in the context of the protests of April 2018:

> We can consider values as those beliefs, attitudes, and goals by which we direct our lives, having freely chosen them from among several alternatives after careful reflection and having incorporated them into our actual behavior. This concept of value means accepting that the exercise of freedom and the rational ability to guide one's personal life in society are traits common to all human beings. It also requires mutual willingness to engage in dialogue, to ask questions of others, and to understand them. Thus, it requires an attitude of accepting that others have exactly the same right as I do to express their ideas and be understood.
>
> *(p. 150)*

This ability to analyze reality critically and to leave students free to engage in their own learning processes is challenged and discouraged under authoritarian regimes, which do not allow citizens to express their ideas freely, especially if they contradict the regimes' effort to dominate people.

On the basis of my experience as a professor and the analysis of interviews I've read and conducted with student leaders from various majors at our university, I conclude that the current generation needs a great deal of accompaniment that stresses formation in values, as well as spaces that allow them time for reflection on the reality of the country, reflection that is essential for achieving the liberating mission that the university is called to fulfill. The role of professors as mediators in the students' learning processes and their efforts to develop critical thinking through training in various disciplines have been determining factors in the accompaniment they have provided the students during their recent struggles.

Take the feminist student leader Madelaine Caracas who believes that the UCA has always been a space "where you can speak freely and where they give you space to express yourself" and freely engage in student organization. Moreover, she stresses that her professors helped her develop her leadership ability because they believed in her and in what she could contribute to the discussions of various subjects.

> I had many opportunities to express myself and feel confident at the UCA. My professors always believed that I was someone who had something to say. I feel that all my professors provided encouragement before, during, and after the protests. ... I appreciate the idea of the university that exists at the UCA, which takes seriously its responsibility to provide a space for dialogue, a space for criticism, and a space for learning.
> *(M. Caracas, personal communication, November 11, 2020)*

Caracas stresses also that the UCA was the only university where the administration and professors closely accompanied the students during that process of struggle. Such accompaniment was rarely provided to the students of other universities who organized in various student movements. Similarly, Lesther Alemán, a communications student at the UCA and leader of the Nicaraguan University Alliance (AUN), comments that both classroom discussions and the professors' views on various issues helped to awaken in students genuine concern about their generation's commitment to Nicaraguan society. The university represented the possibility of thinking about a concrete transformation of reality.

> Since I was coming from a public school, the university was for me a dose of reality, a bath of reality that impelled me to become a citizen committed to justice, truth, and the common good. The university helps me understand that I am being manipulated; it allows me to gain another perspective on my reality. The professors influenced me, and discussions of reality with the different professors stimulated ideas in me and made it possible for me to question the system, not as an anarchist, but within the legal framework.
> *(L. Alemán, personal communication, November 10, 2020)*

Lesther recalls that a particular teacher prompted him to ask questions about reality and about his future profession by insisting that "journalism is a vocation of risk because it gets close to the truth and whoever criticizes power cannot be a friend of power."

Such freedom, however, is not something that is experienced in the public universities, where professors must now keep a low profile in order not to be fired. A student leader from the UNAN-Managua, who requested anonymity for fear of reprisals, has witnessed firsthand the ethical struggles of the professors at the public universities.

> We had a teacher who taught us all the basic subjects of my field and who, out of loyalty to the students whom he trained and who were later expelled, resigned from the university. He wrote me an email and said he was very proud of what we are doing today. I have another teacher who tried to help me recover my grades; he told me that he could not support things that were indefensible and that he understood us perfectly. Other professors supported us with [cell phone] minutes or moral support, but not in a visible way.
> *(Anonymous, personal communication, November 14, 2019)*

According to this student leader, most of the professors in the public universities have a marked leaning toward the governing party; he stated that there are very few professors who are supportive of the actions of the students who led the student struggle at his university.

Repression of the students has been so severe that, of the six students I interviewed from the UNAN-Managua, only two are still enrolled. The other four said that their records were deleted from the system so that they could neither continue in their academic programs nor obtain the documents they needed to enroll in another university. As a result, they were forced to start from square one, enrolling in a new major at another school. This is not new. Ricardo Baltodano recalls that political indoctrination and self-censorship intensified at the universities after the FSLN government came to power in 2007.

> The margin of autonomy was completely lost with the rise to power of the FSLN in 2007. From 2007 on, they began to enter with their claws bared, impeding and blocking and condemning all actions of freedom of thought. What is happening to you in this university is happening at the UNAN-León, and you are seeing it also in the newspapers. You try to stay informed, but you know you must censor yourself. Self-censorship is at work, I think, even in the UCA, but I believe that at the UCA there are still certain freedoms. That is how we see it from outside. They dared to bring in some philosophers that the regime did not like, and even they faced restrictions on expressing their ideas. In other words, freedom of

> thought and academic freedom have been limited for the sake of receiving the 6%, even in the best of cases. In the worst cases, there are sanctions and harassment, because already there are people who fear persecution.
> *(R. Baltodano, personal communication, October 8, 2019)*

Baltodano believes that fear of repression continues to be the principal barrier preventing professors from openly engaging in educational processes where academic freedom is fully exercised.

> My time in prison was a form of terrorism. The [student] leaders remain outside the UPOLI, all of them; none of them could return. Even though they were not expelled, fear prevents them from returning. So now you have students who are somewhat passive, but who have not been tamed. At the present juncture, what is needed is not everybody, but just four valiant souls so that the others can follow them. But it is those valiant ones who have been prevented from returning.
> *(R. Baltodano, personal communication, October 8, 2019)*

The professors' commitment to achieving structural changes that will allow universities to fulfill their political mission as institutions at the service of society (and more specifically, of the oppressed majorities) has at first glance been counterproductive. Instead of reflecting academic freedom, it has brought job insecurity and physical danger for the professors themselves, and it has harmed university autonomy. State repression is being felt by professors who work in private as well as public universities. The university's mission, of course, is carried out and becomes tangible through the work of the professors, who must have a minimum of autonomy in order to do their work and so make that mission a reality.

Holistic accompaniment of student leaders and of any university students engaged in the struggles is especially needed as a response to the problem of political indoctrination and clientelism that permeates public universities in Nicaragua, where the teaching is based not on analysis of reality but on the vision and interests of a political party. Faced with such a situation, professors must do their best to bolster the hope, enthusiasm, knowledge, and values of university students as they carve a path for a pedagogy of accompaniment. Through their various disciplines the professors can contribute to genuine solutions to the problems that afflict Nicaraguan youth. The students, for their part, must develop their capacity for future-oriented critical analysis and so help to rescue university autonomy and promote respect for human rights in a country where defending them has become a crime.

Conclusion

Holistic accompaniment has become an unattainable dream, especially today in the public universities of Nicaragua. It is almost unthinkable that a research topic or a creative project will be approved in those universities if it is mainly concerned with the current sociopolitical reality of the country. The situation of many colleagues in public universities with whom I have been able to speak with is quite desperate. I know firsthand cases of students and professors who have not been able to do academic work that relates to the April 2018 protests or the current Covid-19 pandemic. In the public universities, it is impossible to research public issues that contradict the discourse of Nicaragua's self-styled "good governance." Classes of investigative journalism have been eliminated from many programs of study because investigating can quickly become a crime in this country, especially if it contradicts the discourse of the public administration. All these factors condition what can or cannot be taught in the classroom. If such conditions exist, we cannot speak of academic freedom, and even less can we speak of accompanying the students and trying to change the reality they experience in their families, their communities, and the country in general. On the other hand, universities such as the UCA, where it is still possible to carry out research and produce studies on the national reality, are under siege by the National Police. For the reasons mentioned earlier, even though the professors make an effort to link their students with the national reality, they cannot do so beyond the gates of the university. Whenever there have been human rights campaigns or photographic exhibitions, I have noticed an increase in the number of police on patrol outside the spaces where these activities were held. That is why it has become an ever-greater challenge for the professors to do their work freely and independently.

The interviews I analyzed and conducted for this chapter explain how educational accompaniment of student struggles has functioned during three periods of our recent history. According to the student leaders in those periods, such accompaniment was fundamental in helping university students to deal with the problems they faced in their struggles; without it, they would have found it much more difficult to realize their objectives. The professors have sought to accompany their students in various ways, such as by close monitoring of the learning processes, attentive listening to the reality the students are experiencing, empathy for the various problems they encounter in the struggle, and concern for their socio-emotional state. Such work is seldom visible, but it provides support that the students remember and appreciate as important for their holistic formation. Consequently, in order to fulfill the university's liberating mission in society, great dedication must always be shown for this vital function of providing integral accompaniment, for without it student leaders will have far fewer possibilities of carrying out their mission of transforming reality.

Professors are needed and will continue to be needed who can speak openly and honestly in the classroom about the issues that are most critical for society and about the contribution that the different disciplines can make to restoring the rights of all Nicaraguan citizens. It is not enough to teach a discipline if it does not make students better members of society. Academic freedom and freedom of thought are necessary for classroom discussions that will empower students to contribute to and transform society. In the universities, we have thousands of young people who want to use their studies to contribute to the positive transformation of the country, but for that to happen, the professors in the public and private universities must be allowed to discuss social problems. They should not be denied the possibility of doing research and producing studies on certain topics that affect the whole population, and they should not become victims of verbal, physical, or psychological aggression if they do so. At the present time, society has become increasingly polarized, and the lack of analysis of reality in the universities will have direct consequences for future decision-making about the kind of society Nicaragua needs to be.

The universities must continue to fight to be spaces where professors can accompany their students in an integral manner. Such accompaniment is needed now and will always be needed so that young people can discover the mission that our national reality demands of them and then commit themselves to it. Amid adversity, we must continue to fight for a university where reality can be discussed honestly and where we can work to transform it positively. If such freedom is not allowed and if the assaults continue against those who, between fear and hope, try to stay true to their mission, then we will have failed in our liberating mission to accompany the oppressed majorities, those whom Ignacio Ellacuría, S.J. called the "unjustly dehumanized."

Notes

1 *Escritos Universitarios*, published in 1999 by UCA Editores, brings together Ellacuría's ideas about what a Jesuit university should be in the context of the reality of Central American reality in the 1980s. Unfortunately, almost 40 years later, the same reality still prevails in many countries of the region, especially in Nicaragua.
2 Pope Francis in the encyclical *Laudato Si'* uses the term "our common home" to refer to the natural world, where all living beings co-exist and mutually support one another.
3 Article 30 of the Political Constitution of the Republic of Nicaragua states that "Nicaraguans have the right to express their thoughts freely in public or private, individually or collectively, in speech, in writing, or by any other means." (Asamblea Nacional, 1987).
4 Regarding allowed absences, article 54 of the UCA's Regulations of the Undergraduate Student Academic Order (2020) establishes that "the maximum percentage is twenty percent." (Universidad Centroamericana, 2020).
5 Carlos Tünnermann in discussion with the author, October 8, 2019. Tünnermann was a student leader in the 1950s and later became an education expert and Secretary General of the UNAN-León.
6 Joaquín Solís was later president of the UNAN-Managua.
7 Students from the Centro Universitario de la Universidad Nacional (CUUN) in León organized the annual march to welcome the first-year students. However, this time the organizers said that it was in honor of those killed in a recent incident known as "El Chaparral," where the wounded, including among others, the founder of the FSLN and recent college drop-out turned guerrilla leader, Carlos Fonseca Amador. They decided that for the July 23, 1959 march, as a protest, instead of a farcical march this time it would look like a funeral. Suddenly, and although the march had obtained the mandatory permission from the police, Somoza's National Guard started shooting at the students. There were four dead and almost 50 wounded.

8 Dr. Fiallos was president of the UNAN-León from 1957 to 1964.
9 The two developments that most contradict the spirit of the Law of University Autonomy in Nicaragua are the arbitrary dismissal of professors and the elimination of entrance requirements in public universities. More information can be found at https://confidencial.com.ni/rectora-de-la-unan-leon-ordena-despido-de-15-profesores-por-no-plegarse-al-fsln/.
10 Lludely Aburto in discussion with the author, November 13, 2020. Aburto was national vice president of UNITE from 1990 to 1992.
11 The reference is the case of Zoilamérica Narváez, Daniel Ortega's daughter-in-law, who accused him in 1998 of having sexually abused her for several years.
12 In public schools and universities, especially the UNAN-León and the UNAN-Managua, teachers and professors who openly participated in the students' struggles were fired. Further information can be found at the following links: (1) https://www.laprensa.com.ni/2018/08/05/nacionales/2456573-unan-managua-y-el-ministerio-de-educacion-se-deshacen-de-the-critical-professors-of-the-government; (2) https://www.elnuevodiario.com.ni/nacionales/472708-denuncian-despidos-docentes-unan-managua/.

References

Asamblea Nacional. (1987). *Constitución Política de la República de Nicaragua*. Managua: Asamblea Nacional. La Gaceta, Diario Oficial, 30 de abril de 1987.

Asamblea Nacional. (1990). Ley No. 89: *Ley de Autonomía de las Instituciones de Educación Superior*. Managua: Asamblea Nacional. *La Gaceta, Diario Oficial*, 20 de abril de 1990, (77).

Ellacuría, I. (1999). *Escritos Universitarios*. San Salvador: UCA Editores.

Solís-Cortez, C. (2015). "El acompañamiento ignaciano desde la gestión educativa. Trabajo de obtención de grado," Maestría en Gestión Directiva de Instituciones Educativas. Tlaquepaque, Jalisco: ITESO.

Tünnerman, C. (2012). *La Universidad: Búsqueda Permanente*. Managua: HISPAMER.

Universidad Centroamericana. (2020). "Reglamento del régimen académico estudiantil de grado." Managua: Autor.

4
AN ETHNOGRAPHY OF THE CLASSROOM AND THE DAILY EFFECTS OF REPRESSION

Arquímedes González

The 2018 and 2019 context in Nicaragua: state repression and university resistance

I've arrived at the classroom a few minutes before the start of the "Informative News Story and Interview Workshop" that I'm giving to my second-year students in the Communications Department of the College of Humanities at the Universidad Centroamericana (UCA) in Managua, Nicaragua. Promptly the students enter the classroom and greet me with smiles. As I watch them choose their desks and place their backpacks on the seats, I make a silent wish that this day I will be able to teach the complete class. Every day it becomes more difficult just to get to the university. There are protests, roadblocks, clashes in the streets, and an atmosphere of uncertainty and fear. I was only six years old when the Sandinista insurrection brought down the Somoza dictatorship, but I still remember the barricades in the streets and the National Guard soldiers kicking down house doors and beating those who opposed the regime. Today's young people, who know that history only from the accounts and anecdotes of their parents, are experiencing something similar firsthand. I grieve that this generation must undergo the same tribulations as that earlier generation suffered 40 years ago.

I am a journalist. For many years, I have practiced this profession in Nicaragua in various print media, and I have witnessed many social tensions, but what is happening right now exceeds everything imaginable. I have also published several works of fiction, including short stories and novels, but current events in Nicaragua seem more unreal than anything I have written. Sometimes I wonder if there is any value in continuing to teach my students, but my doubts are allayed when I recall the words of Ignacio Ellacuría, S.J.:

DOI: 10.4324/9781003198925-7

The university can provide the best objective analyses of reality, it can facilitate the discovery and the implementation of practices for confronting the different problems of reality, it can prepare the analytical frameworks, and it can help to find and apply solutions. To raise awareness, it can reduce irrational fears precisely by showing them to be unfounded, and it can show the reasonableness of the goals ideally being sought by de-ideologizing the attacks against them.

(1975: p. 78)

I believe that Ellacuría's ideas about the role of universities and teachers are still valid and important. Whether in face-to-face classrooms or in virtual ones, we teachers must help our students to develop their knowledge so that they can broaden their analytical horizons while they are here at the university and so that, after graduating, they will successfully meet the challenges they will face in their different lines of work.

The students sit down. Many of them stay near the door as if fearing an imminent earthquake. Some move their legs nervously, like telegraphs sending messages in code. There was a time when most of them came wearing formal shoes. Today they wear running shoes, T-shirts, and baggy pants. You can see that in their backpacks, they carry very few items, only what is necessary. Some have even stopped using backpacks to avoid being identified by the authorities as students. Two or three mobile phones ring. The students apologize, saying that the callers are their parents or some other relative asking if they've arrived at the campus safely, what time they will leave, and how long it will be before they return home.

Immediately others check their phones to see what the social networks are saying. None of them uploads a selfie or posts something funny, as students used to do in the past. Today they are constantly seeking information. As I take attendance, I hear some murmurs. The students seem impatient. I know that some of them have taken part in the many marches and protests that have spread across the country in recent months, while others also have used the social networks to speak out about what is happening.

Despite the dangers they face, of the 39 students enrolled in this workshop, only two are absent today. This is a real surprise—a surprise and a praiseworthy feat on the students' part because of the transportation problems throughout the city. Many times I have feared that I would reach the classroom and find it empty, but they are always here, confounding all my worry. Their presence inspires me and gives me great joy. I explain the next assignment and tell them when it is due: they are to write a short news article that is at least two pages in length and includes photographs. Immediately I see them react in feigned shock. "Two pages!" says someone, as if alarmed. Yes, I explain, in these times when few people are reading the news, it is important to develop the ability to write thoroughly.

The students then take out their newspapers. It is pleasant to hear papers rustling and to see how they all fix their eyes on the news in the papers, a medium that many say is doomed to disappear. This is how the workshop begins, by informing ourselves about events in the country and the world. Staying informed helps us to know and understand what is happening now and what we can expect to happen. As I listen to the comments of each student about the news of the day, I am delighted that they are interested in knowing the latest developments in Nicaragua, especially in this difficult period we are all experiencing.

As I teach the class, I become aware that some of them keep checking their phones. In my student days, we exchanged little notes, commenting on some gossip or telling a joke, but today everything has changed. My students' thumbs are very skilled, swiftly opening and closing applications and answering messages; their eyes are raised and lowered quickly as they try to pay attention to two things at the same time.

I hear some distant detonations. I wish I were dreaming. I wish this was not true. In earlier times, such explosions would mean the beginning of religious festivities, such as the feast of La Purísima, celebrated on December 7th throughout the country, or the feast of Saint Dominic Guzmán, celebrated on August 1st and 10th in Managua. Today the blasts mean that all of us have to prepare to escape as soon as possible. At the sound of the explosions, the students' attitude changes. A look of concern appears in their eyes, and their countenance reflects the fear, the pain, and the sadness of these days. They look scared again. You can even sense a quickening of their heartbeat; they are too young to be going through traumatic experiences of this type.

I turn around to write on the board and hear their murmurs rising. As I turn toward them again, I see their looks of pained expectancy. I assume that by now they know the route to take to exit as soon as possible. Sensing that we will have to end this session abruptly, I waste no time in telling them about journalistic techniques for gathering information, the need to present a variety of sources, the value of figures to explain the context of an event, and the importance of writing down correctly the names, surnames, and titles of the persons interviewed.

"Prof," says one of the students, interrupting my discourse.

I know that tone of voice well. I have heard it often these days. It is what one hears the second before the alarm clock goes off in the morning. While its softness masks the fear from which it rises, it has all the urgency of an ambulance siren. As I look around, I see the students nervously and hastily gathering their things. This scene has been repeated so many times in recent weeks that it has become a normal ritual. The students who remained near the door are the first to get up.

"They're attacking the university," several of my students tell me in unison as they confusedly stuff their books, newspapers, pens, phones, and plastic water bottles into their backpacks. I notice that in some of the backpacks, the students have T-shirts, masks, bandanas, and even banners.

"The whole thing again has taken on the color of ants,"[1] someone comments.
"We have to be clever so the vultures[2] don't catch us again," warns another.
"Or the paranormals,"[3] cracks still another.

Through the window, I observe that dozens of students are rushing through the corridors, leaving the classrooms sadly empty, plunged into painful silence. No, my permission is not needed for my students to leave the classroom. Cell phones immediately ring in a digital concert with all types of tones. Again, their mothers and fathers are worried because they've heard already that repression has returned to the streets. The students' friends are telling them what's happening and advising them about the best way to leave campus to avoid trouble. As I'm being left alone in the classroom, I tell my students to take care, and I wonder whether I will ever see them again.

As I step out into the hallway, I hear some louder explosions. The students quicken their pace and gather in small groups, exchanging ideas about what to do and how to escape unharmed. Most of them are already holding plastic bottles filled with water because they know firsthand the damage that tear gas can cause to their eyes. Some of them are already wearing headbands and masks to avoid being identified. Others have changed their shirts to outwit the agents who have already "tagged" them, as they say, by taking photos of them when they were entering the university. Still others unfurl the blue and white flags they have in their backpacks and run with them through the corridors until they are out of sight.

While making my way to the university gate, I reflect that today we at least had some time to advance a little in class, but I still wonder whether my students will in the long run continue studying this profession. Since April 2018, dozens of journalists and communicators who were reporting on events for the independent media have been arrested, beaten, or threatened; their equipment has been destroyed, damaged, or confiscated.

This short description of an interrupted class at the Universidad Centroamericana in Managua helps us understand that since April 2018, the violence in Nicaragua has seriously affected the learning environment. Students are immersed in a socio-political crisis that pervades the entire educational system. The whole learning process is disrupted during the days or weeks when classes are suspended because of the dangers involved in reaching the campus. Continuing to teach and to learn requires adjusting to the "rhythm" marked by repression, taking advantage of the rare moments of tranquility, adapting to difficult circumstances, and refusing to surrender to fear.

Challenges and responses in the classroom

In one class, while I was explaining the importance of communications and media studies for strengthening democracies, a student said to me, "Prof, I'm seeing on the social networks that they're harassing some journalists who are covering a march. Why are reporters and the media always hounded and viewed with suspicion?"

This time the class was progressing smoothly.

While I was responding to the student's question, I noticed that the group seemed more relaxed. They were commenting on typical young people's affairs, but always talking about the past; they said nothing of the future because no one could know what might happen that day or the next. They spoke about their trips outside the capital, their adventures at the beach in previous years, or the birthday party for one of their companions that was sure to be postponed. They were not talking about having fun today, but about how they used to have fun or about the party they would miss in the coming days. Still, I often caught them smiling and laughing again. No adversity was capable of erasing the smiles and the laughter of these young people who radiate hope and use humor as an effective antidote to sadness.

Some of them, though, were staying very quiet during class.

When I asked one of them what was wrong, he replied, "Prof, the problem is that I have a relative detained by the police, and my family is very worried."

Another student explained why she had missed several classes:

> Prof, I haven't been able to come to class because I live in Masaya, about thirty kilometers from here. There are tranques[4] every day, and it has been difficult to find transport. My family fears that in a few days I won't be able to get to Managua because of the protests, and they prefer that I stay home.

"Prof," another student confessed, "I'm worried because I don't know if my parents will be able to continue paying the university fees because they lost their jobs, and now we're having a hard time financially."

"Prof," commented another,

> This situation we're in doesn't allow me to concentrate on my studies. I'm always nervous about what might happen to me or my friends. I fear for the safety of my family. I'm afraid even to go out in the street.

Still another revealed: "Prof, I had to change my name on the networks and delete most of my photos and comments and all the messages from my friends."

As class ended and I left the students, telling them that I hoped everything would work out for the best, I saw a few other students who had overheard the conversations come over to them and offer encouragement. In fact, they had not been left on their own even during class. Other students immediately started sending them friendly messages through WhatsApp and SMS.

Deep down, I understood that my students were no longer the often naive, romantic, and self-absorbed individuals as presented on social networks. Suddenly they were adults committed to protecting and encouraging one another and to changing the tragic course of a country where the number of dead and injured kept growing. They were also worried because at all the university's gates the National Police had posted detachments of riot police armed with rifles, helmets, and shields. The officers often detained and interrogated the students as they left the campus, demanding to see their IDs and then photographing them.

"Imagine, prof, they asked me what I was coming to do at the university," said one student.

"They forced me to hand over my cell phone so they could look at the photos and messages I had," said another.

"They threatened to arrest me just because I complained that they were taking my backpack from me," said still another.

"My parents are worried about me," said one young man. "They say that they're going to make me leave this university because there are always protests around it."

While listening to the concerns and complaints of the students about the abuse and mistreatment they had suffered at the hands of the police, I took out the class materials, some markers, and an eraser. As the hour for the start of class approached, I wrote on the board some ideas I wanted to share with them. The classroom was full of the students' voices and noises; after several weeks of suspended face-to-face classes, I was happy to see them and talk with them again. The university was coming back to life, for the students are its heart and soul.

I kept thinking about the student's first question and how clearly he asked it. I am teaching young people 16 or 17 years of age on average. At that age, I was thinking about my next baseball game and knew little of the world around me. Back then, of course, there was no internet. All communication was by word of mouth, and that made getting information more difficult. Today we have instantaneous news. Information reaches us so fast that there's no time to reflect on what's happening and why it's happening, much less to understand what the short- and long-term consequences will be for us.

Returning to that first question, about why reporters are harassed, I explained to the students that the strong pressure placed on journalists and communicators and the forced closure of media outlets started not in April 2018 but many years before. An extensive report published on the news portal "Confidencial"[5] estimates that since 2007, the first year of Ortega's return to power, 20 different news media have been shuttered in Nicaragua. Most strikingly, 12 of them were closed just in the two years 2018 and 2019. Thirteen of the 20 were radio stations or programs, making clear the great influence and importance that medium still has today as a conveyer of messages to the public. According to the report in "Confidencial," more than half the media that have ceased to operate in the last 13 years closed down because they decided that their workers were running too great a risk. Some of those forced to close in the last two years did so because of the increased pressure on journalists since the start of the anti-government protests.

Since April 2018, more than 60 journalists,[6] after experiencing constant harassment and death threats, have decided to leave the country to preserve their lives. Many in the government thought that their departure would silence them once and for all, but they were surprised when these journalists continued their labors from abroad and persevered in their mission of taking the pulse of their country. Their work in exile gave rise to a variety of online media such as Nicaragua Investiga, Despacho 505, Portavoz Ciudadano, Galería News, Agenda Propia, Nicaragua Actual, República 18, and Actualidad con Dino Andino. Other news media were reborn, such as 100% Noticias, Esta Semana y Esta Noche, Café con Voz, Radio Darío, and Voces en Libertad, which use platforms such as YouTube, Facebook, Twitter, and even WhatsApp and Instagram to transmit their reports. If the intention of the regime's media censorship in 2018 and 2019 was to put an end to the independent media of Nicaragua, it failed.

This new context of Nicaraguan journalism reminded me of the courageous catacombs journalism during the Somoza dictatorship,[7] when reporters had to broadcast from churches because of the risks they ran in the streets or in their studios. Today's audiences are not limited to always buying the classic printed newspaper, tuning in to the same radio station, or watching the regular newscast at a certain hour. Thousands of people now receive a constant flow of information from social networks and digital platforms that are relatively immune to censorship. Secure against forced shutdowns, the new media are highly mobile and can be literally carried in one's pocket; cell phones are used to transmit written, video, and audio messages through social networks. In the short time since April 2018, the media in Nicaragua have undergone a profound transformation, virtually reinventing themselves: they have gone from relying on conventional platforms and fixed transmission locations to using new digital platforms and virtual spaces that authorities have a harder time censoring. As in the times of Somoza, a new era of courageous journalism has emerged, but the catacombs today are not the same church-protected sanctuaries as in yesteryear. The safe places now are the social networks: Nicaragua has given birth to a catacombs journalism that is digitally enabled.

So many horrors happened in those months of repression that it was difficult even to make sense of them or to comprehend which events were most deplorable as seen through the independent media. Every day there were fresh reports of clashes, deaths, and pleas for help from people arrested. Classes were often suspended for weeks, during which I truly missed my students. I needed their smiles, their questions, their comments, the bustle of classrooms and corridors. I wanted to see them daily, hear them speak, appreciate their vision of the world, and learn from them.

In the midst of the political conflict, I found myself thinking constantly about my communications students. Were they really studying, or were they more concerned about the situation in the country, the problems of their friends and families? When classes resumed and I saw how they reacted in the classroom, I concluded that they were indeed learning, although in a rushed and stressful way. They had one eye on the course material and the other on what the protests in the streets were achieving. I also reflected on the larger question of motivation. Would they be inspired to study? I felt convinced they would, because they now understood more clearly the importance of their role as communicators and journalists; they realized that by becoming professionals, they would be able to help transform society for the better. Thus, the challenge for me as a teacher was to persuade my students to concentrate more on their studies and to impart to them the skills they would need for this perilous profession.

The 2018 crisis opened space for new forms of teaching in Nicaragua

The last time I was able to see my students in person, we were halfway through the class when a murmur could be heard advancing down the hallways. We all looked out. It was a spontaneous march of students within the UCA, one of the last places in the country where young people could still express themselves freely. By that time, just walking in the streets with a blue and white flag meant running the risk of being arrested and prosecuted. My students immediately went out into the hallway and applauded the demonstrators. Ten minutes later, the UCA was surrounded by dozens of anti-riot agents and several police patrols that were sounding their sirens in order to silence the voices of the protesters. Classes were suspended once again, but my students decided to wait in the classroom because if they left immediately, they would likely be detained by the police.

When the conflict intensified in April 2018, the UCA canceled in-person classes, and later in the year, it developed virtual forms of instruction. A special Virtual Academic Cycle was offered from September 27 to December 14, 2018, in an effort to help students advance in their studies and at the same time to provide them support in view of the insecurity that existed throughout the country. The UCA's Virtual Learning Environment (EVA) had been an option even before April 2018, but it was not used much by the students. The teachers would upload files with the course curricula and study guides, but as long as in-person classes were possible, few students felt any need to access the EVA. Now, in this moment of crisis, it has assumed crucial importance.

We teachers had previously received several months of training from the UCA's online education specialists on methods for teaching classes online, but my own practical experience in virtual education was minimal. I had to watch tutorials on YouTube to learn the digital tools at our disposal. My students were a great help to me during online classes because even remotely they could show me how to solve sound problems, split the screen, or share videos for the group. For them, these virtual classes were something quite natural. From the first day of online teaching, I felt as though I was in the classroom again. At the beginning of each class, a majority of the students would tune into the videoconference, but some had difficulties and limitations with the online instruction. The internet connection from their homes was not always adequate, or they had only mobile phones, when they really needed computers and Wi-Fi access.

Though the students were not together physically, the camaraderie among them was the same as always. Nothing, neither the distances nor the sad events unfolding in the country, had been able to diminish their bonds of friendship. When someone made a joke, they would send an image like this: 😂. When I asked them if they had understood a point in class, many responded "yes" by sending a funny face: 😊. When I praised the work of someone who had done very well in an exam, the following icon appeared: 👏. When I asked them a question and they remained silent, some indicated that they were thinking: 🤔. Their chat among themselves often took the form of mysterious signs, such as ✧, ♥, :c, :(, Xd, :0, <3, X2, :p, u.u, and :D. Simply to understand and enjoy their exchanges, I had to quickly learn the complex constellation of signs and icons of the new digital communication that they had mastered.

At one point, I heard some opinions expressed that made me stray from the topics I had proposed to develop in class.

"We need a president for everybody, not just for a party," texted one student, and several others offered their own views.

"Politics is piggish,[8] prof," concluded another student and received all kinds of support.

The topic of the virtual session that day was the importance of writing short news articles in two or more versions. I explained to them that journalists should not settle for just one version of an event. They should seek out as many statements as possible from the persons involved, and then they should contrast, compare, and analyze the statements in order to understand and report what happened as clearly as possible. I made it clear to them that journalists should take nothing for granted. They should always raise doubts, ask questions, and consider every possibility. The only commitment of journalists is to the truth, and although the truth is subjective, their job is to get as close to it as possible. I explained to them that no journalist should be beholden to the government or to the political party in power. The primary responsibility of journalists is to transmit the facts as completely as possible. Their audience is what should matter to them most, and their reputation is what they should most try to preserve.

Often the virtual classes lasted longer than the stipulated time, and I was delighted with that because the students then felt more relaxed and could express themselves better.

"Prof, I feel safer now studying from home," one told me.

"The online classes are better because that way we don't expose ourselves," stated another. "My parents always worry when they know I have to go to campus."

"I've found a lot of benefit in the online classes," commented another. "I like them because that way I can talk directly to you and send you emails. And I don't have to waste time traveling to the university every day."

"That's not the case with me," complained one student. "I miss my classmates. I miss going to the food court and having lunch with my friends. I miss walking around the campus and seeing all the students. I miss everything!"

After this exchange of experiences, I returned to the class material, talking to them about the article by Colombian editor and writer Javier Darío Restrepo, "Journalistic Objectivity: Utopia and Reality," which explains that reporters must consult various sources before publishing an article. I also made mention of Argentine journalist Leila Guerriero and her commitment to the truth. I then recommended the "Manual of Journalistic Style," which was published in 2018 by Public Media of Ecuador; it insists on the need for journalists always to seek out and interview all those involved in any news story, regardless of their position, economic class, level of education, gender, religion, or political affiliation. Whatever points I was making, the current political situation kept reinserting itself, time and again, in the online classroom as if it were a ghost that could not rest in peace.

In face-to-face classes, it was easier for my students to speak their mind on politics; they did so with great fluency and vigor. It was also easier for me to redirect the class to the educational material that had to be covered. When we started teaching through virtual classes, however, there was a change in the students' manner. They would comment briefly on political matters, but now they did so with such intense and constant criticism that it was harder for me to bring them back to the subject matter of the class. They asked me my opinion and sometimes even insisted on knowing my views about the harsh reality we were living through. They were constantly asking me about what I expected to happen in the short or the long run. Indeed, their questioning presented me with another personal challenge: how to avoid political polarization in the classroom.

As we have seen in this chapter, the students were looking not only for someone to teach them about the field they were studying, which in my case was communications. They also needed a guide, someone who would help them understand what was happening around them because they felt quite lost in the face of the heartrending events that were tearing apart the social fabric of Nicaragua.[9] Before April 2018, my classes were never so persistently interrupted by the need to explain the political reality. This new situation was a challenge for me as a teacher because I had to constantly insist on pursuing the objectives of the course and persuading my students to focus on their studies.

Conclusions

As I exposed my students to the examples of well-known and respected journalists about the obligation to seek information from all sources and insisted on the need to consult different journalistic manuals, I saw their faces cloud over with doubt and concern. All this theory about freedom of speech and the duties of journalists in reporting the news seemed to them hardly applicable to the

Nicaraguan reality. I took in what their facial expressions were saying, and I created space for the glances they exchanged among themselves. Later I listened as they spoke out, one by one:

> And how are we going to complete our articles if we live in a dictatorship? What can we journalists do if we are always denied official information and no government representative wants to talk to us?
> For me, this is like going to my attacker to ask him why he attacked me. There's definitely not enough security for us to go to all the places we need to go to consult different sources.
> At the present time no journalistic work can be done in this country.
> I'm afraid to go out on the street and identify myself as a journalist. The level of persecution against journalists is extreme.
> If we know already that nobody is going to tell us anything, why should we bother to find out the government's version?

With these remarks that revealed their fear but also their indignation, my students summed up in a few precise words the collapse of our democratic system, the suppression of the freedom of press and the right to information, the disillusionment with politics and politicians, and the lack of spaces for debate in the country. How could I refute or contradict any of their statements, which were only too true?

I explained that, unfortunately, there were very few countries in which the work of journalists and communicators was properly respected. It was estimated that between 2011 and 2018 at least 834 journalists were killed around the world. In Nicaragua, one only had to recall the terrible deaths of the journalists Pedro Joaquín Chamorro,[10] María José Bravo,[11] and most recently Ángel Gahona.[12] This profession will always be subject to political and economic pressures, although the experience of Nicaragua since April 2018 has been unlike anything seen in many decades. What is most important for journalists and communicators in the media, I told my students, is to put up stiff resistance. We knew about the tenacity of the newspaper La Prensa, which kept informing the public even when the government refused to let them import paper for more than a year. We were familiar with the work of media operations like Confidencial, Esta Semana, and Esta Noche, which continued their journalistic labors even after their facilities were overrun. Reporters Miguel Mora and Lucía Pineda Ubau, director and chief editor of 100% Noticias, respectively, spent several months unjustly imprisoned, but when they regained their freedom, they were not discouraged; they simply migrated to other digital platforms and continued their mission.

Data from the Violeta Barrios Chamorro Foundation (2020), which ceased operations in February 2021 due to the Law of Foreign Agents, show that since the citizens' uprising of April 2018, there have been reports of at least two attacks every day against journalists and the media; despite the attacks, they have continued their work of reporting, defying the attempts to censor and suppress the media.

By end of the class, however, I was feeling that my students perhaps needed to pay heed to their valid and sensible sense of prudence before seeking out different sources for the journalistic pieces they had to hand in. They shouldn't just listen to a foolish teacher who was inculcating in them wildly romantic and possibly naive ideas of journalistic commitment. Since even seasoned journalists were afraid to expose themselves to dangerous situations, I could understand my students' concerns perfectly. I had no choice but to encourage them and give them advice on how to proceed in their work, while being careful and protecting themselves. To my surprise, a few weeks later, I received all the assignments, and they all included various sources. That was more than I had expected. Some went to the police, who refused to talk to them. Some went to government officials who would not receive them, and others went to question a politician who wouldn't even open the door. Most of the official sources refused to provide statements or to answer questions put to them in person, by phone, or through social networks, but my students in the Information Note and Interview Workshop had the persistence, the courage, the commitment, and the determination to seek out alternate versions, to keep on asking questions, and to seek out a variety of sources in order to produce a solid journalistic piece that would be worthy of any professional journalist. The fact that many of the persons consulted did not respond to my students' questions did not mean defeat for them, nor did it leave them disheartened. They considered that they had won the battle because they had done honor to this hazardous profession by listening to all the voices possible, regardless of race, sex, position, political thought, economic status, or religious belief.

I also realized that my fears and doubts about my students and the future of this profession were unfounded. They weren't too young for this challenge. They were more prepared than I thought they were to confront the harsh adversities to which Nicaraguan journalism was being subjected. They had not followed the wrong vocation. They showed me that this profession was something they carried in their blood. After reading their work, I happily understood the valuable lesson my students had taught me: it was a lesson to trust their persistence, integrity, and courage, and their dedication to what in the future would be their profession. Even before graduating, they had already advanced far toward the day when they would be helping to make this society more just and more peaceful.

This chapter has addressed the question of whether the students can develop their theoretical and practical media and communication skills and do their work and assignments in a climate of repression. Most of them did indeed complete their work, but it was clear that they had to make a supreme effort to meet their goals because of the worries and distractions that the ongoing socio-political crisis was causing for them and their families. In this chapter, I have also attempted to describe how a professor and his students interacted in class within the context of the conflict that Nicaragua is now experiencing. Since April 2018, as we have seen, the students formed potent support groups to resist the repression and overcome the challenges of living in an unfree society. In turn, the students seek in their professor's words of assurance and perhaps words of solace; they seek a message of hope and encouragement about their country's uncertain future.

Notes

1. Colloquial expression describing something that has become dangerous.
2. A word used by young Nicaraguans to identify riot police because of the color of their uniforms.
3. A word used to identify members of the paramilitary forces.
4. A popular expression indicating barricades blocking passage on a street; they are built as a means of protest and pressure on the government, as well as protection.
5. Confidencial (2020). Daniel Ortega's government has closed 20 media outlets in Nicaragua. Retrieved from https://confidencial.com.ni/nacion/gobierno-ha-ordenado-cierre-de-medios-de-comunicacion-en-nicaragua/.
6. OndaLocal, (2019). Almost 60 Nicaraguan journalists have gone into in exile. Retrieved from https://ondalocal.com.ni/noticias/565-casi-60-periodistas-nicaraguenses-en-el-exilio/.
7. Tünnermann, C. (1981). "The Contribution of Journalism to National Liberation: Inaugural Lecture of the Fourth Congress of the Union of Journalists of Nicaragua," p. 125.
8. The Spanish word is *chancha*, a colloquial word meaning "pig"; it is also used as an adjective to describe something corrupt.
9. See for example, Karla Lara's (this volume) call for the important role of "holistic accompaniment."
10. Pedro Joaquin Chamorro, director of the newspaper *La Prensa* and critic of the dictatorship of Anastasio Somoza Debayle, was assassinated in Managua on January 10, 1978.
11. María José Bravo, reporter for *La Prensa*, was killed on November 9, 2004, while covering municipal elections in Juigalpa.
12. Ángel Gahona, director of a local independent TV station, was killed in Bluefields on April 21, 2018, while broadcasting the protests against the social security pension reforms.

References

Ellacuría, I, (1975). "Diez años después, ¿es posible una universidad distinta?", Escritos universitarios. San Salvador: UCA Editores, p. 78. Retrieved from https://www.uca.edu.sv/centro-documentacion-virtual/wp-content/uploads/2015/03/C27-c24-.pdf

Fundación Violeta Barrios de Chamorro, (2020). Informe de violaciones a la libertad de prensa. Retrieved from https://www.violetachamorro.org/biblioteca/publicaciones/149-informe-de-violaciones-a-la-libertad-de-prensa-jul/

5
RHIZOMATIC SOLIDARITY FOR (RE) FLOURISHING

UCA Graduate Perspectives on Education, Social Change, and Persistence Amid Repression

Fiore Bran Aragón

Introduction: we are roots that have been uprooted but not burned

On the afternoon of April 18, 2018, I was trying to return to the university after work to join the demonstrations with my friends, but it was impossible to enter the UCA. At around 5 PM, the campus was surrounded by riot police and paramilitary forces. After trying several times without success, I went home. That morning, I had been talking about the demonstrations with my friends, some of whom were organizing the events in which many others took part. All of us believed that such activity was a right and a duty because we wanted a change. The raging fire in the Indio Maíz Biological Reserve, which the government had let get out of control, had kindled a blaze of social rebellion in Managua and throughout the country. Young people took to the streets to demand a stop to corruption and injustice; they wanted a stop to the neglect that was killing not only many wild animals in the reserve but also, if more slowly, our people and our communities. We became a generation on fire, driven by both the fire of repression and the fury of our resistance. But none of us was prepared for what was to come. In a matter of days, our lives were changed by a chain of events that blur in my memory: the rebellion in the streets throughout the country, the autoconvocado movement of students, and the consequent repression, slaughter, and exile. Fortunately, on the night of April 18, none of my friends died, but neither we students nor the teachers were at all prepared for what was to come. Now, three years later, many of us are far from home. In the words of my friend Lila, we are like roots that have been uprooted, but I think not burned. We persist still.

In this chapter, I discuss the role of the Universidad Centroamericana (UCA) as an educational institution promoting social change and solidarity in Nicaragua in the context of the April 2018 uprising. To this end, I share my own experience as a UCA graduate, in dialogue with three other graduates of the

Humanities College of my cohort (2018–2019) who have been involved in the struggle for social justice in the country. All of us, my interlocutors and I, were part of the 10% of young people (15–24 years old) who have access to higher education in Nicaragua,[1] and of the still smaller group of students who decided to pursue a career in humanities and social sciences in a country where it is discouraged to "thinking differently."[2]

For the three graduates I interviewed,[3] the UCA has been a space that provided us with interactions, experiences, and education that led us to a life of working for social change. It has also been a place for intense grief, truncated dreams, and unresolved questions about the larger university community in Nicaragua. In my conversations with my fellow graduates, we reflected on our experiences during the uprising that began in April 2018 and on our lives in the years that have followed. In these pages, I want to revisit that past to try to understand our present situation and discern the future possibilities for the mission of the UCA in Nicaragua. These reflections are analyzed using Ignacio Ellacuría, S.J.'s proposals regarding the mission of the Jesuit university in Central America, applying the concept of rhizome as an image of thought according to Deleuze and Guattari,[4] in an analysis of the socio-political context of Nicaragua and its impact on higher education. Together with my interlocutors, I reflect on the possibility of a rhizomatic solidarity that will allow the university to flourish even under repression.

I begin by describing the April 2018 uprising from an ethnographic perspective, contrasting social movement theories with the unfolding events in Nicaragua. In the following section, I reflect on the role of critical higher education in developing the type of ethico-political questioning that motivated the young university students in 2018 and that has been fundamental for the experience of my interlocutors. The third section considers the assessments of my fellow graduates regarding the challenges facing the UCA as an institution that educates for social change, viewed especially from the perspective of Ellacuría's argument[5] about the three fundamental functions of Jesuit universities in Central America: teaching, research, and *proyección social*. In conclusion, I stress the urgency of a multisectoral, intergenerational dialogue in the university community for the sake of developing a rhizomatic solidarity that will strengthen the mission of the UCA in Nicaragua. I end by joining with the other graduates in making a heartfelt call for international solidarity with the UCA in its current situation.

This text would not have been possible without the cooperation of my colleagues Josué, Lila, and Gabriel,[6] all of whom were close to me in humanities classes and on the streets of Managua. They very generously agreed to share their experiences with me. The processes of training and reflection that led us to get involved in the April 2018 uprising were different for each of us. Josué told me that his progression was "from the classroom to the street," while for Lila, it was more from the benches of the *pasarela*[7] to the streets of the city. Gabriel, for his part, took advantage of both opportunities for action-oriented research within the university and the spaces outside the campus. I will explain these processes in the following sections.

Given the present context of a repressive, neoliberal dictatorship, it is not easy to be young and to talk about education and social change in Nicaragua. The repression has driven many of us to become exiles and refugees, while those who remain live in the shadow of the Ortega-Murillo regime. Some activist students and graduates of the UCA, fearing reprisals, preferred not to talk to me about their experiences for this study. While the panorama I present draws only on the experiences of humanities graduates, their perspective extends beyond their personal experiences and reflects the collective struggle in which they engaged with many others.

Three years after the April 2018 uprising

When I began to think about writing this chapter, I contacted several colleagues with whom I had shared the brighter and the darker moments not only of the April uprising but also of the prior days, when the fire in the Indio Maíz Biological Reserve had forced us out onto the streets to protest. At that time, being under fire created solidarity among us young people, who were optimistic but politically naive: we believed we could topple a bloody dictatorship by peaceful means, as if we were living under a constitutional government in a democratic state. When I speak with my colleagues today, I can hear their despair and confusion. Some have taken refuge in safe houses outside of Managua, while others live far from their families, awaiting the rulings of asylum courts. Some say that the uprising was just not worth it. Personally, I do feel somewhat disillusioned with the dream we had three years ago, but I still believe that a deeper kind of social change is possible, and that higher education must play a fundamental role in that process.

In April 2018, Nicaragua returned to the front pages of newspapers around the world because of internal turmoil similar to that of the 1970s. As had happened in 1979 during the uprising against the Somoza dictatorship, a large part of the population, including many young people, surged onto the streets to demand justice and to reclaim the public spaces and the symbols of resistance that had been arrogated by the government in April 2018.[8] At first, this massive mobilization, which spread like a wildfire, had no name, but soon we began to call ourselves the "autoconvocados" to emphasize the anarchic, rhizomatic, and egalitarian character of the movement, in which communication took place mainly through the social media. In the beginning, we were mostly students, but soon we were joined by young women and men from the barrios and the rural communities, as well as by teachers, mothers, and countless other Nicaraguans who were fed up with inequality and poverty. We were protesting the brutal repression of the Ortega government, which was especially harmful to marginal populations, both human and non-human.[9] Shortly after the start of the demonstrations, we began to give names to these events, whence the terms "April Uprising,"[10] "Rebellion,"[11] and "Revolution."[12]

The causes of the uprising were many, and they existed long before the protests of April 2018. Among the factors that roused the university students to protest were several events revealing government corruption and social inequality that affected young people both directly and indirectly. The most important developments preceding the uprising were the government's gross mismanagement of a forest fire in the Indio Maíz Biological Reserve and its proposed reform of the pension system, which would have increased the contributions of workers and employers and reduced benefits by 5%.[13] Another triggering event was the imminent approval of a law that allowed the government to "review" usage of social media, which the government considered a negative influence and danger to social stability. Shortly before the demonstrations began, the monthly journal *Envío* warned that this proposed "gag law" would threaten the free flow of information and opinion on social media. By installing free Wi-Fi in the parks of Managua, Vice President Rosario Murillo was attempting to "rope in" the supposedly alienated and apolitical youth of the city,[14] but by the beginning of 2018 her plan seemed to have gotten out of hand. Young people were using social media not only to share information about relevant national and international political events but to organize protests. The situation was like that of the 2013 Occupy-INSS movement, in which young protesters joined retirees, occupied the offices of the National Institute of Social Security (INSS), and demanded social security benefits for pensioners, all of which also ended in government repression.[15]

University students have played an important role in organizing the protest movements. As I mentioned before, higher education in Nicaragua is a privilege accessible to few, and being able to study humanities or social sciences is an even greater privilege.[16] In April 2018, many students pursuing these fields at various universities took to the streets in support of the uprising: they organized demonstrations, collectives, and even study groups. In the months that followed, it became evident that, while all of us protesters were in danger, the students in the public universities faced greater risks, such as mass expulsions[17] and persecution. There were even armed attacks on the campuses, with the complicity of the school presidents[18]; these assaults in some cases ended with the arrest and murder of students.[19] Those of us studying at the UCA benefited from at least a small zone free of violence on the campus, where we were relatively protected from repression.

In addition to feeling relatively safe on campus, we UCA students were receiving a more liberal education and enjoyed more academic freedom than most of our peers at the public universities. In the humanities college of the UCA, we were exposed to ideas and principles that helped us engage with the national and regional reality; we learned to debate and to disagree cordially; we could speak about the national context without fear of censorship or repression. Some of us had mentors who encouraged us to research the social problems that concerned us or to become involved in initiatives for social justice. I cannot state that this was the experience of the entire student body, but this was definitely the type of education that shaped my life at the UCA and influenced the conception of human rights that I share with my interlocutors.

Free nation and life!

> Achieving a critical education has been a long process for me, and I would not have succeeded without my mentor and my fellow students. Those women saved me, literally, from the riot police, but they also saved me in a figurative sense: with them I could discuss and question so many things. I started out with questions about my family's silences and the history of abuse in my own life, but soon I was moved to take to the streets on March 8, 2018, International Women's Day, and on November 25, 2017, International Day for the Elimination of Violence Against Women. I felt rage against Ortega for being a rapist and a dictator, because he was abusing Nicaragua in the same way he had abused women in his own family ... My anger also fueled my desire to change the system that had allowed Ortega to rule for so long.
>
> *(Lila, UCA graduate in psychology)*

According to Martha Nussbaum, democracy needs the humanities because the humanities help people to develop the ability to think critically, to argue astutely, and to acknowledge the inherent rights and dignity of all persons.[20] But precisely because the humanities and the social sciences cultivate those qualities, they are threatened by the current model of neoliberal education, which has little appreciation for any knowledge not clearly linked to financial profit and business efficiency.[21] In Nicaragua, public universities have been subjected to constant threats by the Ortega government, which has expelled any students and teachers who questioned government policy.[22] At a more structural level, the government has been intent on promoting fields of study exclusively focused on developing the technical skills essential for the national economy; it has simultaneously reduced the budget for humanities faculties and has restricted their academic freedom.[23] This tendency to diminish the role of the humanities in general education is evident also in public secondary education, where the teaching of humanities is limited to a few hours per semester. Meanwhile the students are indoctrinated with texts that applaud the government and avoid any topics that might generate debate about the national reality and the Ortega-Murillo regime.[24] This type of secondary education (or miseducation) negatively affects the quality of higher education and the civic formation of young Nicaraguans.[25]

Althusser argued that public school education functions as an "ideological apparatus of the state"; it serves to reproduce the relations of work and power that sustain an inequitable system of production that operates to the disadvantage of the majority.[26] Although Ortega claims to be on the left and boasts of free public education in Nicaragua, the education offered deviates very little from the capitalist model, which reproduces an uncritical workforce by means of textbooks filled with political propaganda.[27] Private universities in Nicaragua are subject to the dynamics of academic capitalism, but at least some of them give students access to alternative worldviews and help them to learn to dialogue, to think critically, and to analyze the more complex aspects of their social reality. In my own experience, the UCA was a university that possessed these characteristics; it was an institution that formed students to work for social change even in a context of political repression. The teaching, research, and *proyección social* of this Jesuit university helped us "grandchildren of the revolution"[28] to develop the habit of ethico-political questioning, which we took from the classrooms to the streets of Managua, and then to the entire nation. To understand the context of our generation's questioning, we need to reflect on the debate that took place between the adults of the revolutionary vanguard and the young students of the postwar years.

In 2016, an intergenerational debate arose among groups located in Managua about the nature of politics and different ways to be politically active in contemporary Nicaragua; it took place mainly on social media (Twitter, digital journals like *Confidencial*, and some independent blogs). Researchers and journalists of the older revolutionary generation were persistently accusing young people of being conservative and apathetic and of being mostly interested in "family and religious practices."[29] Several young bloggers decided to challenge the adults about their ways of doing politics: they proposed new forms of activism for social change, which would involve critical education, *autoconvocado* community organizing, public spaces for open dialogue and artistic presentations, and honest criticism on social media.[30] These new forms of activism, they argued, would encourage debate and change about many topics that were not on the revolutionary agenda of the 1980s, such as sexual and reproductive rights, sexual diversity, ecology, and the rights of native peoples and people of African descent.[31]

The uprising in April 2018 revealed that young people were not all apathetic but simply had different interests and preferred other forms of activism. Our modes of engagement were not inspired by the "New Man" ideal that had motivated the Sandinista Revolution.[32] More importantly, we did not consider armed struggle to be the means for achieving the Nicaragua we desired. In a 2016 blog post, Ernesto Valle wrote that for him good education and decent work were more important for effecting social change than engaging in armed struggle:

> They label us 'individualists' because we value education as a way of getting ahead and contributing to the country. … They say we are passive because our parents never tire of telling us that waging an armed assault on a government is not worth it.[33]

That was the very same advice my parents gave me, and that was why they were gripped with fear when I took to the streets. And I think that was why they also agreed with our new form of protest: no weapons.

But how do you mount a rebellion without weapons? I propose understanding this rebellion as a collective, popular uprising with an emancipatory and rhizomatic character.[34] Rhizome means a mass of roots in Greek and is applied by philosophers to understand a situation from multiple, non-hierarchical entry and exit points. This rhizomatic characteristic can be seen in the spaces of resistance and self-determination within national and transnational power structures,[35] with a view to "cultivating autonomous forms of living and political association."[36] What most characterizes this type of popular uprising is rhizomatic solidarity, which I understand, following Deleuze and Guattari, to be solidarity consisting in situated, micropolitical, horizontal, and dialogical practices that allow it to persist under repression[37] and that dispense with the forms of representation and hierarchy typical of other forms of collaboration. An uprising inspired by and based on acts of rhizomatic solidarity pursues an objective that is different from that of civil disobedience, as well as from that of the classical revolutionary politics, whose vanguard is a political party seeking to seize power from the state.[38] The mobilizations of April 2018 displayed the characteristics of this understanding of uprising inspired by rhizomatic solidarity: they brought together in a public space a variety of actors, primarily young students, who inspired one another on social media and were thus called the "autoconvocados." These mobilizations not only opened public debate about human rights[39] and new ways of organizing, but they also seriously questioned the prevailing political paradigm, which held that the *caudillo* and the vanguard party[40] were essential for changing the status quo.

We university students had no weapons and little "political" experience in the classical sense; we were studying at college in order to become professionals who could "contribute to the country," as Ernesto Valle wrote. But we were also much involved in *proyección social* or community initiatives that promoted education, health, art, environmental conservation, human rights, and spirituality. Moreover, we were connected to the rest of the world through social media, which opened a window for us to the great variety of unarmed social movements, such as the Arab Spring and Occupy Wall Street, that had managed to disrupt the centers of political power in other parts of the world.[41] Some of us had already had experiences of social mobilization of greater scope in movements such as Occupy INSS in 2013 and the marches on Managua organized by the *Campesinos'* Anti-canal Movement in 2017. Not all the young Nicaraguans who occupied the streets and built the barricades in April 2018 had had the same experiences, but many of them were connected with the larger world and keenly interested in understanding how to adapt global struggles for justice to local struggles, and vice versa.

Our own interest in these struggles began on the university campus and in exchanges among fellow students in the classroom. The experiences of Josué, Gabriel, and Lila reflect how their formation in the UCA motivated them to participate in the April civic uprising. As I mentioned above, Josué moved out into the streets "from the classroom" while Lila's advance was from the *pasarela* benches; for Gabriel, it was social research that led him to involvement in social and political action.

Josué had already graduated with a law degree, but since he still had connections with the university community, he joined the students in the streets. During his undergraduate years, he had been a student representative and an activist for human rights and the LGBTQ struggle. When I asked him about his experience at the UCA, he told me that he had had "good teachers and bad teachers," but that he had been inspired to fight for justice in all his courses and in the opportunities he had to practice law. When I asked him why he had decided to join the protests, he told me a story about his days as a student representative. He had once been told by a teacher, "known for his ties with the government," that he should make an important decision without consulting his classmates; the reason, the teacher said, was that "a leader must make decisions if the people don't know what they want." For Josué, that *dedazo*[42] form of democracy made him reflect on how Nicaragua was being governed and on the importance of understanding human and civil rights in order to be able to challenge that type of governance. This was one of his motivations for joining the protests. He also joined to make the LGBTQ population more visible in the streets. He said that he had not previously felt that he was in a "totally safe space being a gay man" when outside the university. By taking to the streets, Josué believed that he was taking part of the united struggle for democracy while also giving evidence of the contributions of sexual diversity to the struggle and to society as a whole. In our conversation, Josué explained that one of the most important issues for the young protesters was the *dedazo* manner of doing politics in Nicaragua: favoring certain individuals and enforcing decisions with threats and violence. He stressed that these undemocratic tendencies had penetrated deeply into many areas of politics and life, even the classrooms.

Unlike Josué, whose ethico-political questioning began in the classrooms, Lila was moved to join the April uprising through the many opportunities she had for dialogue with peers and professors about postwar social psychology, social justice in Central America, and various types of feminism. These conversations, which took place both inside and outside the UCA, led her to read and reflect about "intersectionality"[43] in order to understand the full complexity of the national reality: "I realized that all our struggles are interconnected and that we have to work together." That conviction about the need to "work together" motivated her to march with other sectors "such as women, LGBTIQ+ persons, Afro and indigenous peoples, children, and so on. All of us were together there, confronting the *caudillo*, and we were agents of change." For Lila, the protests represented an opportunity to join with historically "disregarded or despised" sectors of the Nicaraguan people, so that history could be written in another way, without *caudillos* and with people practicing solidarity in the streets.

The April 2018 uprising forms part of a long legacy of student protests, but this particular uprising was unique in at least two ways: (1) it was autoconvocado through organizing strategies developed on social media,[44] including the spaces for dialogue mentioned by Lila; and (2) it raised ethical questions about the political culture of *caudillismo* and the strong-arm militancy evidenced in the slogan, "Free Nation or Death!" (Patria Libre o Morir).[45] In my conversations with Lila, Josué, and Gabriel, it became clear to me that all of us were part of a generation that had grown disillusioned with the politics of postwar Central America.[46] We had heard from our elders many anecdotes like the one narrated by Ernesto Valle on his blog, about how armed struggle was not worth it. We were consequently searching for meaning in other projects, including in education, which could guarantee us economic stability and provide us the knowledge we need to work for our country and our families.

Perhaps none of us when entering the UCA thought much about how the university community would contribute to our formation, but my interlocutors agreed with me that our experience at the university and the relationships we forged there, both in classes and outside, had given us a passion for social justice. We began to question the ethics of the revolutionary slogan, "Free Nation or Die" preferring instead to use "Patria libre y vivir" (Free Nation and Live), which we shouted in the April 2018 marches. This new, slogan defined our insurgency as a commitment to political practice that was based on values like horizontality, mutual care, full participation, autonomy, and making visible the sectors and demands long silenced in Nicaragua's official history. By going out into the streets, we young people had in a way turned that history in new direction[47]: we had recruited new actors and adopted new ways of proceeding. Although it is still difficult to know what impact this movement will have on the political culture of the nation, or whether university autonomy will survive the dictatorship, we feel certain that Nicaragua will always have young people willing to work for social change and justice.

Achievements and challenges for the UCA

> I believe that the UCA, even in 2018, continued to nourish a vision of human rights and to work for social justice, and this was made evident in its actions. There's no need for me to say much, but I remember how the university gave refuge to many people in the midst of the chaos of the May 30th march, because I was there. And I have to say that I always felt protected and safe at the UCA—as a student, an activist, and a gay person. I always felt I was fully accepted and able to question and disagree.
>
> *(Josué, graduate in law)*

According to Ignacio Ellacuría, S.J., a Jesuit university is called to respond to the historical reality of its time. As a center for formation and intellectual work, its mission is to teach students, carry out research, and develop a vision and projects of proyección social in ways that challenge the dominant system and offer alternatives that are "liberating" and "humanizing."[48] My interlocutors and I agree that the UCA, in different ways and to a different degree, helped to form us for "liberation," not only in the meaning we gave that word during the 2018 uprising but also in the way we understand our professional work. When discussing our experiences, we highlighted the ones that had most affected us. For Josué, it was the formation that had occurred in the classrooms and in his practicums; for Lila, it was the social service project that had aroused her interest in the feminist cause; and for Gabriel, it had been a combination of research opportunities and discussions outside the classroom. Thus, each of them highlighted one of the three aspects that Ellacuría considered as essential to the mission of the university.

Teaching: "seeing the world differently" and "finding my vocation"

In recounting his experience of studying law at the UCA, Josué explained that the UCA had "taught [him] how to exercise [his] profession as a humanistic service." Many factors had contributed to his formation experience, but Josué stressed the classroom teaching and the way his formal education was related to his activism. These were the essential elements that helped him to "see the world differently" and to choose to become a mediator. For him, everything began with two classes, theological reflection and introduction to gender studies, which taught him about other ways of understanding spirituality, his sexuality, and his rights. The discussion in these classes helped Josué to reflect on his own sexuality as a gay man and to accept it "with greater freedom." The process was facilitated by feeling safe to express himself on campus and in class.

As part of his formation, Josué worked as a paralegal in a human rights center and promoted LGBTQ rights at the university, and in both activities, he received professional support from his teachers. These activities helped him decide on his "vocation" since it was during this time that he discovered the importance of mediation as an alternative, peaceful way of resolving conflicts. Josué described his mediation work as his way of adding a "grain of sand for social change" because he could use it to facilitate dialogue and help resolve legal conflicts for persons "who had no way to pay for a lawyer." His "vocation" to be a mediator also motivated him to get involved in the uprising: he thought it was "a powerful thing that people were taking to the streets peacefully" and that everyone was practicing participatory democracy in a way that was radically different from the *dedazo* democracy with which Nicaragua was being governed.

Proyección Social: "from saying to doing" and "being part of the change"

When Lila began studying psychology, she was interested in dedicating herself to clinical work. She had decided to study at the UCA "because they told me it was prestigious, and some of my relatives had studied there." During her studies, however, she became more interested in gender studies, social psychology, and feminism because they connected to her life experience. While she learned a lot in classes, she felt that the most important formation she received had taken place in the student-run spaces for dialogue, in her meetings with female classmates and teachers, and in the social service she performed at the Ignacio Martín-Baró Psychosocial Development Center. During her social service, she began to do more research so that she could provide care for adult survivors of childhood sexual abuse, and she recalled an important event in her own life: "I remembered that I also had been abused as a child, and that I had dissociated from it."

That discovery disturbed Lila, so that shortly after completing her social service, she decided to seek professional help. She received emotional support from a couple of teachers and from female classmates, with whom she attended mutual support groups that were feminist-oriented. Lila now feels "healthy" and "reconnected with life." She is interested in continuing to study sexual abuse and other forms of violence against women in Nicaragua from a historical and social psychology perspective. She found that the experience of service learning changed her life in a positive way because it allowed her to reflect on her own life and to work to heal the wounds of sexual abuse while collaborating with others engaged in the same process. Her experience during service learning led her to do further research on postwar social psychology, which she discussed with her friends. She also reflected on how sexual abuse was intertwined with other forms of systemic violence in Nicaragua. Studying the long history of political violence against women and children[49] helped to inform and motivate her activism.

Calling herself a "diverse feminist activist," Lila has helped to organize activities and marches to commemorate International Women's Day (March 8th) and other events related to feminist struggles for the last six years. Because of her experience as an activist and psychologist, she took part in the April uprising in order to join forces with those who had been historically "silenced" but now were making their voice heard on the streets. She stated that the government repression that began on the night of April 18, 2018, was not a surprise for feminist activists like her, who had often been harassed by the police before. Lila was still uncertain about the ultimate impact of the protests on the future of national politics, but she was happy "to have been part of the change." Her involvement in the struggle was in large part due to her formation as a psychologist at the UCA and to the accompaniment of "so many important women"—teachers, friends, therapists—both inside and outside the classroom.

Research: a "decentralized" vision that reveals "many Nicaraguas"

After attending the Jesuit high school in Managua, Gabriel attended the UCA, where he obtained a degree in sociology. Like Lila, he enrolled at the UCA because he considered it prestigious, but also because he wanted to study "something related to social problems." The formation he received at the UCA made him question his earlier vision of reality. Especially helpful in this regard were the mentoring of his tutor and the conversations he had outside the classroom with members of his study group. He said that he had arrived at the university as an "idealistic" young man: "I believed that I could change things from my own perspective and do so quickly." But his encounters with his classmates, most of whom were working adults, helped him to see things from other perspectives. His fellow students were "people from the city and from rural areas; they were of different religions and ages; they had different gender identities and different political visions." After class, he always stayed to converse with classmates about what they had learned in class, to reflect on social problems, and to talk about their lives. Those conversations made him realize that "the world was more complicated" and social problems more intractable than he had formerly believed. They also made him question the history of Nicaragua and the ideas he had been taught at home, for he came from a "Sandinista family," where everything the government did was extolled. Learning about other perspectives was an enriching experience for Gabriel, one that motivated him to learn more about "the many Nicaraguas" that existed besides the one he knew. He wanted to know more about the rural, Indigenous, and migrant "Nicaraguas" that were discussed in his classes.

Thus, when the opportunity presented itself, Gabriel applied for an internship as a research student at the UCA's Education Institute (IDEUCA), which is now part of the Social Sciences Interdisciplinary Institute. He later became a fellow at a center dedicated to rural development. These experiences in research and praxis allowed him to study the more worrisome aspects of the national reality with interdisciplinary lenses. More importantly, they provided Gabriel with an important opportunity to question the "Managua-centric" version of reality that "we sometimes reproduce in the classroom unwittingly or out of ignorance." This questioning led him to become interested in problems related to environmental protection and to join the *Campesinos'* Anti-Canal Movement, which was protesting the proposed construction of an interoceanic canal through Nicaragua.

Despite his family's opposition, Gabriel took part in the April protests because he now had a broader vision of national problems thanks to his research experience. "By then," he told me, "I was quite aware of how serious the government's human rights violations were, especially in the rural areas." Another reason for joining the protests was that many of his friends and colleagues were also involved: "I felt I had to take part because of what was happening to the others. I was not directly affected by the repression, but other people I knew and communities I knew were affected." Even though the repression had not affected Gabriel directly, his decision to join the collective struggle was a result of his training as a sociologist: he had learned to see reality from "a perspective of tolerance and horizontality," and he had come to understand "the need for collective struggles" thanks to his discussions with colleagues and his work with communities outside of Managua. When asked what he meant by "horizontality," he explained that he was referring to the collective and egalitarian nature of the protests: "All the people, though quite diverse, came out together. ... It began with us students, perhaps because we had a little more experience with dialogue and tolerance, but we also learned from the others, especially from the *campesinos*." Gabriel said that one of the most important things he had learned at the UCA was the practice of dialogue, which took the form not only of dialogue with his classmates but also dialogue with scholarly studies and his fellow researchers.

> As was the case for my colleagues, I also found that the UCA helped me to 'decentralize' my way of viewing reality and to realize that the personal is political. It also helped me to orient my professional work to the service of others. All these lessons guided me in my choice of vocation, and they still guide my human rights activism and my preference for action-oriented research.

As the UCA has facilitated these experiences and insights for us, it has been facing state repression as well. Given the neoliberal context and the current dictatorship in Nicaragua, the UCA is under a constant state of siege, and threats of violence are constantly made against the university community. Moreover, as a means of economic retaliation, the government has since 2018 reduced its assistance to the university by more than 60%.[50] This sharp reduction in funds has especially affected students who depend on scholarships to attend the university; it also threatens to reduce the university's resources and its ability to contribute to social change through its threefold function of teaching, research, and proyección social.

From islands to rhizomes

> For me the UCA is an island that has remained strong in its determination to fight for social justice and to care for its students in a way that other universities have not. That is admirable, but if the UCA wants to connect with the rest of Nicaragua, I think that it must first try to build better bridges among those who belong to its family in order to generate greater trust, and it must continue to work on creating interdisciplinary, intergenerational work projects. ... If we graduates and students don't know what's

actually happening with the university and don't have more opportunity for dialogue, how are we going to support their work, and how are they going to support ours?

(Gabriel, graduate in sociology)

All of my interlocutors participated in the April 2018 uprising as a result of their formation at the UCA, but they sometimes felt that they were not fully supported by the university in their efforts to organize. For example, near the end of our conversation, Gabriel said that, although he took to the streets "thanks to the university," he also thought that "the university was at fault." When I asked him to explain what he meant, he told me that he was "thankful to the university" for the formation he had received and for making the campus a safe place for dialogue. The students were mistaken, though, when they "naively assumed that off campus the situation was going to be the same." "The university was at fault" because "we were not ready: we didn't have much experience in organizing. Perhaps if we had had an organized student movement earlier, we wouldn't have made some of the mistakes we did." These comments make me stop and think about the challenges that the UCA faces regarding the politization of its students, especially in a context of state violence.

During her years as a student before 2018, Lila told me, the UCA had limited the spaces and activities on campus where the government could be directly criticized; the objective was to avoid "radical politicization" of the university. She acknowledged that this policy changed in April 2018 because of the role assumed by the UCA in the protests. Even since then, however, she and her fellow students have not felt fully supported by the university in their efforts to organize political activities on campus, such as student forums, meetings, and marches. Lila admitted that the UCA has legitimate fears for security reasons, but she regretted that the students were not given the institutional support they needed for "organizing a movement from the grassroots," as circumstances had demanded during the April uprising.

Gabriel maintained that there is a kind of "knowledge gap" about why no student movement had existed at the UCA before 2018. Some students had expressed their desire to organize a movement during the protests, but by that time, "the university was fearful that we might organize ourselves as an autonomous sector." In an effort to understand better this lack of organization, Gabriel began to investigate the reasons for the prior lack of a student movement or student representation at the UCA. He found that the UCA had stopped having democratically elected student representatives in the 1990s, after the demonstrations for the restoration of the 6%. At that time the university student movement throughout the country was almost completely controlled by the FSLN.[51] Studying these historical developments helped Gabriel understand why there had been no student movement at the UCA. He still believed, however, that students should "know that history" and that spaces for dialogue among all the members of the university community needed to be opened up for that purpose. Gabriel also seemed to be asking the UCA for unconditional support for political activities, but such support might not be possible in the current situation of government repression against the university. Moreover, the students and graduates who agree with Gabriel's demands want something that goes beyond the mission of the Jesuit university as described by Ellacuría. What is needed, therefore, is an intergenerational, multisectoral dialogue for the purpose of understanding (1) the possibilities and the limits of the university's accompaniment of its students, (2) the history of student movements at the UCA, and (3) the type of accompaniment desired and needed by the students in the present socio-political situation.

Like Gabriel, Josué also thought that there is a need for dialogue in the university community for the sake of strengthening "solidarity" among teachers, students, administrators, and other workers. Such dialogue would treat the needs and demands of different sectors, and it would be geared to "making decisions" in a more consensual way. Gabriel's experience had taught him that the UCA, despite significant efforts, still lacked the mechanisms for promoting a multisectoral dialogue that would unify the efforts of all and strengthen the solidarity that emerged spontaneously during the protests. In his words:

> April brought us together as a university community. There was a sense of equality among students, teachers, and other workers who were out in the streets. As a university and as a country we felt a spirit of solidarity. But this same spirit needs to be made evident in the mechanisms for dialogue within the university. ... Previously there were some suggestion boxes on campus, but nobody was collecting and reading the notes that the students put in them. In the end people used them just to leave jokes and garbage. For me that was evidence of a tremendous lack of dialogue, and that led us more or less to where we are now. The problem is not just the university: it is in the whole of society. We Nicaraguans fail to dialogue, and then we fight.

Josué was here referring to the lack of dialogue that is characteristic of Nicaraguan society, but he believed that the university must strive to generate internal discussion that leads to social change. To achieve that, it would not only have to create spaces for dialogue about the challenges and demands of different sectors but also make decisions in a more consensual manner.[52] Lila also mentioned the importance of dialogue for strengthening solidarity within the university community and for creating support networks to confront the challenges the university faces because of the repression. She explained that in the UCA, there are "families," but these "families" are "islands" disconnected from one another—just as the UCA is an "island" detached from the rest of higher education in Nicaragua. She put it this way:

> In the UCA there are many families. I experienced this in my department, with my fellow students and some teachers. They supported each other.

> And I saw the same thing at the research center where I worked. Amid all the challenges, there was a sense of community, and you felt accompanied. Between those families, however, there was not the same communication. ... Even for the end-of-year parties, each sector had its own separate event. In my view, that didn't help us to know about the needs and the interests of each sector. ... The repression made everything worse because it generated fear about who was with Ortega and who wasn't.

Here Lila commented on how the experience of community before the start of repression differed from what it was afterward. Before the repression, it was easier to have a "family" made up of teachers and fellow students, and her closeness with them made the UCA feel like a "home." But the fear generated by government repression reduced the opportunities for dialogue, so that the various sectors of the university community had little knowledge about the needs and demands of other sectors. Lila considered such dialogue to be necessary, but she thought it would be a challenge while the university is still under fire:

> What makes things difficult is that the UCA is itself like an island that continues to protect its students from the repression of the regime as far as it can. That is something no state university or no other private university is doing. But I think that it's urgent to have dialogue among the different sectors and between young people and adults so that these "families" stop being islands and so that the UCA itself stops being an island in this struggle in Nicaragua.

Putting Lila's invitation to dialogue into practice is a challenge. It means "understanding history," as Gabriel tried to do, and "listening to one another," as Josué proposed. Lila urged students and teachers to build bridges among all the "island families" to reaffirm the internal solidarity of the university community. Only in this way will the UCA community have the strength it needs to overcome the challenges it faces as a result of the neoliberal policies and the repression of the regime. Such internal dialogue and bridge-building would help the UCA to develop further the type of rhizomatic solidarity that manifested itself on the streets of Nicaragua during the 2018 uprising. It could even serve as a model that would inspire the international community to consider new forms of solidarity with the UCA and all the people of Nicaragua.

Conclusion: "You will flourish, Nicaragua!"

> The children descend from the volcano / descend like the lava / with their bouquets of flowers / just as roots descend.
>
> *(Claribel Alegría)*[53]

The last time I saw Lila was almost two years ago. We met in the central plaza of Antigua Guatemala, and we sat down on a bench to talk. It was strange to be there, in a place where the Hispanic elites had declared the independence of Central America centuries before. The independence they declared was only that of their class. The great majority in the region, including the young, continued to experience the hard reality of inequality, unemployment, racism, and lack of full citizenship.[54] There, in that resonant place, Lila and I sat down to talk and to remember April, and also to tell each other about our lives as migrants. Exile had been more bitter for her than for me. Despite everything, I had the privilege of finding a safe home. After much laughing and crying as we shared our memories of April, I asked her if she thought the uprising was worth it. She told me that she still wasn't sure because all of us are roots that remain uprooted. Nevertheless, she hoped that we would some day flourish, whether in Nicaragua or in exile. Together, we talked about Claribel Alegría's poem, a line of which opens this section; we found ourselves commenting on the roots of hope and the possibility of flourishing or flowering. The refrain "You will flourish, Nicaragua!" was very popular during the uprising; it was painted on the streets, embroidered onto shirts, and endlessly echoed on social media. It had never really occurred to me that we could flourish elsewhere, far from our roots, far from Nicaragua. They have pulled up our roots, Lila said, but they have not burned them. We could therefore still hope to flourish and bring a little bit of Nicaragua to wherever we went.

When I feel discouraged about the current state of Nicaragua, my hope is renewed when I remember that my roots run deep and that we can flourish even far from home. But I also know that those who remain in the country must also flourish, and to do that they need safe spaces that are bastions of resistance, places where democracy can be discussed and practiced. That is why the UCA is such an important space and must not be abandoned. If it is to survive the repression, it requires international solidarity. As Ellacuría once said, we need more "eyes"[55]; we need the helping hands of different international actors, especially other academic communities, in order to achieve the level of sympathy and support that will allow the UCA to continue to provide abundant space for social change in Nicaragua during and after the dictatorship.

Long live the students!

Notes

1 Duriez González, 2016, quoted in José Luis Rocha. *Provocation and Protest: University Students in Nicaragua's Uprising.* Chicago: LACASA Chicago Press: 173.
2 Rafael Lucio Gil. "Autonomía y libertad de cátedra en la educación superior." *El Nuevo Diario*, 2015. https://www.elnuevodiario.com.ni/opinion/380130-autonomia-libertad-catedra-educacion-superior/.
3 I conducted three semi-structured interviews, each lasting approximately 60 minutes. The conversations with my interlocutors also continued later through emails, text messages, and informal conversations.

4 Gilles Deleuze and Félix Guattari. *Rizoma*. Valencia: Pre-Textos, 2016.
5 Ignacio Ellacuría. *Escritos universitarios*. San Salvador: UCA Editores, 1999: 112.
6 Josué, Lila, and Gabriel are pseudonyms, adopted to protect the identity of the interviewees, given the human rights situation in Nicaragua. Since all three participated in the April uprising, the pseudonyms are necessary to guarantee their safety.
7 The *pasarela* is the walkway that traverses the center of the university campus. With its many benches and trees, it has traditionally been a meeting space for students after class. It also serves as an assembly point for those preparing to go to marches and demonstrations.
8 Irene Agudelo and Jessica Martínez. "Revueltas de abril: narrativas, redes y espacios en disputa" in *Nicaragua 2018. La Insurrección cívica de Abril*, 21–72. Managua: Universidad Centroamericana, 2020: 27.
9 By "non-human" populations I mean the species of flora and fauna negatively affected by the projects promoted by the Ortega government, such as the interoceanic canal that would threaten the integrity and the sovereignty of Lake Nicaragua and the protected areas around it. See Nicaraguan Center for Human Rights. *Concesión del canal interoceánico en Nicaragua: grave impacto en los derechos humanos. Comunidades campesinas movilizadas resisten*. Managua: Autor, 2016.
10 Fiore Bran Aragón and Jennifer Goett. "¡Matria Libre y Vivir! Youth Activism and Nicaragua's 2018 Insurrection" *Journal of Latin American and Caribbean Anthropology*, Special Issue: Generations and Change in Central America, 2020: 1–20.
11 José Luis Rocha. *Provocation and Protest: University Students in Nicaragua's Uprising*. Chicago: LACASA Chicago Press, 2019: 130.
12 Fabrice Le Lous. "Enrieth Martínez de la Coalición Universitaria: Esto es una Revolución." *La Prensa*. https://www.laprensa.com.ni/2018/06/03/suplemento/la-prensa-domingo/2428873-enrieth-martinez-de-la-coalicion-universitaria-esta-es-una-revolucion.
13 José Luis Rocha. "El tigre nica en la rebelión de abril." *Envío 434*, May 2018. https://www.envio.org.ni/articulo/5480.
14 Equipo Envío. "Nicaragua. El cerco se estrecha, y en la mira las redes sociales." *Envío 433*, April 2018. https://www.envio.org.ni/articulo/5465.
15 Luciana Chamorro and Emilia Yang. "Movilización social y tácticas de control en el neosandinismo: El caso de #OcupaINSS." *Cahiers des Amériques Latines 87*, 2018: 91–115.
16 According to a study by the National Agency for the Promotion of Investment, of the 175,000 university students in the country in 2017, only 11.5% were studying humanities and social sciences. See PRONicaragua. *Estudio de población universitaria 2017*. Managua, 2017.
17 Keyling Romero and Franklin Villavicencio. "Los universitarios expulsados por la dictadura de Daniel Ortega." *Niú*, 2019. https://niu.com.ni/los-universitarios-expulsados-por-la-dictadura/.
18 Franklin Villavicencio and Claudia Tijerino. "Los estudiantes no tienen paz después de las balas." *Niú*, December 10, 2018. https://niu.com.ni/los-estudiantes-no-tienen-paz-despues-de-las-balas/.
19 Joshua Partlow. "'They Are Shooting at a Church': Inside the 15-Hour Siege by Nicaraguan Paramilitaries on University Students." *Washington Post*, July 18, 2018. https://www.washingtonpost.com/world/students-in-nicaragua-trapped-in-church-amid-gunfire-by-pro-government-militias/2018/07/14/c7f04512-86e3-11e8-9e06-4db52ac42e05_story.html.
20 Martha Nussbaum. *Not for Profit. Why Democracy Needs the Humanities*. New Jersey: Princeton University Press, 2010, 24–26.

21 See Chapter 3 in this volume, "The Impact of Neoliberal Reform and Repression on Higher Education in Nicaragua," by Wendi Bellanger.
22 Keyling Romero and Franklin Villavicencio, 2019.
23 *Encuentro*, 40 (79) (2008): 4–62. https://www.uca.edu.ni/2/images/Revista-Encuentro/Revistas/e79/79-completo.pdf.
24 "Régimen de Daniel Ortega pretende adoctrinar a estudiantes de escuelas públicas." *100% Noticias*, February 17, 2020. https://100noticias.com.ni/nacionales/98735-regimen-daniel-ortega-pretende-adoctrinar-estudian/. See also the Social Science Curriculum in Nicaragua: https://nicaraguaeduca.mined.gob.ni/index.php/mup-secundaria-regular/.
25 See Chapter 3 in this volume, by Wendi Bellanger.
26 Louis Althusser. "Ideology and Ideological State Apparatuses" in Slavoj Žižek, ed. *Mapping Ideology*. New York: Verso, 1994: 100–140.
27 Elthon Rivera. "La involución de la educación superior en Nicaragua desde 2018." *Confidencial*, January 18, 2021. https://confidencial.com.ni/opinion/la-involucion-de-la-educacion-superior-en-nicaragua-desde-2018/. See also Nicaraguan Foundation for Social and Economic Development. *La calidad de la educación en Nicaragua, ¿Goza la niñez de las mismas oportunidades?* Managua: Autor, 2017. https://funides.com/publicaciones/la-calidad-de-la-educacion-en-nicaragua/.
28 Sergio Ramírez. "Los nietos de la revolución. Jóvenes lúcidos y sin artimañas políticas luchan por la democracia en Nicaragua." *El País*. May 29, 2018. https://elpais.com/elpais/2018/05/29/opinion/1527603461_596779.html.
29 Elvira Cuadra and Leonor Zúniga. "Jóvenes y Cultura Política en Nicaragua. La generación del 2000." Managua: Centro de Investigaciones de la Comunicación, 2011. https://cinco.org.ni/archive/348.pdf. See also Sofía Montenegro. "La masculinidad hegemónica en los jóvenes de la posrevolución." Managua: Centro de Investigaciones de la Comunicación, 2016. https://cinco.org.ni/archive/569.pdf.
30 Alberto Sánchez Arguello. "Nicaragua, generación millennial y yo." *Confidencial*, June 7, 2016. https://confidencial.com.ni/opinion/jovenes/nicaragua-generacion-millenial/.
31 Cymene Howe. *Intimate activism: The Struggle for Sexual Rights in Postrevolutionary Nicaragua*. North Carolina: Duke University Press, 2013. See also Zachary Wilmort. "Revolution for Whom? Miskitos and Sandinistas in Revolutionary Nicaragua, 1979-1986." Paper presented at the 2017 American Sociological Association Annual Meeting in Montreal. https://www.academia.edu/34621709/Revolution_for_Whom_Miskitos_and_Sandinistas_in_Revolutionary_Nicaragua_1979_1986.
32 Ileana Rodríguez. "La construcción del pueblo y las masas como subalternos: 'Hombrecito' / Hombre nuevo" in Juan Pablo Gómez and Camilo Antillón, eds. *Antología Del Pensamiento Crítico Nicaragüense Contemporáneo*. Colección Antologías Del Pensamiento Social Latinoamericano y Caribeño. Argentina: CLACSO, 2016, 269–284.
33 Ernesto Valle, quoted in Alberto Sánchez Arguello. "Nicaragua, generación millennial y yo." *Confidencial*.
34 Deleuze and Guattari. *Rizoma*. Valencia: Pre-Textos, 2016.
35 Saul Newman. "What Is an Insurrection? Destituent Power and Ontological Anarchy in Agamben and Stirner." *Political Studies 65*, 2 (June 2017): 284–99. https://doi.org/10.1177/0032321716654498.
36 Ibidem, 297.
37 "As opposed to a structure, which is defined by a set of points and positions, of binary relations between those points, and of biunivocal relations between those positions,

the rhizome is made up only of lines: of lines of segmentarity and of stratification as dimensions, but also as a line of flight or deterritorialization." In Gilles Deleuze and Félix Guattari. *Rizoma*. Valencia: Pre-Textos, 2016, 48.
38 Irene Agudelo and Jessica Martínez. 2020. "Revueltas de abril: narrativas, redes y espacios en disputa."
39 For example, feminist movements, LGBTIQ communities, and *campesinos* marched together for the first time to demand the recognition of identity, land, and the rights to self-determination, along with demands for democratization and justice. See Jennifer Goett. "Beyond Left and Right: Grassroots Social Movements and Nicaragua's Civic Insurrection." *LASA Forum 49* (4): 25–31, 2018.
40 Emilio Álvarez Montalván. *Cultura política Nicaragüense*. Managua: Colección Presidencial Enrique Bolaños, 2006, 88–92.
41 Bran Aragón and Goett. "¡Matria Libre y Vivir! Youth Activism and Nicaragua's 2018 Insurrection", 2020.
42 In Nicaragua the phrase *al dedazo* ("by fingerprint") denotes the appointment of a person to a public position with no regard for democratic procedure. Such appointments are said to be "dedocratic."
43 Here Lila uses "intersectionality" as understood by Crenshaw: it is a lens through which one can see where power originates, interlocks, and intersects. See Kimberle Crenshaw. "Demarginalizing the Intersection of Race and Sex: A Black Feminist Critique of Antidiscrimination Doctrine, Feminist Theory and Antiracist Politics," *University of Chicago Legal Forum:* 1 (1989): 139–167. http://chicagounbound.uchicago.edu/uclf/vol1989/iss1/.
44 José Luis Rocha. *Provocation and Protest: University Students in Nicaragua 's Uprising*. Chicago: LACASA Chicago Press, 2019: x.
45 Fiore Bran Aragón and Jennifer Goett. 2021: 16.
46 Irina Carlota Silber. *Everyday Revolutionaries. Gender, violence, and disillusionment in postwar El Salvador*. New Jersey: Rutgers University Press, 2011. See also Ralph Sprenkels. "El trabajo de la memoria en Centroamérica. Cinco propuestas heurísticas en torno a las guerras en El Salvador, Guatemala y Nicaragua." *Revista de Historia de la Universidad de Costa Rica*, 76:13–46, 2017.
47 Walter Benjamin. *Illuminations*. New York: Schocken Books, 1968, 261–263.
48 Ignacio Ellacuría. *Escritos universitarios*. San Salvador: UCA Editores, 1999, 99–114.
49 Abbie Fields. "Enfrentando los silencios: ¿Es posible construir una memoria 'pública' de la violencia sexual 'privada'?" Paper presented at the VI Central American Congress of Cultural Studies in Managua.
50 "UCA denuncia recorte de fondos del 6%, como castigo por su posición crítica." *Despacho 505*. December 22, 2020. https://www.despacho505.com/uca-denuncia-recorte-de-fondos-del-6-como-castigo-por-su-posicion-critica/.
51 Augusto Morales. "NICARAGUA.- La lucha contra UNEN y los desafíos de los grupos estudiantiles de oposición." *Revista de Centroamérica*, June 18, 2019. https://revistadecentroamerica.org/index.php/nicaragua/26-nicaragua-la-lucha-contra-unen-y-los-desafios-de-los-grupos-estudiantiles-de-oposicion.
52 For example, a question that came up in my conversation with Josué was why the UCA decided to continue with the construction of a food court in 2018, even after the protests. The food court was part of a plan that had existed before the April uprising, but Josué thought it was important to question how much a food court contributes to the university during a period of repression.
53 "Flores del Volcán," by Claribel Alegría. *Pasos Inciertos*. Antología personal. Madrid: Visor Libros, 2015.
54 Carlos Sandoval García. *Centroamérica desgarrada. Demandas y expectativas de jóvenes residentes en zonas empobrecidas*. Argentina: CLACSO, 2020.
55 Ignacio Ellacuría. *Escritos universitarios*. San Salvador: UCA Editores, 1999, 306.

References

Agudelo, Irene and Jessica Martínez. "April Riots: Disputed Narratives, Networks and Spaces." In *Nicaragua 2018. The Civic Insurrection of April*. Managua: Central American University, 2020: 21–72.
Althusser, Louis. "Ideology and ideological state Apparatuses." In *Mapping Ideology*, edited by Slavoj Zizek. New York: Verso, 1994: 100–140.
Álvarez Montalván, Emilio. *Nicaraguan political culture*. Managua: Enrique Bolaños Presidential Collection, 2006.
Benjamin, Walter. *Illuminations*. New York: Schocken Books, 1968.
Bran Aragón, Fiore and Jennifer Goett. "Free Matria and Live! Youth Activism and Nicaragua's 2018 Insurrection." *Journal of Latin American and Caribbean Anthropology*, Special Issue Generations and Change in Central America (2021): 1–20. DOI: 10.1111/jlca.12531
Chamorro, Luciana and Emilia Yang. "Social Mobilization and Control Tactics in Neo-Sandinism: The Case of #OcupaINSS." *Cahiers des Amériques Latines*, 87 (2018): 91–115.
Crenshaw, Kimberle. "Demarginalizing the Intersection of Race and Sex: A Black Feminist Critique of Antidiscrimination Doctrine, Feminist Theory and Antiracist Politics." *University of Chicago Legal Forum: 1 1989*, 1 (1989): 139–167. http://chicagounbound.uchicago.edu/uclf/vol1989/iss1/
Cuadra, Elvira and Leonor Zúniga. *Youth and Political Culture in Nicaragua. The Generation of 2000*. Managua: Communication Research Center, 2011. https://cinco.org.ni/archive/348.pdf
Daniel Ortega's regime intends to indoctrinate public school students. *100% Noticias*, February 17, 2020. https://100noticias.com.ni/nacionales/98735-regimen-daniel-ortega-pretende-adoctrinar-estudian/
Deleuze, Gilles and Félix Guattari. *Rhizome*. Valencia: Pre-Texts, 2016.
Ellacuría, Ignacio. *University Writings*. San Salvador: UCA Editores, 1999.
Encuentro, 40(79) (2008): 4–62. https://www.uca.edu.ni/2/images/Revista-Encuentro/Revistas/e79/79-completo.pdf
Envío. "Nicaragua. The Fence Tightens, and Social Networks Are in the Sights." *Envío*. 433, April, 2018. https://www.envio.org.ni/articulo/5465
Fields, Abbie. "Facing the Silences: Is it Possible to Build a Public Memory of Private Sexual Violence?" Paper presented at the *VI Central American Congress of Cultural Studies in Managua*, 2017.
Goett, Jennifer. "Beyond Left and Right: Grassroots Social Movements and Nicaragua's Civic Insurrection." *LASA Forum*, 49(4) (2018): 25–31.
Howe, Cymene. *Intimate Activism: The Struggle for Sexual Rights in Postrevolutionary Nicaragua*. North Carolina: Duke University Press, 2013.
Joy, Claribel. *Uncertain Steps. Personal Anthology*. Madrid: Book Viewer, 2015.
Le Lous, Fabrice. "Enrieth Martínez of the University Coalition: This Is a Revolution." *La Prensa*, 2018. https://www.laprensa.com.ni/2018/06/03/suplemento/la-prensa-domingo/2428873-enrieth-martinez-de-la-coalicion-universitaria-esta-es-una-revolucion
Ministry of Education (MINED). "Macro Regular Secondary Pedagogical Unit." n.d. https://nicaraguaeduca.mined.gob.ni/index.php/mup-secundaria-regular/
Montenegro, Sofia. *Hegemonic Masculinity in post-Revolution Youth*. Managua: Communication Research Center, 2016. https://cinco.org.ni/archive/569.pdf

Morales, Augusto. "NICARAGUA. – The Fight against UNEN and the Challenges of Opposition Student Groups." *Revista de Centroamérica*, June 18, 2019. https://revistadecentroamerica.org/index.php/nicaragua/26-nicaragua-la-lucha-contra-unen-y-los-desafios-de-los-grupo-estudiantiles-de-opposition

Newman, Saul. "What Is an Insurrection? Destituent Power and Ontological Anarchy in Agamben and Stirner." *Political Studies*, 65 (2) (2017): 284–299. DOI: 10.1177/0032321716654498

Nicaraguan Center for Human Rights. *Concession of the Interoceanic Canal in Nicaragua: Serious Impact on Human Rights. Mobilized Peasant Communities Resist*. Managua: Author, 2016.

Nicaraguan Foundation for Social and Economic Development. *The Quality of Education in Nicaragua. Do Children Enjoy the Same Opportunities?* Managua: Author, 2017. https://funides.com/publicaciones/la-calidad-de-la-educacion-en-nicaragua/

Nussbaum, Martha. *Not for Profit. Why Democracy Needs the Humanities*. New Jersey: Princeton University Press, 2010, 24–26.

Partlow, Joshua. "'They Are Shooting at a Church': Inside the 15-Hour Siege by Nicaraguan Paramilitaries on University Students." *Washington Post*, July 18, 2018. https://www.washingtonpost.com/world/students-in-nicaragua-trapped-in-church-amid-gunfire-by-pro-government-militias/2018/07/14/c7f04512-86e3-11e8-9e06-4db52ac42e05_story.html

PRONicaragua. *Study of the University Population 2017*. Managua: Author, 2017. http://pronicaragua.gob.ni/media/ckeditor/2018/05/07/estudio-de-poblacion-universitario-2017.pdf

Ramírez, Sergio. "The Grandchildren of the Revolution. Lucid Young People without Political Tricks Fight for Democracy in Nicaragua." *The country*, May 29, 2018. https://elpais.com/elpais/2018/05/29/opinion/1527603461_596779.html

Rivera, Elthon. "The Involution of Higher Education in Nicaragua since 2018." *Confidencial*, January 18, 2021. https://confidencial.com.ni/opinion/la-involucion-de-la-educacion-superior-en-nicaragua-desde-2018/

Romero, Keyling and Franklin Villavicencio. "The University Students Expelled by the Dictatorship of Daniel Ortega." *Niú*, 2019. https://niu.com.ni/los-universitarios-expulsados-por-la-dictadura/

Rocha, José Luis. "The Nicaraguan Tiger in the April Rebellion." *Shipment 434*, May, 2018. https://www.envio.org.ni/articulo/5480

Rocha, José Luis. *Provocation and Protest: University Students in Nicaragua's Uprising*. Chicago: LACASA Chicago Press, 2019.

Rodriguez, Ileana. "The Construction of the People and the Masses as Subaltern: Hombrecito / Hombre nuevo." In Juan Pablo Gómez and Camilo Antillón, eds. *Anthology of Contemporary Nicaraguan Critical Thought*. Collection Anthologies of Latin American and Caribbean Social Thought. Argentina: CLACSO, 2016, 269–284.

Sánchez Arguello, Alberto. "Nicaragua, millennial generation and me." *Confidencial*, June 7, 2016. https://confidencial.com.ni/opinion/jovenes/nicaragua-generacion-millenial/

Sandoval García, Carlos. *Central America Torn Apart. Demands and Expectations of Young Residents in Impoverished Areas*. Argentina: CLACSO, 2020.

Silber, Irina Carlota. *Everyday Revolutionaries. Gender, Violence, and Disillusionment in Postwar El Salvador*. New Jersey: Rutgers University Press, 2011.

Sprenkels, Ralph. "Memory Work in Central America. Five Heuristic Proposals around the Wars in El Salvador, Guatemala and Nicaragua." *History Magazine of the University of Costa Rica*, 76 (2017): 13–46.

UCA denounces cut of funds of 6%, as punishment for its critical position. *Dispatch 505*. December 22, 2020. https://www.despacho505.com/uca-denuncia-recorte-de-fondos-del-6-como-castigo-por-su-posicion-critica/

Villavicencio, Franklin and Claudia Tijerino. "The Students Have No Peace after the Bullets." *Niu*, December 10, 2018. https://niu.com.ni/los-estudiantes-no-tienen-paz-despues-de-las-balas/

Wilmort, Zachary. "Revolution for Whom? Miskitos and Sandinistas in Revolutionary Nicaragua, 1979–1986." Paper presented at the *2017 American Sociological Association Annual Meeting in Montreal*. 2017. https://www.academia.edu/34621709/Revolution_for_Whom_Miskitos_and_Sandinistas_in_Revolutionary_Nicaragua_1979_1986

PART 3
Solidarity and Implications beyond Nicaragua

6
CYBORG SOLIDARITY WITH NICARAGUA AND DIGITAL/ ANALOGUE ENTANGLEMENTS

Andrew Gorvetzian

Introduction: the problems that confront us all

In April 2018, I spent my last days in Nicaragua witnessing students protest the state's mismanagement of the fire in Indio Maiz, a crucial biological reserve in the southern autonomous region. The Sandinista government rejected an offer of aid from Costa Rica and prohibited journalists and environmental groups from accessing the reserve, adding to the protestors' indignation. Young people were unwilling to sit back and watch the fire burn unchecked. They gathered in front of the gates of the UCA at dusk, with signs and songs demanding that the government act to put out the fire whose smoke had begun to form a thin veil over the city. My last night at the UCA, on April 14th, I stood at the university gates and watched the protestors gather in increasing numbers, when a friend came and stood next to me. "It feels different this time," she said, as the chants meshed with the beeping horns and roars of bus engines from the packed street. I left Nicaragua the following day for a scheduled work trip in the United States. I was planning to return to the UCA three weeks later. Three days after leaving, the first protestor was killed by government paramilitary forces. Now almost three years later, I have yet to return to the UCA.

Nicaragua has been caught in a series of crises: the ongoing state repression that started with the April 2018 uprising, an environmental crisis due to extractivist practices, and the global coronavirus pandemic. Throughout it all, I've been on the sidelines, following social media, looking for news, and bearing witness to these crises from afar. However, as global borders closed in March 2020 and I transitioned to teaching on Zoom in New Mexico, I felt a similar sense of the precarity that the 2018 crisis in Nicaragua had provoked, only this time the crisis did not affect one country, but rather the entire world. These dual crises showed me that although the 2018 crisis in Nicaragua was the result of social, political, and historical factors unique to the country's history, it was illustrative of global

DOI: 10.4324/9781003198925-10

patterns rife with problems that are confronting all of us. Grappling with that precarity demands solidarity that is multivocal, intercultural, intergenerational, and interdisciplinary, what Anna Tsing (2015: 19) calls "collaborative survival" in response to omnipresent precarity.

This chapter explores such collaboration through what I call *cyborg solidarity*, a way to think about solidarity that emerges out of the entanglement of the digital and analog self in a precarious world. Following Donna Haraway, a cyborg is a hybrid of biology and high-tech culture with no ontological separation in our knowledge of machine and organism (1991: 178). A cyborg challenges the persistent dualisms of Western traditions and the hubris of totalizing theories, opting instead for an "intimate experience" of the deconstruction and reconstruction of boundaries.[1] Relatedly, Anna Tsing argues that labor and ecological precarity are no longer the exception to the way the world works, but rather "is the condition of our time" (2015: 20). The condition of precarity, in its most fundamental sense, requires us to be vulnerable to others, to be open to flux and the possibility of transformation, contamination, and reassembling of self in response to our encounters. Though we experience that precarity in deeply unequal ways, this flux makes new life itself possible. Cyborg solidarity leverages the facility granted by rapid communication to question Western teleology grounded in the promise of unfettered progress and the primacy of the individual and asks that we reorient ourselves toward an ethics based on *relations of care* that emerge "when one allows oneself to be affected by the faces of others" (Mbembe 2018: 176).[2] Solidarity at its core is allowing ourselves to be affected by others and entails a mutual recognition of vulnerability born of precarity deriving from structural factors. Juliet Hooker writes how solidarity arises in response to structural conditions that require collaboration based not on shared national or racial identity; rather, solidarity emerges from the geographical, social, political spaces that we share in which individual actions have inevitable consequences on the lives of others (2009: 170). Cyborg solidarity argues that we need to expand our idea of shared space, as the entangling of digital and analogue worlds has radically shifted how we connect to one another. In response to global precarity that we all experience in unequal ways, cyborg solidarity asks that we act from where we are physically with an awareness of how the digital world has expanded our notions of shared space. This expansion of shared space connects us with others living in different realities that we cannot fully understand but that nonetheless affect us and forms the grounds for daily solidarity with others that is necessary to address global problems that confront us all.

Through autoethnographic narratives combined with historical analysis, I explore cyborg solidarity in an interconnected, fragmented, and unequal world where the edges between the analogue/digital and local/global have become entangled. These vignettes attempt to capture how I lived the Nicaraguan crisis primarily through a computer and cell phone screen and the disorientation that resulted from the experience. Sara Ahmed writes that "moments of disorientation are vital" (2008: 157–158) because they break the lines of how the world should be and can offer new reasons for hope from subsequent reorientations. Personal narratives are well suited for understanding cyborg solidarity emerging from disorientation because personal narratives are socially constructed, and as a result "… idiosyncratic experiences become co-narrated according to *local* narrative formats, *recognizable* types of situations and people, and prevailing moral frameworks, which inevitably constrain representation and interpretation" (Ochs and Capps 2001: 55). I had been living in Nicaragua from 2016 until April 2018, when I left the country for a scheduled work trip to the United States days before the crisis broke out. Watching the violence erupt in Nicaragua, a place that had been home for me for the past two years, through a screen in Seattle, Washington, was a disorienting experience, as my living through the crisis that was faraway geographically yet so intimate emotionally and psychologically did not fit into the local narrative formats of where my body was. The disorientation I experienced as a result of digital intimacy with a faraway conflict in a place that was at that time my home forced me to "rethink the phenomenality of space" and made me question my familiarity with the world (Ahmed 2008: 7). By telling my story through these vignettes, I hope to trace how the crisis caused severe disorientation that required me to find my way toward "feeling at home" again as a result of the crisis and continue to be in solidarity even if only at a distance.[3]

Feeling my way back home taught me that engaging in solidarity encompasses work that is political and collaborative, global yet deeply personal. Practicing solidarity occurs in a "patchy" space that allows us to view the precarious state of the world as a "mosaic of open-ended assemblages of entangled ways of life, with each further opening into a mosaic of temporal rhythms and spatial arcs" (Tsing 2015: 4). These patches challenge local narrative formats that would constrain representation and interpretation of what cyborg solidarity is and why it matters. Digital connections allow us to transcend space and time in ways unimaginable just a few decades ago, engendering new entanglements and collaborations. Cyborg solidarity functions as a tool for rethinking "ways of being in line/aligned with others" as we confront the problems that face us all (Ahmed 2008: 15). We experience the problems differently, but in collaborating across differences that "emerge from histories of extermination, imperialism, and all the rest," we can create "contaminated diversity" that allows for new directions to emerge from the collaboration of different worlds (Tsing 2015: 27–29). A patchy conceptualization of the world means that we can now bear intimate witness to the lives of people from geographically distant locations through screens. It also makes it clear that the fire in Indio Maiz, which was the spark that set off the crisis in Nicaragua in 2018, is connected to the wildfires in California and the Amazon and Australia, and as Ryan Jobson (2020) has written, these fires represent the problems that "confront us all." We experience precarity in unequal and distinct ways, but we are all nevertheless exposed to it and made vulnerable in that exposure. Cyborg solidarity requires us to see the connections between apparently disparate places, and to then make use of those connections as a means of creating spaces for collaboration that address global problems.

Progress is not guaranteed, and though we set out to find new ways of collaborating, we may also just replicate hegemonic structures and practices. But in leveraging the power of international, intercultural, and intergenerational scholarship, we seek "a stance that is hopeful and active, that seeks to struggle for a better future knowing that a better future is not guaranteed" (Ellacuría 1999: 64).

My story of cyborg solidarity begins exactly one year before the crisis in Nicaragua began in April 2018, during an event at the Universidad Centroamericana that would prove to be a harbinger of the things to come.

One year before: women defend their territory in Nicaragua

On the evening of April 19, 2017, I headed to the Xabier Gorostiaga Auditorium in the heart of the UCA campus. Lottie Cunningham, a Miskitu lawyer and activist from the Northern Caribbean, Haydee Castillo, an activist from the Segovia region, Francisca Ramirez, a leader of the campesinos anti-canal movement, and Dolene Miller, a Creole activist from Bluefields in the Southern Caribbean were set to speak to a packed room. Dr. Jorge Huete, the vice president of the UCA, opened the event highlighting the need for the UCA to be a space for public dialogue for the people of Nicaragua. The women expressed deep gratitude to the UCA for providing the space that brought civil society, academics, and activists together to work for social change in Nicaragua.[4]

Lottie Cunningham outlined the stakes of their presence on the stage, "We have received death threats, but we fight against the fear by making our struggle visible." The struggle involved exploitation of their land by the State through threats, the displacement of entire villages, and struggles in the Inter-American courts to have their lands recognized. They spoke of the spiritual connection to that land, without which they would cease to exist as a people. They lamented the abuses of the government and the corruption of the Sandinista party, asking: "What would Sandino say if he saw the Sandinistas today? He wouldn't recognize them and what they are doing to the people of Nicaragua."

When their presentations ended, a question-and-answer session began. A man from Puerto Cabezas on the Caribbean Coast who had traveled 15 hours by bus to Managua for the event, did not ask a question, but rather shared the testimony of his confrontation with the colonos (settlers) on his land.[5] He declared, "We are a multiethnic Nicaragua, we don't have weapons, but our ancestors taught us to resist our foes." More testimonies followed, and as the energy reached a climactic end in a burst of applause, a colleague of mine, a professor from the Social Sciences department, turned to me: "I feel the same way I did at the end of the 1980s," the tumultuous time when the Sandinistas lost their grip on power.

I had no idea that night that exactly a year later, the energy, anxiety, fear, anger, and hope that filled that space would erupt in the crisis of April 2018. In retrospect, that night was a "configuration pregnant with tensions" that would "crystalize into a monad ... a revolutionary chance in the fight for the oppressed past" (Benjamin, Arendt, & Zohn 1986: 263) that also showed the importance of networks that allowed for the UCA to be an "island for critical thought and dialogue" in the increasingly repressive political environment in Nicaragua (Jose Idiáquez, S.J., personal communication, January 18, 2021). In part, the UCA could provide this space because Jesuit universities across the globe share a commitment to critical social analysis at the service of social justice and inclusion. Forming a wider network of solidarity means that discussions of local conflicts and issues can take place with the strength from advocacy and solidarity in a global network, which would be crucial when the crisis broke out in 2018 and is a significant driving force of this book.[6]

That night in the auditorium challenged the historical and political narrative in Nicaragua that focused on the role of Managua and the Pacific side of the country with a history of Pacific coast and mestizo strong-arm leadership. This history focused on the heroic figures of Sandinista leaders Sergio Ramirez and Daniel Ortega and the "Group of Twelve" who formed the public face of the revolution that attracted solidarity from around the world in the 1980s. However, that revolution pursued policies toward the Miskitu people that represented the "blackest chapter" in the history of the Caribbean Coast. The Sandinistas carried out brutal campaigns of forced relocation that became "the greatest collective trauma" in Miskitu history (Kinzer 2007: 253, 261). The night was a culmination of a process decades in the making, that of community-based, multicultural movements struggling for autonomous rights "under conditions of prolonged violence" since the defeat of the Sandinista government in the 1989 elections (Goett 2017: 3). In one auditorium, the discontents of multiple social movements found a space to air their grievances and call for multiethnic civic resistance to government repression. Following Hooker (2019: 24), the discontent was heterogenous in ideological and ethnic terms, as peasants resisted the interoceanic canal and Black Indigenous activists resisted threats to autonomy. Yet they shared a common fear stemming from a settler state with increasingly centralized decision-making power concentrated in Managua and the State, and the threat that this represented to the land itself (Simmons 2019).

The night brought to memory a struggle that went deeper in Nicaragua's history, beyond the Sandinistas in the 1970s and 1980s and to Sandino himself and the fight he led against the U.S. marines who were occupying the country from 1912 to 1933.[7] To understand the civic resistance that young people, campesinos, women, and Indigenous people in Nicaragua tapped into in the 2018 uprising, it is important to remember that history, as it shows that past acts of solidarity between scholars from the United States and people in Nicaragua have provided important collaborative spaces for these stories to be told. Civic resistance and solidarity in Nicaragua are not new issues and recalling past stories of struggle is necessary for continuing onward in new sites of struggle and collaboration.

Margaret Randall's classic oral history *Sandino's Daughters* (1994) opened new spaces for women to share their stories in a time when the narratives of the Sandinistas focused primarily on the male actors.[8] One testimonio came from Maria Lidia, a campesina from Chinandega who went to the mountains in Segovia and fought alongside Augusto Sandino and the Sandinistas against the occupying U.S. marines in the 1920s. She shares her stories of her time with Sandino, drawing a connection between that struggle for autonomy and the autonomy of the land: "I'll tell you, my Segovia, those pine trees, those mountains were our friends, do you know? That's the way it was for us with Sandino." (Randall 1994: 11). For Maria, the revolutionary struggle for national autonomy could not be decoupled from the land itself, and Lottie, Francisca, Haydee, and Dolene echoed that sentiment a century later that night at the UCA. Multiple feminist scholars (Randall 1994; Rodríguez 1996; Montoya 2012, Randall and Yanz 1981) describe how one of the legacies of the women Sandinistas in the 1980s was the birth of a feminist consciousness that opened a new front of social struggle. When the 1990 election ousted the Sandinistas, there was more freedom among women to question contradictions and power structures in a way that wasn't possible when the Sandinistas were in power. This freedom expanded when the "revolution" itself was over, as there was no longer the need to "repeat the party line" (Randall 1994: 35). The event at the UCA that night and its showcasing of the power of women organizing social movements is a sign of how the Sandinista revolution allowed for a revolutionary consciousness to be born in the 1980s, and that women and other groups that had been marginalized by the leadership of the Sandinista party maintained this spirit of questioning the status quo even after the revolution "ended" in 1989. Through the work of Randall, we can see how collaborative spaces in post-revolutionary Nicaragua allow for new narratives of resistance and social struggle to emerge, grounded in the history of Nicaragua and adapted to the current socio-political moment.

Randall offered a powerful example of the spaces for dialogue that can be opened up through acts of solidarity between people in the United States and Nicaragua, and we can continue this spirit of collaboration through projects like this one, which allow for new forms of working in solidarity with one another across time and space in our patchy, entangled world. That spirit of resistance was on full display on April 19, 2017, in the auditorium at the UCA, even if no one at the time knew what that resistance would lead to a year later. As we will see, young people in Nicaragua who led the civic uprising in the streets inherited the legacy of the Sandinista Revolution by demonstrating a "commitment to active participation in their own lives, whether this be through political struggles in the public or the private arena. This commitment, and their belief in their capacity to affect the forces that shape their lives and society" (Montoya 2012: 202). They did so in a world where the digital world was as real as the analogue, where the line between the technological and the organic had meshed so much that it became impossible to understand one without the other, enacting historically rooted resistance in the cyborg present.

The 2018 Nicaraguan uprising: activism in cyberspace

On April 15, 2018, Father Chepe (José Idiáquez, S.J.) and I were on a plane to Seattle. When we landed, his phone erupted with hundreds of WhatsApp messages. A student protestor had entered the classroom of Edwin Castro, the President of the Sandinista National Assembly, one of the most powerful people in the Nicaraguan government who also taught law classes at the UCA. The student derided Castro over the mismanagement of the fire in Indio Maiz in addition to the suspension of public Wi-Fi in the parks and the threats to control access to social media platforms. The chaos of that scene had shaken many within the university and contributed to the general sense of tension throughout the country. As we arrived at our friend, co-author, mentor, and colleague Serena's house for what we had planned to be a writing retreat for our book documenting Garifuna resistance to invasive state policies on the Caribbean Coast of the country, the news coming out of Nicaragua showed a rapidly deteriorating situation. Proposed social security cuts had added further fuel to the already combustible situation.[9] Images of elderly protestors who had been beaten by the Juventud Sandinista and pro-government shock squads flooded social media. A little over 24 hours after arriving in Seattle, Father Chepe returned to Nicaragua, and Serena and I set to work on organizing a solidarity campaign to bring as much international attention as we could to the situation that the UCA faced.[10] The network that allowed for the UCA to host the Mujeres en Defensa de su Territorio event a year earlier became even more crucial in confronting the onslaught of government repression.

We solicited statements of support from Jesuit universities in the United States., and from the newly formed International Association of Jesuit Universities, gathering 20 signed statements from the presidents of Jesuit Universities across the country and the first public statement from IAJU. We also worked with the Jesuits of the Western province of the United States to have these translated statements and denunciations of the violence read on the floor of the U.S. House of Representatives. Rep. Juan Vargas of California read these statements, contextualizing the violence in the history of the assassination of Ignacio Ellacuría, Amando López, Ignacio Martín-Baró, Segundo Montes, Juan Ramón Moreno, Joaquín López y López, Celina, and Elba Ramos on the UCA El Salvador campus in November of 1989 at the hands of the far-right military. That event changed the political calculus in the United States and allowed them to finally exercise their power in ushering in the end of that conflict after a decade of sustained support to the far-right governments and counterinsurgency movements across Central America.[11] Being reminded of that history imbued the moment with a sobering acknowledgment of the risk in Ellacuría's call for the university to be a critical voice on behalf of the marginalized that never relented in the face of the most severe repression.

In order to understand the role that cyborg solidarity played in the crisis in 2018 and how it informs ongoing efforts today requires looking at the historical roots of the digitalization of the world and the fracturing of revolutionary movements like the Sandinistas as many former revolutionaries left the political party to form interest-based social movements. After the electoral defeat of the Sandinistas in 1989, the Sandinista spirit of civic resistance moved away from the nation-state and was channeled into social movements such as the *campesino* movement, feminist movements, and the struggles for recognition and respect of Indigenous and Black autonomy on the Caribbean Coast (Field 1999; Montoya 2012; Soto 2013; Goett 2017).[12] These social struggles labored under the government of Violeta Chamorro and successive right-leaning governments whose policies thoroughly planted Nicaragua into the wave of neoliberal economic policies that fueled the rapid rise of globalization in the aftermath of the Cold War and the fall of the Soviet Union.[13]

The fracturing of social movements and the shift of solidarity efforts in Latin America in the context of neoliberal globalization took place alongside the expansion of networks, technology, and personal devices that dramatically altered how people consume media and organize themselves, a term Hill (2013) calls "cyberactivism." Hill (2013) and Wolfson (2014) describe the Zapatista movement in Chiapas as among the first to combine their movement for autonomy with a networked organizational structure aimed at promoting participatory democratic governance through the use of personal devices as communication tools in the 1990s. The Zapatistas and other groups provide an example of the potential power of digital technology and the networking of social movements across the globe, a new way for human beings to connect with one another that Escobar argues is an "altogether novel framework of interaction—a relational model in which all receivers are also potentially emitters, a novel space of dialogic interaction" (2008: 269–270).

The potential for new "dialogic interactions" on digital platforms boded well for resisting the threats of neoliberal globalization when combined with the sentiment that lay at the heart of the earlier solidarity movements. This entanglement produces cyborg activists. Perales (2005), a Spanish writer and member of the solidarity movement with Nicaragua in the 1980s, writes of the solidarity efforts in the 1980s as ushering in "the new globalization," one based not on the unfettered expansion of global markets and supply chains that characterizes neoliberalism, but rather one that sought to "construct an interdependence of social actors, an alliance of values, struggles and proposals." An important part of this forging of alliances based on the interdependence of social actors depended on "powerful sentimental bonds" that fueled the initial waves of solidarity work in Central America in the 1980s. Those sentimental bonds comprise the organic part of the solidary cyborg, while our increasing dependence upon their computers and personal devices as a means of organizing themselves and disseminating information across the globe would comprise the machine side. The power of those bonds in the increasingly digital world showed the potential for new ways of cyborgs connecting with one another. One of the seminal events of this new type of globalized solidarity occurred at the 1999 Seattle WTO Protests or Battle of Seattle, which saw thousands of activists from around the world come together to protest the meeting of the World Trade Organization. Lievrouw describes this moment as a "watershed moment," while noting that the watershed "may have at least as much to do with mainstream media becoming aware of cyberactivism as with changes amongst activists" (2011, cited in Hill 2013: 21). While the Battle of Seattle showed the potential for cyberactivism in bringing people from across the world in acts of resistance that transcended the borders of nation-states, the Arab Spring in 2011 showed how powerful this marriage between social networks and social actors had become in threatening the power of the nation-state (Castells 2012). The cyborg was proving to be a powerful agent in global struggles for social change, as the 2018 crisis in Nicaragua would demonstrate.

The crisis continues in Nicaragua: the horror in your hand

On May 30, 2018, Mother's Day in Nicaragua, there was a mass mobilization planned. Hundreds of thousands of people poured into the streets of Managua, including families, elders, young people, and children. I was in Seattle, but my partner and many of my friends were in that march. As they passed by the UCA, shots rang out from nearby. Government snipers had opened fire on the marchers, causing scenes of chaos and violence. Father Chepe and the UCA decided to open the gates of the university to let demonstrators into the safety of the campus. Thousands of people fled into the UCA, and for a few hours, the campus turned into a field hospital as it tried to safely transport people back home. Father Chepe denounced Ortega and Murillo in a widely watched video. In the background of the interview, medics tended to the unmoving body of a young man wounded in the chaos. I watched these events unfold on my phone, through videos on Facebook Live and panicked WhatsApp messages from friends fleeing the march. The horror on my screen contrasted starkly with where I was on Seattle U's campus. Groups of students buzzed with the infectious energy of spring quarter, with the sun out and shining after months of gray skies. Rhododendron bushes bloomed brilliantly, and a group of senior students walked by dressed in colorful dresses and tidy suits, on their way to ceremonies honoring the end of their college careers. As I ran back to Serena's office to check in about the unfolding events, I felt complete disorientation, as my fear contrasted so drastically with the scene that surrounded me. On one Jesuit university campus, well-dressed students went to a celebration. On another, families fled gunfire and sought refuge inside the university's gates. Such were the contradictions of that period. My body moved through my old university campus, but my heart, mind, and work were consumed entirely by the events in Nicaragua. We watched events such as the first national dialogue on Facebook live, though the video was cut out after Ortega and Murillo stormed out, and we were left with just the audio of the students chanting "asesinos, asesinos." I felt the fear through WhatsApp groups as students I had worked with from the Caribbean Coast sent horrified messages to one another asking if the internet was going to be cut off, messages I read as I sat on the shore of Elliott Bay in the center of Seattle. I heard bullets in the background of Facetime calls with my partner as she sheltered in the apartment we shared. I cried at the video of Valeska Aleman-Sandoval, who said goodbye to her parents under the barrage of bullets at the siege of the UNAN,[14] *in tears as she told her parents "All I wanted to do was to defend my country." Those contradictions inspired horror as much as they inspired relief. Horror as we watched events in real time and relief that we could connect to loved ones and hear that they were ok in the next moment. The violence felt intensely intimate, even as my body was far away from any physical harm.*

In their analysis of the power of social networks in the 2018 crisis in Nicaragua, Agudelo and Cruz draw parallels with the Arab Spring. Both events showed how the use of social media allowed for conversations online to "interrupt the monologue of the powerful" (2020: 41, citing Reguillo 2017). Those conversations online, and the actions they inspired in the streets, showed how for young people "the virtual world is not a separate reality: what is virtual is also real" (Martinez-Cruz 2020: 42). The entangling of the virtual and the analogue world would prove to have ontological implications in the ways in which people in geographically disparate sites experienced the Nicaraguan crisis of 2018. The disorientation emerging from the exposure to the vulnerability of others through personal devices required a reorientation of how we relate to one another, how we recognize one another's vulnerability, and how we react accordingly in solidarity from wherever we are. Such reorientation is a fundamental piece of cyborg solidarity. In the face of global precarity, we need to collaborate across geographic, historical, racial, and national difference with an openness to the indeterminacy of such encounters. We need to be hopeful that in the shifting assemblages of life we find the tools we will need to address the problems that confront us all.

The 2018 Nicaraguan crisis occurred 20 years after the Battle of Seattle, a watershed moment that supposedly opened our eyes to the potential for cyberactivism. Yet, we continue to be surprised by the seeming spontaneity of mass mobilization that appear to materialize out of nowhere and threaten the foundations of powerful institutions. The crisis of April 2018 in Nicaragua is one of those cases. Agudelo and Cruz (2020: 67) attribute this characterization of the apparent spontaneity of the movement to a "state-centric" and "partisan-centric" worldview that the media and the academy have had a role in reproducing. This worldview led to widespread views of young people in Nicaragua as apathetic, selfish, and uninterested in politics, caring more about what was on with their phones than in the "real world."[15] Many labeled the millennial generation of Nicaraguans as the antithesis to their more heroic young predecessors of the 1970s and 1980s. That they would take the same risks that the young people in the 1980s did was unthinkable. And yet, young people in 2018 were organizing online and protesting in the streets, exposing themselves to the barrage of police bullets in the hope of a better Nicaragua. Trouillot (2015: 82) wrote about how the Haitian Revolution was an unthinkable event for the European powers in the eighteenth century because it challenged the "ontological and political assumptions of the most radical writers of the Enlightenment." For many, that the oft-maligned, "selfish" youth of Nicaragua would go into the streets in 2018 was also unthinkable, outside the ontological assumptions of possibility (Agudelo and Cruz 2020). That it was young people who led the protests in the streets that they organized in digital space thus requires an ontological shift, a reorientation to a world in which the events that occurred in the digital world would alter the way in which we experienced the analogue world.

What these analyses of the supposedly indifferent young people missed was that "the new generations usually respond to a conceptualization of politics as an everyday phenomenon, from their way of using social media, to inhabiting public space, and relating to one another as peers" (Agudelo and Cruz 2020: 33). The everyday experience of politics turned into an everyday confrontation with the horror of the violence that the Nicaraguan state unleashed on its people in 2018 through Facebook live streams and WhatsApp messages. This cyborg experience of the crisis, the fact that so many experienced violence through cell phone screens in geographically disparate places, meant that "the horror was in our hand" whether one was in Nicaragua or Seattle (ibid: 39). To have that horror in the palm of your hand was to confront the violence inflicted on people who are real human beings with faces, names, and personal histories (Cavarero 2009: 41). It was to experience vulnerability and exposure to death whether one was in Seattle or Managua, to "be affected by the faces of others" (Mbembe 2018: 176). Cyborg solidarity requires the recognition of mutual vulnerability, and that to live is to live exposed to precarity, including to death itself (Mbembe 2018: 176).

That intimacy with acts of violence, shared on the same platforms through the screens in the hands of people in Managua and in Seattle, gave an intense urgency to the need to act against that violence. Despite the geographic distance between my body and the events in Nicaragua, the affective phenomenon of such intimate witnessing of violence changed the way I understood my body and my Self in space and time. Cell phones and computer screens became the window into the suffering of others. Centering the power of screens expands Juliet Hookers discussion on solidarity in Latin America. She argues that political solidarity occurs daily, even momentarily, with friends and with strangers. What underpins solidarity is not mutual identification based on nation or race, but rather shared geographical, social, and political spaces. Cyborg solidarity, with its emphasis on the power of digital space on how we move through the world, thus expands Hooker's notion of shared space in which "actions have unavoidable consequences on the lives of others that also inhabit such locales" (Hooker 2009: 170). We all share that digital space through the phones we hold in our hands, and so need to practice daily solidarity mindful that our actions there affect others in geographically disparate locations, connected as we are through the digital space we share.

Ahmed (2008: 165) describes how because of the tactile nature of hands, how they touch things, how they hold things, how they let things go makes them "crucial sites in stories of disorientation." Disorientation is a slippage, a rupture of the way things aligned before that opens "another angle on the world" (Ahmed 2008: 170–171). While the intimacy of the horror in your hand brought thousands of people across the world who followed the Nicaraguan crisis in 2018 into close proximity with human suffering, it provided the thrust of real-world organizing activity in geographically disparate places and provoked real-world consequences (Thomas 2019: 143). During the crisis, the appearance of horrific online videos would generate huge marches the following day in Managua and throughout the country (Agudelo and Cruz 2020: 42). People in Nicaragua, and our group in Seattle, witnessed horrors on the same digital landscape, and that shared experience demanded that we respond from our respective places in solidarity with one another. In Nicaragua, that meant putting one's body on the line alongside thousands of others in the streets. For our group in Seattle, it meant working as hard as we could to ensure that international attention was on those actions, bringing as much recognition as possible to the situation in Nicaragua. We were not the only group doing so. Social media accounts showed vigils, teach ins, marches, and other acts of solidarity across the world. These events occurred in Madrid, New York, Toronto, Vancouver, Miami, Albuquerque, Singapore, Berlin, Seattle, San Francisco, San Salvador, San José, Costa Rica, and elsewhere, and ranged from four or five attendees to concerts and mass rallies. I hosted or attended such events in Seattle, New York, San Jose, Costa Rica, and New Mexico in 2018 and saw the emanations of anguish, pain, and solidarity that people across the country and world channeled into collaborations and actions to support those struggling for a new reality in Nicaragua. That is the power of cyborg solidarity. Analogue events in one corner of the globe erupt through digital wavelengths, and the intimacy of witnessing the pain of the other on a screen generates acts of solidarity across the world.

It's important to stress that that common bond did little, if anything, to close the gap between our immensely different physical experiences of the conflict. In Seattle and at other events we weren't in as much physical danger, whereas our Nicaraguan friends were exposed to physical danger daily. The fusion of the virtual and the analogue worlds that allows us to experience the horror in our hand allows for new ways of recognizing the pain of others, but it does little to change the dramatic inequalities that heighten the precarity with which many in Nicaragua continue to live. But it does mean that we can recognize our mutual vulnerability in a global state of precarity where "life on earth seems at stake" (Tsing 2015: 25) and thus informs the work that needs to be done going forward. In that space, our collaborative survival means we embrace working across those differences and recognize that we are contaminated by our histories. Counterintuitively, it is that contamination of diversity that opens new possibilities (ibid: 29). It gives us a chance to reorient.

Conclusion: Cyborg solidarity in an entangled yet unequal world

To use the word dictatorship in a way that described a reality that I knew, that of Nicaragua, and to see the devastation that it wrought on people I knew and loved lent a different weight to words like dictatorship and authoritarianism. They were not abstract concepts discussed in a classroom, as they had been for most of my life living in the United States. Rather, they were descriptors of a visceral and dangerous reality. But it is important to remember that the problems of climate change, digital platforms, and authoritarianism are problems that affect us all. Though it felt strange to use terms like authoritarianism to describe the situation in Nicaragua, they have become apt descriptors of the political situation here in the United States under Trump, demonstrated so viscerally in the events of January 6, 2021.

In 2018, I spoke to my parents about authoritarianism in Nicaragua. While they and many others with whom I spoke about the crisis listened with deep sympathy about the challenges in Nicaragua, those terms still felt like they belonged far away from the reality of the United States. On January 6, 2021, I held my mom's hand in horror as the events at the U.S. Capitol transpired on the TV in front of us.[16] Authoritarian attacks on democracy and coup attempts were no longer concepts foreign to U.S. political discourse, but rather the only words appropriate to describe the events of that day and all that had preceded it. In 2018, authoritarianism was a concept to describe what was occurring in Nicaragua; in 2021, it described what occurred in the United States. Authoritarianism and threats to democracy are problems that face us all.

The inequalities in terms of how political turmoil affects the wider public in the United States and Nicaragua are massive. The United States still has democratic institutions that can resist authoritarian power grabs, while Nicaragua remains mired in a political quagmire with no immediate hope for institutional solutions. Furthermore, the ongoing political turmoil in Nicaragua is due in large part to decades of United States meddling in the affairs of Nicaragua. Baldwin's (1984: 163) assertion that "people are trapped in history and history is trapped in them" points to the limitations of our ability to understand the reality of our counterparts in Nicaragua, especially because the stability that people in the United States have enjoyed is in many ways tied to the actions taken historically against Nicaragua. However, Tsing (2015: 29) reminds us that collaborative survival requires working across difference, pursuing ongoing transformation through such work in spite of (and perhaps due to) the fact that our,

> "selves" are already polluted by histories of encounter; we are mixed up with others before we even begin any new collaboration … The diversity that allows us to enter collaborations emerges from histories of extermination, imperialism, and all the rest. Contamination makes diversity.

In order to practice cyborg solidarity, the recognition of this unity in the threats that we all face while acknowledging the ways our histories limit the possibilities for change will be a vital starting point in identifying strategies for efforts going forward. What can help is an awareness that "the tradition of the oppressed teaches us that the 'state of emergency' in which we live is not the exception but the rule" (Benjamin, Arendt, & Zohn 1986: 257). The events of Nicaragua in 2018 and in the United States in January of 2021 should be viewed through the entanglement of the virtual and analogue worlds and our new ontological stance within that space that allows us to confront global precarity with cyborg solidarity, hopeful that new life can emerge from the entangling of the digital/ analog worlds.

The space at the UCA on the night of April 18, 2017, demonstrated that institutional solidarity can protect physical spaces where crucial dialogues take place in a context that was largely hostile to the democratic exchange of ideas that challenged Ortega's authoritarian rule. That chokehold on democratic discourse has only tightened in the years since the crisis in 2018, making collaborative institutional endeavors that allow for the UCA to continue its work in carving out democratic spaces under the pressure of authoritarian governance as vital as ever.

We were supposed to come together in person to work on this book in a physical workshop, but the coronavirus pandemic forced us to find a new, virtual way to collaborate through a Wenner-Gren Foundation-sponsored workshop. The pandemic pushing us into a virtual space for dialogue subsequently inspired the primary theme of this chapter: that the precarity of our world, and the need for us to be present to one another's vulnerability amid that precarity, forms the basis of solidarity that demands collaboration across difference in the hope of new life going forward. Solidarity as realized through these types of collaborations allows us to work in dialogue across the inequalities and geographic distances that separate us in order to find those common spaces where our distinct perspectives and experiences can allow for new visions of a healthier, more inclusive, more democratic world, with an environment that can sustain generations to come.

The questioning of Western teleology that assumes progress based on the primacy of the individual also means that it is important to recognize "the risk … that the visions of repair that movements imagine, the modes of new relationality they invent, might not make things less broken" (Stuelke 2014: 773). Recognizing that possibility that we might not "make things less broken" is to recognize our mutual vulnerability in working with one another. This position often offers more questions than answers but is an important stance for an act of solidarity to be substantive and resistant to, or at least suspicious of, the assumed altruism of North-South solidarity that may actually replicate previous power imbalances. However, by recognizing the power that our entangled cyborg nature has both for witnessing the suffering of the faraway other, and the concomitant recognition of our shared humanity, we can allow ourselves a little bit of hope for a brighter future in our entangled digital/analog world.

Notes

1 Examples of such dualisms are self/other, mind/body, culture/nature, male/female, civilized/primitive, God/man. The cyborg imagery is useful for contesting totalizing theories that fail to capture most of reality in addition to a reconstruction of

boundaries as mediated by the tools of high tech that allows for "partial connections" with other with others. Partial connections offer a way out of duality as they do not seek a perfect common language, but rather a "powerful infidel heteroglossia" (Haraway 1991: 177–181).
2 The relation of care stems from Frantz Fanon's work with patients who had suffered colonial violence in French Algeria in the 1950s. In response to these wounds, Fanon undertook psychiatric work with his patients that "essentially aim [ed] to restore the patient to his being and his relations with the world" (Mbembe 2018: 144). In order to re-establish ruptured relations with the world, humanity ought to offer "gestures— and thus a relation of care ... when one allows oneself to be affected by the faces of others; when a gesture is related to speech, to silence breaking language" (ibid: 176). This approach based on relations of care is open to "inversions ... of corporeality" that emerge from the constant making, un-making, and re-making of "assemblages of objects-humans and of humans-objects" that merge humans together with objects of technology in today's context (ibid: 164). In other words, the re-establishing of relations with the world that has been violently ruptured through colonial processes of separation can create new assemblages of life not only between human beings, but also between machines and humans.
3 I refer to Nicaragua as my home during this time for multiple reasons. I had a job, I had an apartment, I had a relationship that had just started. Prior to leaving in April 2018, I had plans to remain in the country indefinitely. The crisis upended the "home" that I had been establishing in Nicaragua and had just become comfortable with. However, the crisis also highlighted the ways in which it wasn't my home; I had a U.S. passport, a family in the United States, another home that I could return to. Ahmed (2008: 10) writes that orientation can be a homing device that "might be described as the lived experience of facing at least two directions: toward a home that has been lost, and to a place that is not yet home." As we find our way back home, we can follow certain lines that inherently exclude others. Furthermore, some lines are available to some but not others. While it is important to note that we face problems that confront us all, it is important to note the unequal nature of how these problems affect us differently based on nationality, gender, socio-economic, status, and race.
4 I name the four women intentionally to demonstrate the heterogeneity of the social movements that comprise the civic resistance to the Ortega government since April 2018. That many are led by women who represent the interests of the campesinos, Indigenous, and Creole/Afro-descendant movements is a reflection of the fractal nature of social movements in the wake of the 1990 electoral defeat of the Sandinistas. It also demonstrates the legacy of the Sandinista Revolution, a "commitment, and belief in the capacity to affect the forces that shape their lives and society" (Montoya 2012: 202).
5 Colonos is the Spanish word for settlers, and in this context refers to the conflict between colonos who migrate to the Caribean Coast of the country and settle on land that the Nicaraguan constitution recognizes as the land of the Miskitu and other Indigenous groups. Colonos seek the land with the backing of the Ortega government, and the clashes between colonos and Miskitu has led to a years long conflict (see reporting on confidencial.com.ni and from the Oakland Institute, cited in Cosgrove in this chapter).
6 See vignette on page 125 to understand how these networks can be mobilized for purposes of institutional solidarity.
7 José [Chepe] Idiáquez, S.J. always tells me that one of the most important pieces of Ignatian spirituality involves "bringing to memory" past struggles, both personal and political.
8 Randall was an activist and author from the United States who spent decades of her life involved in solidarity movements with revolutionary struggles in Cuba and Nicaragua.

9   As the fire in the Indio Maíz reserve continued to burn, the Ortega government released a new social security law that would increase the percentage that workers paid into the system throughout their careers, while reducing the benefits they would obtain in retirement. Questions over mismanagement of social security funds had sparked widespread protests in 2013 called OcupaINSS, one of the larger movements against the Ortega regime prior to 2018. See more at https://globalvoices.org/2013/07/18/young-and-old-united-in-nicaraguas-ocupainss-movement/.

10 The book we were working on, *Surviving the Americas: Garifuna Persistence from Nicaragua to New York City*, has now been published, and is connected to the April 2018 crisis as well as this volume. That book was the culmination of multiple years of visits to the Caribbean Coast of Nicaragua in order to understand how the Afro-Indigenous Garifuna communities were dealing with the increasing penetration of neoliberal markets, the threat of loss of their land, and other challenges that the Ortega government presented. From that book, "The crisis revealed that the tensions we had been witnessing on the Caribbean coast had finally exploded in Managua, the capital. Historically, tensions in Nicaragua begin in the rural and more isolated areas, and Managua wakes up at the end. Looking back at our field notes from our years of working together, we realized we had been witnessing a repetition of this historical pattern through our work on the Caribbean coast" (Cosgrove, Idiáquez, Bent, & Gorvetzian 2021: 102).

11 The international outcry in response to the assassinations forced the United States to end their support for the far-right military regime in El Salvador, recognizing that their support was no longer tenable given the brutality of the assassinations. See Teresa Whitfield's 1994 *Paying the Price: Ignacio Ellacuría and the Murdered Jesuits of El Salvador* for a detailed account of this history.

12 By spirit of civic resistance, I refer to what Montoya (2012: 195) argues in her analysis of the legacy of the revolution:
    "The revolution indeed changed subordinate groups' subjectivity in empowering ways. Offering support for this claim must begin by acknowledging that the revolution produced more than state subjects, whether docile or agentive. As the case of El Tule has shown, it also produced ideas of sociability and sharing beyond one's family and community; a language for articulating a sense of historical agency; and a basis for a deeper understanding of class consciousness and organizing, and of national projects.

13 See Cosgrove's chapter in this volume for more detail."

14 The national autonomous university of Nicaragua, a site where students had occupied the campus in resistance to the government paramilitary and police forces. "Operation Clean-up," a brutal assault carried out to clear the students from the campus in July 2018, received widespread media coverage as a Washington Post journalist was trapped in the barrage of bullets. Valeska's video has been watched thousands of times and was shared widely on social media. She fled Nicaragua and sought asylum in the United States, crossing at a checkpoint in El Paso, Texas. Her request for asylum was denied and she was deported back to Nicaragua 17 days later.

15 See Bran-Aragón in this volume for more explanation of this phenomenon, in addition to a more in-depth exploration of how university students experienced the crisis in 2018 and the aftermath that is ongoing.

16 The events in Washington, DC on January 6th were the culmination of a narrative long pushed by Donald Trump and many members of the Republican Party that claimed there was widespread voter fraud in the 2020 U.S. presidential election that cost Trump the presidency, despite little to no evidence of such claims. That morning, Trump gave a speech in front of the White House that was followed by a march to the U.S. Capitol, where rioters breached the defenses of the building and entered the halls of the capitol. While no politicians were killed or injured, multiple police officers died as did some protestors. The riots led to a second impeachment of Trump and as of this writing the planning of the riots continue to be under investigation.

References

Agudelo Builes, I., & Martínez Cruz, J. (2020). Revueltas de abril: Narrativas, redes, y espacios en disputa. In *Abril 2018: La insurrección cívica de abril*. Managua: UCA Editores.
Ahmed, S. (2008). *Queer phenomenology: Orientations, objects, others*. Durham: Duke University Press. DOI: 10.1215/9780822388074.
Baldwin, J. (1984). *Notes of a native son*. Boston: Beacon Press.
Benjamin, W., Arendt, H., & Zohn, H. (1986). *Illuminations*. New York: Schocken Books.
Castells, M. (2012). *Networks of outrage and hope: Social movements in the internet age*. Cambridge: Polity Press.
Cavarero, A. (2009). *Horrorismo: Nombrando la violencia contemporánea*. México: Anthropos.
Cosgrove, S., Idiáquez, J., Joseph Bent, L., & Gorvetzian, A. (2021). *Surviving the Americas: Garifuna persistence from Nicaragua to New York City*. Cincinnati: The University of Cincinnati Press.
Ellacuría, I. (1999). *Escritos universitarios*. San Salvador: UCA Editores.
Escobar, A. (2008). *Territories of difference: Place, movements, life, redes*. Durham: Duke University Press.
Field, L.W. (1999). *The grimace of Macho Ratón: Artisans, identity, and nation in late-twentieth-century western Nicaragua*. Durham: Duke University Press.
Goett, J. (2017). *Black autonomy: Race, gender, and Afro-Nicaraguan activism*. Stanford: Stanford University Press.
Haraway, D.J. (1991). *Simians, cyborgs, and women: The reinvention of nature*. New York: Routledge.
Hill, S. (2013). *Digital revolutions: Activism in the Internet age*. Oxford: New Internationalist. http://public.eblib.com/choice/publicfullrecord.aspx?p=3382537
Hooker, J. (2009). *Race and the Politics of Solidarity*. Oxford: Oxford University Press. DOI: 10.1093/acprof:oso/9780195335361.001.0001
Hooker, J. (2019). Civil society in revolt against the leftist authoritarianism of the Ortega/Murillo regime. *LASA Forum*, 49(4), 23–24.
Jobson, R.C. (2020). The case for letting anthropology burn: Sociocultural anthropology in 2019. *American Anthropologist*, 122(2), 259–271. DOI: 10.1111/aman.13398
Kinzer, S. (2007). *Blood of brothers: Life and war in Nicaragua* (1st David Rockefeller Center for Latin American Studies ed). David Rockefeller Center for Latin American Studies, Cambridge, MA: Harvard University.
Mbembe, A. (2018). *Necropolitics* (S. Corcoran, Trans.). Durham: Duke University Press.
Montoya, R. (2012). *Gendered Scenarios of Revolution Making New Men and New Women in Nicaragua, 1975–2000*. Tuscon: University of Arizona Press.
Ochs, E., & Capps, L. (2001). *Living narrative: Creating lives in everyday storytelling*. Cambridge, MA: Harvard University Press.
Perales, I. (2005). *Revista Envío—Twenty-six Years On: Memories of Solidarity*. https://www.envio.org.ni/articulo/2989
Randall, M. (1994). *Sandino's daughters revisited: Feminism in Nicaragua*. New Brunswick, NJ: Rutgers University Press.
Randall, M., & Yanz, L. (1981). *Sandino's daughters: Testimonies of Nicaraguan women in struggle*. Vancouver, BC: New Star Books.
Rodríguez, I. (1996). *Women, guerrillas, and love: Understanding war in Central America*. Minneapolis: University of Minnesota Press.

Simmons, S. (2019). Grito por Nicaragua, un grito desde la Costa Caribe. *LASA Forum*, *49*(4), 32–36.
Soto, F. (2013). Las historias que contamos. *Confluenza*, *5*(1), 104–120.
Stuelke, P. (2014). The reparative politics of Central America solidarity movement culture. *American Quarterly*, *66*(3), 767–790. DOI: 10.1353/aq.2014.0058
Thomas, P. (2019). *Communication for social change: Context, social movements and the digital*. New Delhi: SAGE Publications India.
Trouillot, M.-R. (2015). *Silencing the past: Power and the production of history*. Boston: Beacon Press.
Tsing, A.L. (2015). *The mushroom at the end of the world: On the possibility of life in capitalist ruins*. Princeton: Princeton University Press.
Whitfield, T. (1994). *Paying the price: Ignacio Ellacuría and the murdered Jesuits of El Salvador*. Philadelphia: Temple University Press.
Wolfson, T. (2014). *Digital rebellion: The birth of the cyber left*. Champaign: University of Illinois Press.

7
UNIVERSITY PARTNERSHIPS AND SOLIDARITY 3.0 WITH NICARAGUA

Serena Cosgrove

> ... strong international relationships offer cover to the UCA, in general, and its *proyección social* [social outreach], in particular; these relationships make it difficult for those in power to attack the institution without justification and help the UCA survive the risks that its social commitments entail.[1]
>
> —*Ignacio Ellacuría (1978)*

Introduction

"I had no idea we had so much in common," exclaimed Marissa Olivares, a sociology professor from the Universidad Centroamericana (UCA) in Managua, as we stepped over sleeping bags, boxes of food, and students preparing protest signs in the humanities college at Seattle University (SU) where I was teaching at the time. "I never imagined that students in the U.S. could be such activists; they're just like my students." One week before Marissa's arrival to Seattle in April 2016, SU students in the college where I taught had occupied the college office demanding a more inclusive humanities curriculum among other anti-racist demands. Though their occupation was an important and much needed move forward—one I likened to visiting liberated zones in El Salvador in the 1980s—I was concerned about how it might appear to an outside visitor. As clarified by her exclamation of pleasure at the occupation, her initial surprise was due to the fact that she never imagined that student activism would be something we'd have in common. In fact, it made her feel even more at home and contributed to strengthening our relationship and collaboration. We had first gotten to know each other—and each other's students—thanks to a 2015 research project we conducted together in Chinandega, Nicaragua about the experiences of grandmothers whose children had emigrated. We had organized the research project and traveled with colleagues and students from both our universities to one of the hottest and most humid parts of Nicaragua to interview older women who were raising

DOI: 10.4324/9781003198925-11

their grandchildren because their children were working abroad. After this collaboration in Nicaragua, we had decided to share the classroom in Seattle. Marissa and I had spent months planning her visit to Seattle University where she would take over my Women in Leadership in Latin America class and teach Margaret Randall's **Sandino's Daughters: Testimonies of Nicaraguan Women in Struggle***. Her visit was a complete success: my students were spellbound by Marissa's teaching: she made an academic book come alive for them as she knew all the women profiled in Randall's book and complemented their stories with her own.*

I recount this story because it exemplifies a number of the characteristics of academic solidarity—such as scholarly and pedagogical collaboration between equals, affection and colleagueship, and motivation to deepen engagement with social justice themes—we've endeavored to cultivate in our partnership as faculty, staff, and students at Seattle University[2] and the UCA in Managua, Nicaragua.[3] This academic solidarity manifests itself through the shared programming of the sister relationship[4] that binds our two universities together, in which we listen to each other, learn from one another, and accompany each other, celebrating our achievements and standing in solidarity in times of hardship. Just as Ignacio Ellacuría, S.J. articulates in the quote that opens this chapter, international solidarity can play an extremely important role for universities serving societies in crisis. The SU-UCA partnership has served to awaken us to the vital importance of solidarity given the differently-positioned challenges facing higher education today from navigating the exigencies of academic capitalism to facing a repressive government as is the case of the UCA presently.

In a germinal lecture about how universities need to be on the side of those who are pushed to the margins of their societies by systemic injustice, Ignacio Ellacuría, S.J.—the martyred president of the UCA in San Salvador, El Salvador who was assassinated over 30 years ago—wrote,

> It is said that the university should not be partial or biased. We believe differently. The university should be free and objective but objectivity and liberty should be partial. And we are freely partial towards the poor majority because they are unjustly oppressed and in them ... lies the truth of reality.[5]

(1999: 304)

With this statement, Ellacuría is not discrediting critical education or objective research; rather the opposite, he is saying that these forces need to be in active service to inclusion and justice for the poor and marginalized. This liberational engagement inspires my pedagogy, service, and research. In fact, I confess that I am not impartial either when it comes to making my contribution to address injustice. I have participated in solidarity actions with Nicaragua since the 1980s. As an undergraduate in Seattle at that time, I joined the Nicaraguan solidarity movement when I saw that the United States was misrepresenting the Sandinista revolution as a communist threat due to misguided and toxic notions of U.S. sovereignty informed by cold war rhetoric. So, in 1984, I joined a Witness for Peace delegation and visited Nicaraguan war zones where U.S.-sponsored counterrevolutionaries or *contras*, as they were called, attacked civilian targets in a "low-intensity conflict" to sway Nicaraguan public opinion away from the revolutionary Sandinista project.[6] After this initial three-week trip, I moved to Nicaragua in 1986, joining the Central America solidarity movement to end U.S. support for the *contras*, which we did achieve as I explain below. However, in hindsight, our political analysis and activism may have been short-sighted. Though U.S. foreign policy shifted regarding Central America, the postwar challenges for the region—such as structural inequality, neoliberal economic policies, high levels of violence, and weak governance and rule of law—have intensified. As I watch what is unfolding in Nicaragua today, I see that actions of solidarity are still needed, but as we envision a new era of solidarity, it's important to incorporate lessons from the past.

This chapter covers three main topics, including a context for solidarity with Nicaragua, a case for renewed efforts, and examples readers and their institutions can consider for their own solidarity with Nicaragua. First, I briefly summarize the current situation in Nicaragua and the repressive nature of the Ortega-Murillo regime.[7] Second, I provide a brief history of the different phases of transnational solidarity with Nicaragua in the twentieth century and then analyze their achievements in the light of scholarship on this topic. And third, I theorize a definition of solidarity that addresses critiques of past solidarity efforts and prepares us for a new era of solidarity, one I am calling *Solidarity 3.0*.

Background

In April of 2018, student protests against the Nicaraguan government's inaction regarding a forest fire started by mestizo settlers in the Indio Maíz Natural Reserve grew when the government proposed cuts to the social security system of the country. State police and paramilitary youth,[8] aligned with the government, responded repressively toward the protesters. For the next six months, the repression continued, targeting youth activists, environmental defenders, feminists, farming families, Indigenous peoples, and Catholic clergy and lay people. It is estimated that between 75,000 and 85,000 Nicaraguans fled the country between 2018 and 2019 (Servicio Jesuita de Migrantes, Costa Rica 2019); as of 2019, at least 325 people had been killed and more than 2,000 injured (CIDH 2019: 165; see also LASA forum 49: 4); and in this same period, more than 700 people were imprisoned and prosecuted (CIDH 2019: 165). As regards public services, such as health and education, 300 health professionals have been fired for serving injured protesters and 144 students have been expelled from the public universities for criticizing the government and participating in protests (CIDH 2019: 165; see also Goett 2019: 25).

By the end of 2018, the repression had sown so much fear that an eerie quiet fell over the country like a dense fog. In 2019, this involved the "criminalization of demonstrators" in which representatives of the Nicaraguan judicial system prosecuted protesters for exercising their civil rights of free speech and association and incarcerated them, punishing them as traitors or *"golpistas"* for attempting to overthrow the government (Goett 2019: 30). Many youth activists have either been killed, jailed, or have left for Costa Rica predominantly. Others have gone to study at universities in Central America and beyond or remain hiding in safe houses across the country. Today, this is the "new" normal of Nicaragua: scaring people into silence or exile through the use of selective violence and sustained harassment of activists, including many of the college students involved in the April 2018 protests. There are moments where the state-sponsored violence spikes again and then the spectral quiet returns, such as when the Nicaraguan government stepped up the repression in response to President Evo Morales' departure from Bolivia in November of 2019.[9] For example, 13 Nicaraguan college students were detained at this time and then prosecuted for treason because they took bottles of water to the mothers of political prisoners and youth killed by the regime. The mothers were on a hunger strike in a church in Masaya, Nicaragua demanding justice for their children.

Of the 60 colleges and universities in the country, only the UCA has called for a cessation of the repression, a return to rule of law, the release of political prisoners, and free elections. Wendi Bellanger's analysis (this volume) of how neoliberal reforms have systematically eroded the autonomy of Nicaraguan universities helps explain why there is so little response from other universities and why the UCA is standing alone and facing so much repression. In today's academic culture of accreditation and evaluation, Nicaraguan universities have become beholden to state audits and dependent on state budget allocations. In retaliation for public statements criticizing government repression and providing support to groups such as the mothers of political prisoners and slain youth, the UCA has been sanctioned with budget cuts, police harassment, and threats against their president. In January of 2019, the government cut half of its funding to the UCA (a quarter of the UCA's overall budget) in reprisal for its oppositional stance; and in 2020, it cut funding in half again. And in 2021, it cut all state funding for the UCA. Furthermore, riot police and dogs regularly surround the university, intimidate students, staff, and faculty coming to the university, and often attempt to provoke the students to justify storming the university gates and the university campus. José (Chepe) Idiáquez, S.J., the president of the UCA, has received multiple death threats and has been granted interim protective measures (*medidas cautelares*) by the Interamerican Human Rights Commission as was Auxiliary Bishop Silvio Jose Baez Ortega of Managua.[10] These factors have led to a crisis of autonomy for the UCA, and autonomy is one of the most crucial characteristics of a university committed to serving the poor and marginalized, especially in times of repression. The UCA's current situation is eloquently evoked by Ellacuría's reflection (1999: 81) on the topic of university autonomy:

> What the university needs is real autonomy, independent self-sufficiency. Independent from what? The answer is easy: independence from all the efforts that the dominant sectors of society use to tame the university.[11]

The Nicaraguan political crisis is a sensitive topic for a number of reasons, one of them being that there is a sobering precedent of state-sponsored violence waged against higher education in the region of Central America. On November 16, 1989, in San Salvador, El Salvador, elite-battalion soldiers, under direct orders from the High Command of the Salvadoran Armed Forces, entered the campus of the UCA "José Simeón Cañas," which is the sister university of the UCA in Managua, and assassinated six Jesuit priests—all professors, administrators, or campus ministers affiliated with the university, including President Ignacio Ellacuría (quoted above and throughout this chapter)—and two women collaborators. I mention this tragic event because it's an example of how a Central American government has treated a university it saw as critical and independent. In Nicaragua, the government, its security forces, and paramilitary youth continue to threaten the UCA.

The immediate challenges facing the UCA are significant, but their vulnerability is exacerbated by the institutional effects of economic, political, and cultural transformations brought about by the neoliberal era. Neoliberal policies have compelled Latin American countries to privatize state industries, cut social spending, and end subsidies, which kept basic goods at affordable prices for poor communities (Gusterson 2017). These policies, in turn, have led to increased poverty, exclusion, and inequality, on the one hand, and the concentration of wealth, on the other. As described in detail by Wendi Bellanger in this volume (and corroborated by other scholars including Hyatt et al. 2015; Gusterson 2017; and Peréz and Montoya 2018 to mention a few), this neoliberal turn has many implications for universities everywhere, but particularly in regions like Central America. Misleadingly couched in a vocabulary of efficiency and effectiveness, these policies have led to what many call the corporatization of higher education or simply put, academic capitalism. The emphasis on quality, efficiency, and control has contributed to the erosion of university autonomy and academic freedom, and in the hands of repressive states, have become tools to pressure universities politically and sanction them with budget cuts when they speak out or oppose these policies or government actions, as exemplified by what the Nicaragua government is doing to the UCA at this time.

This context—a particularly repressive government and the harsh impacts of international policy—animates our understanding and practices of solidarity, in which we commit to accompanying each other in quotidian challenges as well as in efforts to understand and respond to the broader forces that exacerbate poverty and inequality in our respective countries. Solidarity means exclaiming over what we have in common, and it also means thinking together critically, bearing witness to our daily realities, building strong relationships, and collaborating across difference.

Solidarity 1.0 and 2.0

In the 1980s, there were sanctuary churches across North America who received Central Americans fleeing civil and political conflict; these efforts involved transnational collaboration between activists in Central America and supporters in Mexico, the United States, and Canada (Coutin 1993; Perla and Coutin 2010). There were delegations of concerned U.S. citizens traveling regularly to the region, including Nicaragua, El Salvador, Honduras, and Guatemala. Multiple organizations formed in the United States, either founded by Central Americans (see Perla and Coutin 2010) or others, like the solidarity organization, CISPES,[12] who worked in close collaboration with their Salvadoran counterparts on strategy and programming (See Valencia 2018). North American-based activists applied a critical lens to U.S. imperialism critiquing foreign policy, military assistance, development aid, and economic interests in the region; they used this knowledge to educate others and promote empathy and actions of solidarity. Remarkably, the 1980s transnational solidarity movement with Central America wasn't the first one. In the case of Nicaragua, there were two distinct movements of transnational solidarity in the twentieth century: first, there was solidarity with farmer-turned-guerilla-leader, Augusto César Sandino, and his fight against U.S. marines in Nicaragua in the 1920s, and second, the solidarity movement of the 1980s during Nicaragua's counterrevolutionary war.

Solidarity 1.0

In the 1920s, two different groups of North American activists—those protesting U.S. intervention, called "anti-interventionists," and those standing in solidarity with Augusto César Sandino—began to protest President Calvin Coolidge's 1926 decision to send U.S. marines into Nicaragua to protect U.S. interests and prop up authoritarian ruler Anastasio Somoza García (Grossman 2009: 68). Fighting against the U.S. marines and the Nicaraguan National Guard, Sandino enjoyed a wide range of civilian support and for six years, led an intrepid, peasant-based resistance against the U.S. marines (Grossman 2009: 67). Anti-interventionists protested U.S. military intervention but did not actively support Sandino. On the other hand, there were a number of organizations who protested U.S. intervention *and* supported Sandino. These solidarity groups were led by the Workers' Party of America, headquartered in New York City, and there were actions to raise awareness and support for Sandino across the United States (Grossman 2009: 71). Part of this solidarity work was kindled from Nicaragua itself and involved the writing, public relations, and leadership

> of two forgotten Nicaraguan women poets—Carmen Sobalvarro and Aura Rostand… [who] insert[ed] themselves in public discourse … [and] both challenged and participated in Nicaragua's conservative social mores.

Writing strategically as poetisas, these women lyrically promoted early Sandinista ideology and g[a]ve public voice to the cosmopolitan women in Nicaragua and beyond who supported the general.

(Finzer 2021: 457–458)

Ultimately Sandino forced the Nicaraguan government to agree to a cease-fire. This, together with the actions of the U.S.-based movements and civilian supporters from within Nicaragua, successfully pressured the United States to pull out the marines in 1931 (ibid: 75–76). Yes, this was an important achievement, but sadly, this did not keep Somoza from ordering the assassination of Sandino when he came into Managua for negotiations in 1934. I call this Solidarity 1.0.

Solidarity 2.0

The Somoza dynasty continued until 1979 under the leadership of two different generations of Somozas: first Anastasio then his two sons, Luis Somoza Debayle and then Anastasio Somoza Debayle. On July 19, 1979, the Sandinista guerrilla forces—named for the original Sandino—and other leaders from across the political spectrum called a national strike and overthrew Somoza. As well as investing in education and health, "the [Sandinista] government … introduced polices that … aimed at increasing the supply of goods to the countryside, the wages paid to rural workers, and the prices paid to rural producers for their crops" (Harris 1987: 10).[13] The Sandinistas endeavored to sustain their revolution as the United States, under the leadership of President Ronald Reagan with his cold war mentality, armed the former National Guard of the Somoza regime, the *contras*, so they could destabilize the Sandinistas from military camps in neighboring Honduras with the justification that the new Nicaraguan government was a proxy for the Soviet Union and Cuba (see Walker 2003). Meanwhile, there was a broad transnational movement across North America, Europe, South America, and beyond in solidarity with Nicaragua that was comprised of "a heterogeneous collection of groups ranging from nonprofit, campus, church, and community-based organizations, foundations, and ad hoc committees to national-level organizations and transnational advocacy networks" (Perla 2009: 82). Thousands of people in the United States in close collaboration with many Nicaraguan groups protested U.S. military aid to the counterrevolution through organizing in the Global North and sending delegations to Nicaragua; in fact, "… more than 100,000 U.S. citizens travel(ed) to Nicaragua by 1986" (Perla 2009: 84). I was part of this movement of people traveling to Nicaragua during this period. When I moved to Nicaragua in 1986, joining the ecumenical organization, Witness for Peace, I was based in the mountainous region of northern Jinotega, near the Nicaraguan-Honduran border, where I bore witness to the effects of the conflict. Along with teammates located in civilian communities in war zones across the country, we documented human rights abuses and led delegations of

U.S. citizens so they could learn more about the conflict and then lobby lawmakers in the United States. Due to the solidarity efforts of many organizations and thousands of people across multiple continents, the United States was not able to escalate its involvement, nor send troops to Nicaragua (Perla 2009: 94). After the 1990 elections, which the Sandinistas lost to the neoliberal right, the intensity of solidarity efforts did begin to diminish. I call this Solidarity 2.0.

Achievements and limitations

In both of these solidarity movements, the following common elements can be distinguished: articulation of an anti-imperialist critique of the United States; support for a model of organizing committed to human rights and democracy; and implementation of transnational collaboration, direct action, and relationships across geographical distances to keep people safe and advocate for change. The successes of these solidarity movements—getting the United States to pull out the marines in the 1920s and then cut aid to the *contras* in the 1980s—exemplify the impact of transnational solidarity movements, particularly the grassroots power of citizens based in the Global North and other countries to raise awareness and lobby for changes to foreign policy and aid flows that affect people in other parts of the world. These efforts achieved many of their goals, and today, their legacies are evident in the next generation of U.S.-based organizations fighting for Central-American immigrant rights and advocating for immigration policy reform.[14] However, even though some lives were saved and U.S. aid to the *contras* and other human rights abusers in the region slowed, the solidarity movement's hyper-focus on ending U.S. military spending in the region meant that the movement was ill-prepared to support their Central American counterparts in the post-war, neoliberal period.

What is solidarity and what can we learn from the past?

For the purpose of this book, I proffer a definition of solidarity that is radical, transnational, compassionate action that illuminates the local impacts of injustice and endeavors to apply pressure to stop the wrongs through multiple types of actions targeting different actors at local and international levels. Planned and carried out in collaboration with the people most affected by injustice, these actions are the result of shared strategic thinking and leverage personal relationships. We're talking here about love—solidarity as love—it is horizontal, it is mutually transformational, it is global (Brackley 1999). Binford refers to these relationships as *compañerismo* which is more than allyship, it is shoulder to shoulder—*codo a codo*—accompaniment, which

> involves a 'being with' the compañerxs on this uncertain journey, documenting the journey itself, the changing destinations and strategies as well

as the obstacles they confront and the ways they strive to overcome them, and where possible and when called upon to do so, making an effort to move it along.

(Binford 2008: 181)

There was accompaniment and direct witness, such as the work I carried out in Nicaragua in the 1980s, in which volunteers gathered information and checked facts on the ground with claims being made in Washington D.C. Multiple organizations based in the United States—some started by Central Americans—educated the public, advocated for policy change, and organized protests. A cadre of organizations provided direct services to Central American refugees; whereas others, focused on support and technical assistance to Central American NGOs and movements—even the guerrillas in the case of El Salvador and Guatemala and the Sandinistas in the case of Nicaragua—on the ground. Others dedicated themselves to fundraising on behalf of solidarity efforts. These activities were dynamized by the creation of new organizations and partnerships (sister cities, sister parishes, sister islands, to mention a few) and part of the public expression of concern based on respect and connection between people (see Binford 2008; Silber 2007).

In this way, solidarity involves listening to those who are oppressed, learning from them, and accompanying them in their struggle; it also means seeing one's own experiences in global perspective and how we're all interconnected. It involves doing everything possible to raise awareness and support a positive resolution of grievances; this accompaniment or *"acompañamiento,"* as Binford calls it, means that "I am with you in this journey, I accompany you on this road" (2008: 181). Solidarity is deeply interpersonal and powerfully political. By interpersonal, I mean that it is built on relationships between people; it has powerful effects on all involved. Emotions and human connection across difference are an important feature of solidarity; this affection between accomplices or *compañerxs* means that solidarity is an emotional response in one human being toward another that leads to action. In the germinal volume of *Latin American Perspectives* about solidarity movements in and with Latin America, the editors open with a definition of solidarity attributed to the Sandinistas: "solidarity is the tenderness of the people" (Power and Charlip 2009: 3). Though ironic in the light of current events in Nicaragua where some former revolutionary leaders have become authoritarian leaders, this definition that informed Solidarity 2.0 evokes the affective power of solidarity. Furthermore, solidarity isn't just emotional; it is also political and tied to actions and concrete changes, such as change gained through mass mobilization of protesters, cutting military aid, preventing an invasion, and even limited changes for Central American immigration (Stuelke 2014: 773). Nonetheless, solidarity has unprotected flanks: it can be paternalistic, it can be naïve, it can overly focus on the local situation and miss systemic causes. In Stuelke's interrogation of Central American solidarity culture of the 1980s, she argues that the individualized focus on affective solidarity against U.S. imperialism allowed paternalist creep and the avoidance of systemic change (2014).

In fact, many of the neoliberal reforms imposed on Central America in the late 1980s and 1990s by the World Bank and the International Monetary Fund shared similar philosophical and economic foundations to the neoliberal turn in the United States which was implemented through such programs as the war on drugs and crime, exemplified by "three strikes, you're out" policing which overwhelmingly put Black and Brown youth in prison,[15] and spending cuts to social services including welfare, education, health, and housing. These policies have had disastrous effects in both regions, especially for the most vulnerable and marginalized. Stuelke argues that the affective—emotional—and reparative—ameliorative—vision of the Central America solidarity movement needed to have been more critical of structural inequalities and more alert to the global consequences of neoliberalism, which served to:

> ... undercut the movement's ability to connect the Reagan administration's violence abroad to its privatizing domestic rhetoric and policy, or to compel US citizens to change the neoliberal terms by which global power was increasingly organized. Instead, these dramatizations of US imperialist violence offered a vehicle for redeeming the guilty US nation and its citizens, instantiating a reparative vision of the nation's future as a neoliberal multicultural family.
>
> *(2014: 768)*

Not only did these tendencies limit the ability to see the effects of the neoliberal turn in global perspective, but they also meant that the Central America solidarity movement was not prepared for the bigger challenges that presented themselves in the postwar era.

The atomization of solidarity actions can dissipate long-term, radical change efforts. I've seen this in my own life. After I spent two and a half years in Nicaragua and almost five years in El Salvador doing solidarity work in the 1980s, the civil wars were ending in the early 1990s. By that time, I thought of myself as having roots in the region; I'd had a child and was part of an extended network of Salvadoran kinship. I remember making the decision to leave the region and return to school, thinking that I needed new skills to contribute to the period of postwar reconstruction. Obviously, I wouldn't be where I am today—coordinating my academic institution's solidarity efforts—if I hadn't attended graduate school, but the animating idea for myself and many of my Salvadoran friends and colleagues at the time was that the war was over, and it was time to professionalize and contribute from inside the system. I remained committed to Central America but less as a radical and more as a future professional. My own example describes the implicit risk of what can happen to individual solidarity efforts: they can dissipate. Yes, emotions such as love, compassion, and outrage are important drivers of solidarity, connecting people and motivating action, but institutional relationships and critical analysis are key to sustaining systemic change. These are the reasons why institutional partnerships—built through time—can be so important. As individuals come and go, the institutional relationship continues.

Today, critical political analysis and a commitment to inclusive social change have to accompany the emotional call to respond because our globalized world is interconnected at the local, regional, and global levels; it's not just a particular local situation that has to be addressed but the local emergency has to be analyzed against a broader matrix of global economic and political interests: "micro-initiatives run up against macro-obstacles" (Brackley 1999: 3). This summons was Dean Brackley's challenge to U.S. universities on international solidarity commemorating the tenth anniversary of the assassination of the two lay women and the six Jesuits at the UCA in San Salvador in November of 1989; he urged universities in the Global North to consider not just the interconnections but also complicity: "… the very grave social problems of the U.S. are also related to the kind of society we have constructed here which depends on the foreign policies which have distanced us from the poor majorities of other nations and even contributed to their misery" (1999: 4). In support of new formulations of solidarity that are more inclusive, radical, and self-critical and often led by the next generation, Stuelke writes, "… as we seek to remake the world, to reinvent relationality and reciprocity beyond the modes that neoliberalism and imperialism allow, we must remain critical of our own Utopian imaginations. Solidarity needs suspicion too" (2014: 787). Solidarity often begins with the affective connection between people, and it needs to be built and sustained with critical, reflexive analysis, long-term institutional relationships, and commitment to inclusion in transnational perspective.

Solidarity 3.0

The first phases of solidarity with Nicaragua involved two interconnected phenomena: support for an underdog—Sandino in the 1920s and the Sandinistas in the 1980s—and protest against U.S. interventionist policies. Today, in Nicaragua, a former underdog—the Sandinistas or better said, Sandinista leaders Daniel Ortega and Rosario Murillo—has created a dynasty and is implementing strong-arm, authoritarian tactics to remain in power (see Goett 2019; Hooker 2019; and Simmons 2019). However, there is a beleaguered group of visionaries—many of whom are young college students—being punished for calling for rule of law, freedom for political prisoners, and free elections, and they are being treated as traitors for their nonviolent activism. Today's underdogs are college students, parishioners, farmers, feminists, and the organizations—and institutions like the UCA—that represent them. They are, as Bran Aragón cogently theorizes, the "grandchildren" of postwar (Bran Aragón and Goett 2021). These activists and organizations need support; they need Solidarity 3.0.

Solidarity 3.0 with Nicaragua faces some challenges that the past two solidarity movements described above didn't. In the past, solidarity movements protested U.S. intervention; this time the narrative isn't quite so simple. Yes, the United States has played a significant role in Nicaraguan politics over the past two centuries, and yes, the United States continues to impose a neoliberal agenda throughout Central America and beyond, but today, U.S. foreign policy vis-à-vis Nicaragua, in particular, is not the cause of the immediate problem. In fact, the United States had been providing aid to the Nicaraguan government since before the crisis started (Hooker 2019: 24). During this time, though, the U.S. embassy in Nicaragua has been critical of the Ortega-Murillo regime for its human rights abuses, and the U.S. Congress has put sanctions on several Sandinista leaders, making it hard for them to travel or access their savings in the United States. These actions are important for the opposition[16] but not enough to oust the regime. Nonetheless, some researchers, such as Joshua Mayer (2019a, 2019b), argue that international financial institutions supported by the United States, like the International Monetary Fund and the World Bank, have contributed to increased inequality and poverty and the expansion of the power and use of repression against Indigenous peoples, Afro-descendant groups, and poor farmers by forcing the Nicaraguan government to fulfill neoliberal conditions for aid and loans. These measures have contributed to the decline of rule of law and an increase in repressive tactics over recent decades in Nicaragua. Thus, Solidarity 3.0 should not lose sight of how the global economic order has contributed to the current crisis.

Regrettably, this complex analysis does not lend itself to a narrative that is easily explained or affectively mobilized as were the arguments against sending in the marines in the 1920s or stopping aid to the counterrevolution in the 1980s. The solidarity movements of the 1920s and 1980s leveraged a leftist critique of the imperialist abuse of power by the United States; today, many leftists in the United States are reluctant to criticize the Nicaraguan government because of its historical commitment to a revolutionary, socialist project. Goett cogently confirms this: "Some on the [U.S.] Left are reluctant to disavow a leftist state, even one that has become increasingly violent and authoritarian" (2019: 25). There are middle-aged, former solidarity activists who retain a romanticized image of the Sandinistas, and probably even more challenging, many potential activists are loath to criticize a leftist political project in this current political context with many examples of conservative, populist fascism on the rise. A more nuanced political analysis is needed: I—along with the contributors to this book and many others—argue that Nicaragua is showing us that a traditional, Left-Right political analysis is not a sufficient explanatory framework anymore, particularly when there is such a diversity of actors that comprise the opposition. In fact, "… it is impossible to accurately understand the conflict in Nicaragua by viewing it through such outdated ideological lenses," (Hooker 2019: 23). The use of state repression, corruption, and land dispossession exposes a government that is no longer committed to a bottom-up, inclusive democracy serving the poor majorities of the country (Goett 2019: 26). Indigenous groups and Afro-descendant communities on the Caribbean Coast are directly impacted by these forces through the sustained incursion of mestizo settlers onto their lands and the Sandinista cooptation of local leadership (Cosgrove et al. 2021; Mittal and The Oakland Institute 2020) as well as the implementation of paternalistic, extractive models of development that increase dependence and exclusion, respectively (Simmons 2019).

Yet, there are some resonant similarities between a possible Solidarity 3.0 and the solidarity movements of the twentieth century and other social movements today that deserve mention. And here I am heeding the advice of Irina Carlota Silber who calls scholars of Central America activism and solidarity to not only map shifts but also continuities because "not in the past, present, or future does there exist a 'pure' form of activism" (2007: 181) or solidarity. As in the past, transnational grassroots relationships between people, groups, and movements catalyzed increased engagement. The contributors to this book believe that partnerships, such as university partnerships or other types of shared activities between organizations in the Global North and Nicaragua, can help inspire solidarity, especially if they join forces with broader networks, such as the global Jesuit network of universities in the case of SU and the UCA or advocates for Central American migrants with their roots in the solidarity movement of the 1980s. Also, the protests in Nicaragua have been led by high school and college students similar to the environmental youth leaders who are emerging right now like Greta Thunberg and students in the United States advocating for gun control, and most recently the Black Lives Matter protests against white supremacy and systemic racism demanding a dismantling of U.S. policing due to its racist treatment of Black and Brown people. Solidarity can't just be about fighting imperialism; it's about fighting structural inequalities, oppression, and environmental devastation. This new political culture inspires a radical commitment, making it easier to commit to Solidarity 3.0 in which we and our institutions realize that when Ellacuría calls us to a preferential option for the poor, we choose to center the margins, not elites. This choice means being at the service of the people who face systemic violence every day. Their everyday experience inspires our everyday commitment to solidarity.

Yes, there are aspects of the current situation in Nicaragua that make it harder to explain than in past iterations, but there are some factors that didn't exist in the 1930s or 1980s that can help facilitate solidarity today. Social media platforms like Facebook, Instagram, Twitter, and others serve the communication needs of social movements[17] today where "the power of images is paramount … particularly meaningful are images of violent repression by the police or thugs" (Castells 2015: 252) that can be used by youth-led movements from Chile to Nicaragua and beyond. This includes the use of social media and cellular phones to document and disseminate what is going on (Cabalin 2014) as well as using these social media platforms for organizing and protest (Valenzuela et al. 2012). Activists don't have to wait to come to the attention of global news agencies or even national news sources to show what is going on and tweet it, post it, or blog about it. Whereas many social movements have been able to get their stories out through alternative outlets, mainstream news sources haven't been covering Nicaragua in a sustained and rigorous fashion. It is vital to request more coverage and share the coverage that is coming out, such as when Raquel Idiáquez gave an interview to NPR about being unable to leave the United States due to the death threats against her uncle, the president of the UCA (Hajek 2019).

I write this chapter as a professor at Seattle University, a Jesuit university in the United States that is part of a global network of Jesuit universities committed to educating our students for a more just and humane world. Committed to sharing our model with the other universities in our network, SU is taking a set of actions to embody solidarity with the UCA, in particular, and the Nicaraguan people, in general. Neither Seattle University nor I seek congratulation for our solidarity; this is not like the humanitarianism that Fassin critiques in which do-gooders lament the tragedy and then celebrate their generosity (2012: ix). Seattle University understands that it is the UCA that is saving us by showing us what it means to stand up to injustice and retain the vital role of a university committed to those whose rights are disrespected and whose voices are seldom heard on the global stage.

Interuniversity solidarity

Seattle University's Central America Initiative—a vibrant set of partnerships between Seattle University and the three Jesuit universities in Central America—emerged from shared activities between Seattle University and the UCA in Managua, which coalesced after more than 20 years of immersion visits by SU faculty and staff to Nicaragua. Since 2014, SU and the UCA have collaborated on over a hundred projects, such as student exchanges, co-taught courses, guest lectures, and collaborative research. Examples of our shared activities include: student educational and service programming and student exchanges between both universities; extended visits at the highest level integrating UCA and SU provosts, presidents, and chief financial officers; multiple faculty pairings for pedagogical and research collaborations as evidenced by the in-tandem work between Marissa and me; the UCA's invitation to SU president, Fr. Stephen Sundborg, S.J., to give the annual inaugural lecture, "Two Universities: One Jesuit Mission" in March 2014; and Seattle University's 2019 award of an honorary doctorate to UCA president, José (Chepe) Idiáquez, S.J., in recognition of his commitment to the UCA in the face of government repression. Some of these activities came to a halt when the repression started in April 2018. So, we pivoted to help the UCA survive this time of crisis with ongoing actions to support their scholarship, increase their visibility, raise awareness about the situation in Nicaragua, and raise funds for UCA scholarships.

As the coordinator of SU's Central America Initiative, I drew on my experiences of Solidarity 2.0 to encourage SU leadership, faculty, staff, and students to educate themselves about what was happening and denounce what was going on in Nicaragua through the dissemination of information and calls for action to the Jesuit network of colleges and universities in the United States and globally. Many joined us and prepared press statements denouncing the human rights violations, lobbied elected officials to condemn the actions of the Nicaraguan government, and carried out teach-ins. This was when I realized that a critical interrogation of Solidarity 2.0 was needed; this, in turn, led to this present theorization of Solidarity 3.0. I saw that the institutional response—nourished over years—was an important platform for increasing visibility about what was going on in Nicaragua, but that strategic projects for the long-term sustainability and autonomy of the UCA were also needed. This led to further investment of time in fundraising and scholarly publications.

Visibility refers to raising awareness about the situation in Nicaragua as well as increasing the international profile of the UCA to foment increased knowledge and action. Concerned about the death threats to the UCA president and the funding cuts to the UCA and convinced that calling attention to the situation would help protect our partner, SU committed itself to accompanying the UCA as it raised its international profile. Leveraging the scholarly collaborations that had been going on between SU and UCA was a logical next step to support the UCA's scholarly publications at an international level. The more that the UCA is recognized internationally as providing a critical education and carrying out research that highlights invisiblized or marginalized realities the more difficult it becomes for the Nicaraguan government to harm the institution. We've also focused on supporting the UCA's development of a short- and long-term fundraising strategy for the survival and sustainability of the UCA, its educational programs, and student scholarships, particularly for students from under-resourced backgrounds. In the course of these actions, both institutions have learned so much. As I mentioned above, at SU, we have seen our own institutional challenges in global perspective thanks to the UCA, and they, in turn, know that they are not alone, but we have all also realized that there is a need to apply a broader analysis about the hemispheric effects of the neoliberal era and understand how these policies have directly impacted the UCA and endangered university autonomy throughout the Americas. And even further, we have come to see that what may have appeared as different policies applied in Latin America and the United States—cuts in social spending, increased concentration of wealth, and increased exclusion, marginalization, and discrimination in our two different regions—respond to the very same neoliberal architecture that does not prioritize the marginalized, the poor, and the excluded in both our respective regions.

The UCA has declared that they are biased on behalf of human rights and inclusion; they are the only university in Nicaragua that has consistently spoken out for the rights of their students (and all Nicaraguans) to enjoy free speech, the right of association, and the opportunity to participate in fair elections. Today, the crisis in Nicaragua is about an authoritarian government that unjustly targets dissent, refuses to participate in dialogue, and continues to consolidate power. An informed and creative Solidarity 3.0 is needed: a solidarity that is affective, reciprocal, radical, strategic, and self-critical. Solidarity 3.0—and the individuals and institutions who've committed ourselves to bear witness and be accomplices in the struggle—demands a resolution to the present challenges facing the Nicaraguan people and also sees the connections between the politics and economics of neoliberal reform and how the disenfranchisement of people in Nicaragua and the United States are connected.

Final thoughts

Of the scholars who critically analyze the Central American solidarity movement of the 1980s calling out paternalism and lack of strategic vision, they do acknowledge what the movement achieved. They recognize very real human lives were transformed (and saved in some cases) to live another day, to contribute to a more inclusive Central America, and they acknowledge that many policy changes were accomplished (Coutin 1993; Binford 2008; Perla 2008, 2009; Perla and Coutin 2010; and Stuelke 2014). New iterations of solidarity have to incorporate the critiques and then do better. We have to love deeper, risk more, and take a stand with others that acknowledge what connects us and do something to get at the deeper systemic injustices that can remain untouched. Juliet Hooker, in her analysis of the need for political solidarity to overcome racism, advocates for a solidarity that "is seen as arising from the (geographical, social, political) spaces that individuals share and as a result of which their actions have unavoidable consequences on the lives of others that also inhabit such locales" (Hooker 2009: 170). This encourages us to consider what spaces we share and how we are interconnected. We have to connect Deborah Thomas' "Witnessing 2.0" (2019: 2) to our academic Solidarity 3.0. Thomas proffers a bearing witness that moves past eyewitnessing to one that is "embodied practice" and citing Conquergood, is "co-performative" and requires "a commitment to 'shared temporality, bodies on the line, soundscapes of power, dialogic interanimation, political action, and matters of the heart'" (2019: 2) and can lead to radical, transformative change (2019: 3).

In February of 2020, I visited the UCA having been invited to give the opening lecture for the school year. Entitled "The Impact of Exclusion: Global Reflections on War, Conflict, and Poverty," I endeavored to convey my witness to what is happening to the UCA community, in particular, and Nicaragua, more generally, applying a global lens. When I finished speaking, the auditorium filled with applause. I believe this response was due to the fact that my words had been interpreted as accompaniment. The people who came to hear me speak—students, professors, and other Nicaraguan intellectuals—felt seen.

That night as I attempted to sleep in the guest bedroom of the Jesuit residence on the UCA campus, my fear kept me awake: every falling coconut in the garden was a potential intruder, every lull in the noises of tropical insects made my heartbeat quicken: had police or government strongmen come in over the fence as part of a night-time raid? If I could choose, would I rather paramilitary youth enter and kill us or police who would beat us up, maybe kill us, and if we survived, take us to prison? I thought about the Nicaraguan students I knew who had been detained and how they had been tortured by the police and other prisoners trying to show loyalty to the government and possibly get a shorter sentence. I spent the night with all my very real fears for Nicaragua like the sheet covering me—a flor de piel: no sleep for me. This was just one sleepless night for me accompanying people who have been living with repression and threats for multiple years now and who frequently startle awake in the night when a coconut falls on the patio or the cicadas grow quiet in the trees. Though meaningful for my Nicaraguan partners, maybe, my actions won't lead to a regime change, nor will they address the broader systemic issues that circumscribe and limit university autonomy, but they are part of sustained, institutional commitments to accompaniment and social justice. May the UCA's courageous stand and Seattle University's institutional commitment to the UCA inspire others to follow our example. This is our version of Solidarity 3.0 with Nicaragua. How might you and your institution commit to Solidarity 3.0 and follow Fr. Ignacio Ellacuría's call—which he shared ten days before he was killed: "... to keep your eyes on what is happening in Nicaragua and El Salvador and to help us"?[18]

Notes

1 "... fuertes vinculaciones internacionales ofrecen una cobertura a la UCA en general y a su proyección social en particular, hacen más difíciles los ataques irracionales de los poderosos a la institución y facilitan correr los riesgos que la proyección social implica." Originally drafted in 1978 and published in Ellacuría (1999: 151).
2 Seattle University is a private liberal arts university perched on Capitol Hill above downtown Seattle. Its mission is to form leaders for a just and humane world. With about 8,000 students, half undergraduate and half graduate students, Seattle University is a Jesuit university, forming part of a network of more than 200 institutions of higher learning worldwide that embrace the pedagogical approach of critical thinking and engaged learning of the Jesuit order of the Catholic Church.
3 Founded in 1960, the Universidad Centroamericana-Managua, or the UCA as it is called, is one of three Jesuit universities in Central America; it has a historical commitment to the poor majorities of Nicaragua, for which the university received 50% of its budget from the government (this is the part of the 6% state budget allocation that goes to universities in Nicaragua) to support an expansive scholarship program for disadvantaged students. As I explain in this chapter, this funding has been cut by the state.
4 Starting in the 1980s, many cities, town, parishes, and even islands in Central American countries experiencing conflict—such as El Salvador, Guatemala, and Nicaragua—developed "sister" relationships with counterparts in North America and Europe. This became a route for exchange, visits, advocacy, and aid. See Molly Todd (2021) *Long Journey to Justice: El Salvador, the United States, and Struggles against Empire* for an in-depth exploration of this phenomenon in the rural Salvadoran department of Chalatenango.
5 "Suele decirse que la Universidad debe de ser imparcial. Nosotros creemos que no. La universidad debe pretender ser libre y objetiva pero la objetividad y la libertad pueden exigir ser parciales. Y nosotros somos libremente parciales a favor de las

mayorías populares, porque son injustamente oprimidas y porque en ellas, negativa y positivamente, esta la verdad de la realidad." (Excerpt from Ellacuría's November 6, 1989 essay, "El Desafío de las Mayorías Populares" or "The Challenge of the Poor Majority," published in 1999: 304).

6 "Nicaragua suffered for four decades under the brutal U.S.-backed Somoza dictatorship, which the Sandinista Revolution ousted in 1979, leading to another decade of U.S.-funded counterrevolutionary 'contra' war" (Rogers 2018).

7 Many journalists and mainstream news sources now refer to the "Ortega-Murillo regime" due to the amount of power Rosario Murillo, Vice President and wife of Daniel Ortega, wields. See Kai Thaler's 2020 article about Nicaragua in *Foreign Policy*: https://foreignpolicy.com/2020/04/17/ortega-virus-murillo-nicaragua-is-stumbling-into-coronavirus-disaster/

8 The historically pro-Sandinista, mass youth organization, the Juventud Sandinista or Sandinista Youth, is being utilized by the regime to impose heavy handed treatment of the opposition, particularly youth. See the *NACLA* (Jillson 2020) article, "The Anti-Sandinista Youth of Nicaragua," which explains the repressive role that the Sandinista Youth are playing now.

9 See Drazen Joric's Reuters article, "Bolivia's ouster of Morales stirs tensions in left-leaning Nicaragua," as an example of the coverage of this phenomenon.

10 See David Agren's article "Jesuits denounce threats; seek protection for Nicaraguan bishop," *Americas*, June 5, 2018.

11 "Lo que necesita [la universidad] es autonomía real, autosuficiencia independiente. ¿Independiente de qué? La respuesta es fácil: de todo aquello a través de lo cual la sociedad dominante presiona para domesticar a la universidad." (Excerpt from Ellacuría's 1975 essay on the tenth anniversary of the UCA-El Salvador, "Diez años después: ¿es posible una universidad distinta?" or "10 Years Later: Is a different university possible?," published in 1999 page 81.

12 Committee in Solidarity with the People of El Salvador.

13 There is a robust scholarly literature about the Sandinista Revolution, its inception, aims, achievements, contradictions, and limitations. See Quesada's chapter for this history as well as scholars such as Gould (1990), Hale (1994), and many others who have written about the revolutionary period of Nicaraguan history.

14 A number of the organizations created in the 1980s remain active today; in fact, a number of U.S. based organizations, originally founded to promote solidarity with Nicaragua, El Salvador, or Guatemala, work today on immigrant rights and services and immigration policy reform. See Perla and Coutin (2010: 16–17).

15 See Michelle Alexander's *The New Jim Crow: Mass Incarceration in the Age of Colorblindness* for a detailed history and description of the present day, racist and exclusionary effects of these policies and programs in the United States.

16 The opposition in Nicaragua is comprised of a wide range of organizations, including civil society organizations, many private sector businesses, and some churches.

17 I would like to acknowledge SU 2020 International Studies honors graduate, Julia Schwab, whose thesis on the topic of the social protests in Chile introduced me to the scholarly literature on the broader topic of social movements and the social media age.

18 "… y yo les pido a ustedes aquí presentes como personas y tal vez como estamentos oficiales que pongan a sus ojos en Nicaragua y en El Salvador y nos ayuden" (Excerpt from Ellacuría's November 6, 1989 essay, "El Desafío de las Mayorías Populares" or "The Challenge of the Poor Majority," published in 1999, page 306.

References

Agren, David. (2018) Jesuits denounce threats; seek protection for Nicaraguan bishop. *Americas*, June 5. Accessed July 9, 2020: https://www.americamagazine.org/politics-society/2018/06/05/jesuits-denounce-threats-seek-protection-nicaraguan-bishop

Alexander, Michelle, and Cornel West. (2012) *The New Jim Crow: Mass Incarceration in the Age of Colorblindness* (Revised ed.). New York, NY: The New Press.

Binford, Leigh. (2008) Reply: Solidarity: Solidarity and Acompañmiento. *Dialectical Anthropology*, 32, no. 3: 177–182.

Brackley Dean, S.J. (1999) Higher Standards for Higher Education: The Christian University and Solidarity. San Salvador, El Salvador: Universidad Centroamericana José Simeón Cañas. Accessed March 12, 2021: https://onlineministries.creighton.edu/CollaborativeMinistry/brackley.html

Bran Aragón, Fiore Stella, and Jennifer Goett. (2021). "*!Matria libre y vivir!*: Youth Activism and Nicaragua's 2018 Insurrection." *Journal of Latin American and Caribbean Anthropology*, 25, no. 4: 532–551.

Cabalin, C. (2014) Online and Mobilized Students: The Use of Facebook in the Chilean Student Protests. *Comunicar*, 22, no. 43: 25–33.

Castells, M. (2015) *Networks of Outrage and Hope: Social Movements in the Internet Age*. Cambridge, UK: Polity Press.

Comisión Interamericana de Derechos Humanos. (2019) *Migración Forzada de Personas Nicaragüenses a Costa Rica*, Septiembre.

Cosgrove, Serena, José Idiáquez, Leonard Joseph Bent, and Andrew Gorvetzian. (2021) *Surviving the Americas: Garifuna Persistence from Nicaragua to New York City*. Cincinnati: University of Cincinnati Press.

Coutin, Susan Bibler. (1993) *The Culture of Protest: Religious Activism and the U.S. Sanctuary Movement*. Boulder: Westview Press.

Ellacuría, Ignacio. (1999) *Escritos Universitarios*. San Salvador, El Salvador: UCA Editores.

Fassin, Didier. (2012) *Humanitarian Reason: A Moral History of the Present*. Berkeley: University of California Press.

Finzer, Erin S. "Modern Women Intellectuals and the Sandino Rebellion: Carmen Sobalvarro and Aura Rostand." *Latin American Research Review* 56, no. 2 (2021): 457–471. https://doi.org/10.25222/larr.878.

Goett, Jennifer. (2019) Beyond Left and Right: Grassroots Social Movements and Nicaragua's Civic Insurrection. *LASA FORUM*, 49, no. 4: 25–31.

Gould, Jeffrey L. (1990) *To Lead As Equals Rural Protest and Political Consciousness in Chinandega, Nicaragua, 1912-1979*. Chapel Hill: University of North Carolina Press.

Grossman, Richard. (2009) Solidarity with Sandino: The Anti-Intervention and Solidarity Movements in the United States, 1927-1933. *Latin American Perspectives*, 36, no. 6, SOLIDARITY: 67–79, November 2009.

Gusterson, Hugh. (2017) Homework: Toward a Critical Ethnography of the University AES Presidential Address, 2017. *American Ethnologist*, 44, no. 3: 435–450.

Hajek, Danny. (2019) "Pray for Me": Nicaraguan Priest Threatened with Death Reaches out to Niece in U.S. *Morning Edition*, National Public Radio, April 24. Accessed July 12, 2020: https://www.npr.org/2019/04/24/711561210/pray-for-me-nicaraguan-priest-threatened-with-death-reaches-out-to-niece-in-u-s

Hale, Charles R. (1994). *Resistance and Contradiction: Miskitu Indians and the Nicaraguan State, 1894–1987*. Stanford, CA: Stanford University Press.

Harris, Richard L. (1987) The Revolutionary Transformation of Nicaragua. *Latin American Perspectives*, 14, no. 1: 3–18. Thousand Oaks, CA: Sage Publications.

Hooker, Juliet. (2009) *Race and the Politics of Solidarity*. New York: Oxford University Press.

Hooker, Juliet. (2019) Civil Society in Revolt against the Leftist Authoritarianism of the Ortega/Murillo Regime. *LASA FORUM*, 49:4: 23–24.

Hyatt, Susan Brin, Boone W. Shear, and Susan Wright, eds. (2015) *Learning under Neoliberalism: Ethnographies of Governance in Higher Education*. New York and London: Berghahn Books.

Jillson, Chris. (2020) The Anti-Sandinista Youth of Nicaragua. *NACLA*, February 5. Accessed on July 17, 2020: https://nacla.org/news/2020/02/05/anti-sandinista-youth-nicaragua

Joric, Drazen. (2019) Bolivia's Ouster of Morales Stirs Tensions in Left-Leaning Nicaragua. *Reuters*, November 20. Accessed on July 9, 2020: https://www.reuters.com/article/us-nicaragua-politics/bolivias-ouster-of-morales-stirs-tensions-in-left-leaning-nicaragua-idUSKBN1XU2BO

Mayer, Joshua L. (2019a) Growing (through) Dispossession: Development Strategies and Settler Colonization amid Nicaragua's New "Normal." Paper presented at the *Annual Meeting of the American Anthropological Association and Canadian Anthropology Society*, Vancouver, BC, November 20.

Mayer, Joshua L. (2019b) International Institutions, Disavowal, and Dispossession: Nicaragua and Global Assemblages of Settler Colonialism. Unpublished manuscript, last modified March 26. Microsoft Word file.

Mittal, Anuradha, and The Oakland Institute. (2020) Nicaragua's Failed Revolution: The Indigenous Struggle for Saneamiento. Oakland, CA: The Oakland Institute. Accessed on July 11, 2020: www.oaklandinstitute.org

Pérez, Marta, and Ainhoa Montoya. (2018) La insostenibilidad de la Universidad pública neoliberal: hacia una etnografía de la precariedad en la Academia. *Revista de Dialectología y Tradiciones Populares*, LXXIII, n. 1: A1–A16, enero-junio.

Perla, Hector, and Susan Bibler Coutin. (2010) Legacies and Origins of the 1980s US-Central American Sanctuary Movement. *Refuge* (Toronto, English Edition), 26, no. 1: 7–19.

Perla Jr., Héctor. (2008) Si Nicaragua Venció, El Salvador Vencerá: Central American Agency in the Creation of the U.S.: Central American Peace and Solidarity Movement. *Latin American Research Review*, 43, no. 2: 136–158.

Perla Jr., Héctor. (2009) Heirs of Sandino: The Nicaraguan Revolution and the U.S.-Nicaragua Solidarity Movement. *Latin American Perspectives*, 36, 6, SOLIDARITY: 80–100, November.

Power, Margaret, and Julie A. Charlip. (2009) Introduction: On Solidarity. *Latin American Perspectives*, 36, 6, SOLIDARITY: 3–9, November.

Rogers, Tim. (2018) The Unraveling of Nicaragua. *The Atlantic*, June 6. Accessed July 9, 2020: https://www.theatlantic.com/international/archive/2018/06/nicaragua-ortega-protests/562094/

Servicio Jesuita de Migrantes-Costa Rica. (2019) personal communication, November 10.

Silber, Irina Carlota. (2007) Local Capacity Building in "Dysfunctional" Times: Internationals, Revolutionaries, and Activism in Postwar El Salvador. *Women's Studies Quarterly*, 35, no. 3 & 4: 167–183.

Simmons, Shakira. (2019) Grito por Nicaragua, un grito desde la Costa Caribe. *LASA FORUM*, 49, no. 4: 32–36.
Stuelke, Patricia. (2014) The Reparative Politics of Central America Solidarity Movement Culture. *American Quarterly*, 66, no. 3: 767–790.
Thaler, Kai. (2020) Nicaragua is Stumbling into Coronavirus Disaster. *Foreign Policy*, April 17. Accessed July 9, 2020: https://foreignpolicy.com/2020/04/17/ortega-virus-murillo-nicaragua-is-stumbling-into-coronavirus-disaster/
Thomas, Deborah. (2019). *Political Life in the Wake of the Plantation: Sovereignty, Witnessing, Repair*. Durham: Duke University Press.
Todd, Molly. (2021) *Long Journey to Justice: El Salvador, the United States, and Struggles against Empire*. Madison: University of Wisconsin Press (Critical Human Rights Series).
Valencia, Ricardo. (2018) The Making of the White Middle-Class Radical: A Discourse Analysis of the Public Relations of the Committee in Solidarity with the People of El Salvador between 1980 and 1990. Doctoral dissertation, University of Oregon.
Valenzuela, S., A. Arriagada, and A. Scherman. (2012) The Social Media Basis of Youth Protest Behavior: The Case of Chile. *Journal of Communication*, 62, no. 2: 299–314.
Walker, Thomas W. (2003) *Nicaragua: Living in the Shadow of the Eagle* (4th ed). Boulder: Westview Press.

8
LESSONS FROM NICARAGUA FOR A CRITICAL HIGHER EDUCATION

Irina Carlota Silber

Introduction

Throughout this book, the authors have provided us with ethnographic analyses of a leading regional Central American university caught in the crossfires of neoliberal exigencies and persistent violent state repression. Their collaborative intersectional approach, across hierarchies within the institution, and across borders, provides a potent roadmap for transformative and liberatory practices in higher education across our world threatened by corporate models and what many scholars document as the militarization of the university (Chatterjee and Maira 2014).[1] This is a pressing topic, as scholarly research and public conversations on the attacks against and the role, responsibility, and accountability of "the university" for the public good make clear (e.g., Ergül and Coşar 2017). This book beckons us to take seriously a university manifesto, historically informed that unequivocally exposes the forces of repression and a neoliberal-spawned inequality. It does so to battle against complacency or a silencing "academic containment" (Chatterjee and Maira 2014: 22) through a call to action that is rooted in the everyday complicated work and commitments of the university—from presidents and top administrators, accompanying contingent faculty, student activists to intergenerational and international academic solidarity. The authors are unapologetic in the righteousness of this charge that moves from a pedagogy of resistance to participatory research and learning, from alternative knowledge production for the public good to efforts to enact ethical and committed institution building during the most trying and dangerous times. Invoking Ignacio Ellacuría, S.J., they remind us that the role of the university, particularly in times of crisis, is to be "freely partial towards the poor majority"[2] (Ellacuría 1999: 304). Key themes guide us throughout, as we recognize why a manifesto advocating for a liberatory politics of education is needed, how uprisings entangle administrators and students against multiple waves of violence, which are also entwined with a long history of international solidarity and new projects of institutional accompaniment.

I come to this activist project through my positioning as a socio-cultural anthropologist, Argentine-born and U.S.-raised, and as what some may call a "Central Americanist" or at least a "Salvadoranist." I've spent much of my scholarly career committed to forwarding knowledge about El Salvador's armed conflict (1980–1991) and postwar processes that honor the lives and trajectories of everyday insurgents in the rural landscape of El Salvador's northern department, Chalatenango, and their decades-later migration to the United States. I first accompanied joint UCA-Nicaragua and SU faculty and student research as they presented their findings and art projects on the "abuelización" across Nicaragua about how grandmothers had become central caregivers for a host of reasons including economic pressures. From the start, I was struck with the differences in the Central American narratives around postwar for the region. For instance, at the time, in 2016, Nicaragua seemed an exceptional case, outside of policy conversations and framings around the "surge" of migration to the United States from the "Northern Triangle" (Guatemala, El Salvador, and Honduras) understood as resulting from economic despair and uncontainable gang violence. My colleagues were taking note of various other concomitant processes, such as Garifuna persistence in the Caribbean Coast (Cosgrove et al. 2021), the seed of their prescient analyses we've read here.

I also come to this project on universities under fire as an academic based in a public university system that like so many well-documented cases across the United States has endured cycles of economic austerity, shrinking budgets, new mixed funding structures and often shifting priorities as those who study the neoliberal university make clear (e.g., Godrej 2014; Hyatt et al. 2015).[3] And so, I ask, what does it mean to take seriously the call to be partial in favor of "las mayorías populares?" Is there a global blueprint for pursuing this cultural and institutional transformation in a world characterized by continuities of violence and inequality—political, systemic, racialized, gendered, and so on? Comparative examples across Latin America are many: from market-driven and government implemented reforms in Peru and Ecuador that reinscribed power (Benavides et al. 2019) to the repression of university students in Chile who demanded equal access and expansion of public higher education and having a place at the table (Bellei et al. 2014) to the rampant assault of academic freedom in Brazil under the Bolsonaro regime (Lima and Iamamoto 2020).[4]

For the United States, in the wake of the movement for Black Lives, Bianca Williams, Dian Squire, and Frank Tuitt push us to recognize the ways in which a history of white supremacy (colonialism and enslavement) underscores the very logics of the university, what they term "plantation politics" (2021). This puts into stark relief the "connections between historical policies, practices, and discourses in higher education and their new iterations, which are used to control, exploit, and marginalize Black people." (Williams et al. 2021: 3). Their project, attendant to student protests, demands accountability and profound changes to institutionalize liberation, racial equity, and justice. This is resistance with first-generation students, BIPOC students, faculty, and staff, for LGBTQIA+ rights that also interrogates the ableism that roots the university. This is a resistance in tension with narratives that leverage the numbers and the statistics that prove the success of social mobility for students in public universities, as these institutions are often seen as engines for economic change.

With all of this in mind, I suggest that we can find a path forward in the embodied and reciprocal academic solidarity so eloquently and specifically outlined in the preceding chapters by colleagues at the UCA in Managua and Seattle University. While these universities are linked in part by their institutional affinities and missions as Jesuit universities, they model for us possibilities and obligations, of what we can do together—in the name of a university manifesto. Because across the world, many institutions of higher education confront both homegrown repression and international pressures. The UCA in Managua shows us how to pursue a liberatory politics of education. It illuminates the power of a history of solidarity and how we must all push forward with critique and collaboration. All the authors offer us lessons about the risks to critical education, the importance of university autonomy, and highlight the strategies for resisting the harsh consequences of neoliberalism with its marketization and commodification of education (e.g., Hyatt et al. 2015) and repression. This is public scholarship at its best.[5] This is a Nicaraguan story. This is a Central American story. This is a global story.

Mobilizing a University Manifesto

For so many of us, this book project begins with José (Chepe) Idiáquez, S.J.'s transformative leadership and what we hope you've come to see as a new invocation of a University Manifesto, one that builds deeply from his personal, intellectual, and historical relationship with the martyred scholars and Jesuits from the UCA in El Salvador. Specifically, Idiáquez finds inspiration in Ignacio Ellacuría, S.J.'s University Essays (*Ensayos Universitarios*) that expound on the role of knowledge production and the critical function of the university in contexts of war and political polarization that we are in the thick of still. Idiáquez's manifesto, now written and publicly declared, reflects an everyday labor that speaks truth to power in the face of great personal and institutional repression. It signals a call to action justified by the efforts of multisectoral youth, from university students to environmental activists, who reignited a broad social movement. Recall, for instance, Fiore Bran Aragón's analysis of the autoconvocados, a new generation or coalescence of activism in response to a series of failed state responses to diverse issues across generations and landscapes that were a long time coming. Idiáquez's manifesto helps us to focus on what the "quehacer universitario," the university's overarching "task" or mission, should be. Building on Ellacuría, Idiáquez emphasizes that the university task must center on rigor, critical thought, and theory building. It is not about politics, performative or otherwise, or co-opting student resistance. But it is about forming students and pedagogy.

From his years of leadership, Idiáquez offers that in Nicaragua "university youth" are often seen as the harbingers of a family's success, the embodied hope for the future.[6] He saw them, stood by them, well before having to mobilize for their right to breathe. Yet, Idiáquez does not mobilize these hopeful numbers or branding around the university's ability to promote students' economic and social mobility. Rather, he invokes Ellacuría to remind us that the task, the university obligation, is to unmask the oppression lived by the majority. It is *not* about creating "successful" graduates in the capitalist model of hyper-accumulation, which Julie Livingston, writing about development models in Botswana, reminds us is actually a "self-devouring growth" (2019), but rather it is about creating a deep and broad possibility for an open preparation. What does this preparation look like? The concept is agentive—to prepare for a "future action or purpose" (OED 2021). It entails "bring[ing] to a state of mental or spiritual readiness" (OED 2021). This university manifesto invokes a preparation that happens in the intimacy of the classroom, full of an appetite for critical inquiry in the service of building a more just and inclusive society. Ultimately, Idiáquez offers us a liberatory politics of education, grounded not in charismatic leadership but in a humble, nonviolent, horizontal, and intersectional collectivity that calls for an international response. It is only in this making of educational equity and inclusion, indeed what we actually do in our classrooms, that he argues we can realize our full humanity.

Do we only need manifestos in times of crisis?

It is of course cliché, utopic, and redundant to state that youth are the future. Yet, the analysis and stories presented here on the entangled violences of militarization and neoliberalism that strangle institutions such as the UCA in Managua circle back to this very point. Nearly every author grants considerable attention to youth activism and the choices institutions have made regarding academic freedom and cultivating or silencing spaces for free speech, liberty of thought, and expression. The UCA comes to stand in literally and metaphorically as a place of sanctuary. Indeed, it is the incorporation of the perspectives of everyday upper administrators that offers one of the most compelling and nuanced reads of how to implement a university manifesto—one that speaks back to corporate models of investment and strategies. Analysis by the UCA Provost interrogates the meanings of metrics and the politics of evaluation in service of creating an institution where critical thought can find sanctuary.[7]

Wendi Bellanger, Provost of the UCA, offers a compelling critique of the ways in which a focus on access and funding has been complicit in sidelining a critical discussion on institutional autonomy and academic freedom. She argues that the technocratic focus on outcomes, accreditation, and so on works to silence academic freedom, protest, and university autonomy. Across the world of higher education, this feeds into debates around what the "new 21st century student" needs. In the case of Nicaragua, and specifically, the UCA, Bellanger argues that in this elision, "universities are easily absorbed into networks of clientelism put in place by authoritarian governments." This analysis of political clientelism is courageous as it points to the cross-cutting union of university sectors with direct linkages to the FSLN. She argues that this teaches faculty, students, and administrators to learn to play the game. Through a careful consideration of historico-legal processes, Bellanger sheds light on the arc of university autonomy in Nicaragua that she cogently reminds us has spanned different governments and epochs. Like in many other cases across the world, the battle, struggle, advocacy, and organizing centers on funding. In Nicaragua, the rallying cry has focused on the government mandated "6%" upon which academic freedom appears to rest.

She unmasks this framing by brilliantly mapping out issues around evaluation, accreditation, and "quality assurance" that entangle state repression, neoliberal global higher education policy, and the hegemony of academic capitalism. This is a deep critique of the entrepreneurship that is expected now of universities—precisely what Chepe Idiáquez's manifesto contests. Like so many of the chapters, Bellanger offers a reflection on how to contest the fragility or the attack on autonomy, for the UCA particularly, but that has lessons for other cases of government repression across Latin America. Because as the comparative work of Ana Karen Barragán Fernández makes clear, Jesuit university missions are under fire in places such as Universidad Católica Andrés Bello in Venezuela and Universidad Iberoamericana Puebla in Mexico as well.[8] And while the integrity of the Jesuit mission may not ultimately be derailed, resistance to government repression, as in the case of the UCA in Managua, has had significant consequences. Such consequences included acts of violence on campus, threats against university leadership, espionage, and the creation of hate campaigns by governments or pro-government forces (Barragán Fernández 2021).

In the hierarchy of value and analyses of how institutions operate, there is often a felt split, if not often animosity or "faculty contempt" for administrators who are seen as the "enemy" (Rosenberg 2021). This book offers a radical intervention to this framing as it demonstrates the academic solidarity within an institution from administrators, faculty, and students. Indeed, it sheds light on the intrepid, resolute, and positioned gendered leadership of Bellanger as Provost.[9] Without her leadership, one could argue that the UCA would not still be on its feet, however precarious and day to day, with its doors open, with faculty teaching, with students in classrooms (in-person and virtually) enacting the boldness of the university manifesto. Including this perspective makes the critical claim that a university manifesto must be cross-cutting, and that administrative support is fundamental. Chapters penned by high-level administrators expose the institution's vulnerability and underscore the urgency of an international, institutional academic solidarity so that the UCA can continue to lead. Through the support of administrators such as President Idiáquez and Provost Bellanger, the UCA remains the outlier, one of the few that refused to turn in to the government detailed lists of students and faculty, that refused to expel them, and instead raised their voices. The UCA created sanctuary and now suffers and stands in the face of the consequences.

Accompaniment within and outside classroom walls

The literature on student activism and protest, historically and in the current moment, is expansive, for Latin America (e.g., Levy 1991), Central America (e.g., Vrana 2017), and across the world (e.g., Cole and Heinecke 2020). Scholarship on the university tends to focus on student protagonism (e.g., Williams et al. 2021) and student life (Gusterson 2017) as the chapters included in this volume also make clear. However, new research illuminates the critical space of faculty accompaniment within and outside the classroom walls. For the Nicaraguan case, Karla Lara's and Arquímedes González's chapters demonstrate just how crucial this accompaniment has been. Recall that to accompany, accompaniment, in Spanish, for Central America historically, has been of profound importance within and across social groups and causes as Serena Cosgrove's chapter clarifies. Lara and González provide us with concrete and fraught experiences of what it means to accompany students inhabiting the multiple meanings of the term from companion to attendant, from partner to supplementing with (OED 2021). I wonder about thinking musically about the meaning of accompaniment, with song and melody, with the instrument of one's own body on the line (OED 2021).

For Lara, it is crucial to historicize Nicaragua's student accompaniment as she theorizes phases and periods of a pedagogy of accompaniment, what she terms "holistic accompaniment." She focuses on the ways in which professors have been allies across the three most significant periods of student protests in the country's history: the struggle for university autonomy in 1958; the movement to gain 6% of the state budget for universities, which started in 1972; and the uprising that began in April 2018. This pedagogy of accompaniment is exactly what we need to think through on local, regional, and global scales. Particularly important is Lara's recognition of the affective element of this accompaniment, the socio-emotional aspects that must be written into our understanding of student movements. Complementing this ethnographic theory building work is González's chapter that spotlights the particular work of accompaniment in the Department of Communications—a location under particular attack given its academic mission to educate the next generation of journalists who are to expose truths for the public good. González develops a richly textured ethnographic account so that we all can inhabit that space of the classroom and what permeates through its walls. González reveals the potent everyday meanings that he learned to recognize and support—the shift in his students' clothing from shoes and button-down shirts to sneakers and t-shirts so that they could be ready for movement and flight. He beckons us to understand the new space of the activist cell phone in the classroom. What a short while ago it was when instructors demanded that these be silenced, put away, in desks or satchels for the real "learning" to take place. This accompaniment is a recognition that decenters professorial power as González offers the hard work and grit of teaching and learning, of writing under fear, of journalism on the frontlines by youth who are learning a craft and standing up for truth.

For many of us, decades deep into our scholarship in solidarity, perhaps before we had a name for it, the chapters, autoethnographic and theoretical, by Fiore Bran Aragón and Andrew Gorvetzian point to what is to come, to the fruits of the university manifesto. Their chapters are compelling, thematically playing with new conceptualizations of how social movements work, from the metaphor of rhizomic resistance to the cyborg solidarity, across borders, across temporality, across difference, and how the UCA has been key. They show us the losses and the gains, the "horror on the screen" as Gorvetzian explains with the rhododendron bush in the background. Or as Bran Aragón argues about the student persistence that her generation represents—"lo arrancado per no lo quemado." These are no neat, clean, or tidy endings of local and global proportion that defeat the crisis. Their ethico-political exposition also moves us beyond a facile celebration of the UCA or the implementation of a university manifesto. This too is critical and cautions against the still too often circulation of a romance of resistance that is flattening and essentializing. Is it as Sarah Muir argues in *Routine Crisis* (2021) that it is incumbent on us all to think about these always unequally felt incessant crises? In the Argentine case, Muir shows that this is experienced and narrated as financial crises. She urges us to look beyond a Marxist critique and explore how we can think about futures when it all seems so dim and inescapable, with fires burning on all fronts. I offer that Bran Aragón and Gorvetzian's generational analyses and call offer us spaces for imagination.

And that imagining, in narrative and practice, what in my own work I have underscored as a diasporic Salvadoran (Chalateca/o), reflexive insurgent call to "imagínese," to really imagine it, appears now as the importance of recognizing and honoring the hardships of the past in order to envision an equitable and glorious future (Silber 2022). This vision is most clearly threaded in Serena Cosgrove's powerful historical analysis of solidarity with Central America that culminates in her theorizing around solidarity 3.0. Through decolonial research and teaching praxis, and institutional alliances that are rooted in experiences of radical persistence that require radical solidarity, Cosgrove's is not a romantic perspective though it is full of love, affective labor, intimacy, peopled, institutional, horizontal accompaniment in action and thought. She illuminates how solidarity 3.0 seeks to create safe spaces of action and theory to meet the challenges of state repression and a neoliberal crush. This is a history of violence that in the Coda James Quesada eloquently demonstrates is characterized by weak governance and paramilitary violence that facilitates state and paramilitary repression against protestors and other institutions through the centuries. Quesada argues that it is crucial to disrupt the narrative that state violence in Nicaragua ended with the overthrow of the Somoza dynasty in 1979. Rather he calls attention to a more nuanced history of *caudillista* or strong-arm violence that has been used to advance political and economic interests that we can now see have particularly deadly consequences for university autonomy and as a result, have made universities pivotal sites of contestation or cooptation in Nicaragua.[10]

Within this framing, Cosgrove's work heeds Idiáquez's original call to think beyond borders. She offers us a model of inter-university collaboration. She points to the challenges and the successes, in her case of partnerships between the UCA and SU aligned in their Jesuit mission. She urges us all, inherently variously positioned with different relationships of and to power, to take these ideas and lessons and think through them alongside and outside of a politico-religious mission and from the private institution to the public. In doing so, she loops us back to a university manifesto that pushes us beyond deception and disillusionment and toward action. This brings us back to Ignacio Ellacuría, S.J. and his call for social change and proyección social at the service of the poor (1999), as we ask ourselves who are we working for and whom do we serve?

Manifestos and uprisings, solidarity and accompaniment, repression and sanctuary, liberation, these are all keywords entwined, lived, and ethnographically portrayed and theorized in each of these pressing chapters. Taken together, they echo the public scholarship of anthropologists João Biehl and Adriana Petryna (2013) as they intervene in studies of global health. Biehl and Petryna suggest that we consider "ethnography as an early warning system" (2013: 18). They explain,

> People on the ground recognize what's troubling them. And it is somewhere in the middle of their social lives that ethnographic work always begins. Ethnographers are uniquely positioned to see what more categorically minded experts may overlook: namely, the empirical evidence that emerges when people express their most pressing and ordinary concerns, which then open up to complex human stories in time and space. Life stories do not simply begin and end. They are stories of transformation, linking the present to the past and to a possible future.
>
> *(Biehl and Petryna 2013: 18–19)*

In every instance, these chapters highlight the key agents and actors of this "early warning system." They excavate for us so much including how we think about history, the legacies of the revolution, our larger understanding of the region, theories of aftermaths, trauma and persistence, all through a lens that puts "the university" at the center to tell these interlocking stories that call us all to action for Nicaragua and beyond.

Notes

1 Chatterjee and Maira (2014) home in on the American university and how it has become increasingly susceptible to neoliberal influences such as privatization and militarization with dramatic shifts away from public funds to increasing reliance on corporate and private funds. They also focus on the long-held practice of campus resistance among students, faculty, and staff. They discuss this as "the imperial university" locating universities in the United States as agents in maintaining U.S. empire. They write,

> We argue that the state of permanent war that is core to U.S. imperialism and racial statecraft has three fronts: military, cultural, and academic. Our conceptualization of the imperial university links these fronts of war, for the academic battleground is part of the culture wars that emerge in a militarized nation, one that is always presumably under threat, externally or internally.
> (Chatterjee and Maira 2014: 7)

See also Ergül and Coşar (2017) for a comparative model of multinational, multidisciplinary and mutualistic approach as a method of resistance to neoliberalism in itself.
2 "parciales a favor de las mayorías populares."
3 Godrej explains that privatization, at least in the public University of California system:

> rather than being a necessary evil, comes about as the result of deliberate complicity with—and in fact advocacy of—neoliberal disinvestment in the concept of education as a public good by the very people charged with protection and disbursement of this public good. And consequently, education is systematically reframed as a private good existing in the sacred neoliberal realm of individual choice, something therefore to be commodified and paid for by those who have the resources.
> (2014: 126)

4 See also Bascara (2014) for a discussion of the founding of universities under occupation in the Philippines, Hawaii, and Puerto Rico and that negotiation between radicality and conservative politics.
5 This volume is in conversation with texts such as *Learning under Neoliberalism* (Hyatt et al. 2015) that also focuses on what ethnography can bring to light and the role of engaged scholars to "produce possibilities for a more democratic, socially just, egalitarian future" (2015:6). It also builds from the intersectional critiques of activist anthropology (Berry et al. 2017) that hold us all to account through a "fugitive anthropology" that must reimagine the dynamics of research toward social transformation and that does not erase vectors of power, similarities, and differences.
6 An anthropology of childhood reminds us that the very category of youth is historically and culturally contingent, not universally experienced, but valued and conceptualized in particular ways (Lancy 2015). There is also an ample literature on youth and childhood in war (e.g., Scheper-Hughes and Sargent 1998).
7 For a striking comparison see Mendoza and Lisa (2020) for discourse analysis of educational administrators in Peru, Argentina, Mexico, and Chile and the ways in which these administrators echoed the neoliberal values (e.g., quality assurance)

hegemonically circulated by international financial and development organizations such as the World Bank. This volume also heeds Hugh Gusterson's call to repair what has been left out in the ethnographic analysis of the neoliberal university such as administrators, university presidents, budgets, and so on (Gusterson 2017: 437).
8 Barragán Fernández interviewed leaders in three universities experiencing repression and explored the historical mission of Jesuit universities to forward social justice. She quotes the following:

> We believe that our Universities should be eminent in the human sciences, because of the decisive importance they have in planning the change of our society. In our Universities there should be a group of experts in Education, at the service of the educational interests of the community. We cannot forget that at the base of the unjust social structures of Latin American countries is the hurtful inequality of educational opportunities.
> *(Barragán Fernández 2021: 20; Arrupe 1968)*

9 See Cosgrove (2010) for a comparative analysis of gendered leadership in Latin America.
10 See also Feldman (1989) for an early analysis of the relationship between the United States government and repression in Central America that includes international universities, multinational corporations, the U.S. government, and oppressive regimes in Central America.

References

Barragán Fernández, Ana Karen. 2021. "Jesuit Universities in Latin America: Government Repression and Resistance in Venezuela, Nicaragua, and Mexico." Master's Thesis, University of San Francisco.
Bellei, Cristian, Cristian Cabali, and Victor Orellana. (2014) "The 2011 Chilean Student Movement against Neoliberal Educational Policies." *Studies in Higher Education*. DOI: 10.1080/03075079.2014.896179.
Benavides, M., A. Arellano, and J.S. Zárate Vásquez. 2019. "Market- and Government-Based Higher Education Reforms in Latin America: The Cases of Peru and Ecuador, 2008–2016." *High Educ* 77, 1015–1030. doi: 10.1007/s10734-018-0317-3
Berry, Maya J., Claudia Chávez Argüelles, Shanya Cordis, Sarah Ihmoud, and Elizabeth Velásquez Estrada. 2017. "Toward a Fugitive Anthropology: Gender, Race, and Violence in the Field." *Cultural Anthropology* 32(4), 537–565.
Biehl, João, and Adriana Petryna. 2013. "Critical Global Health." In *When People Come First: Critical Studies in Global Health*. Princeton: Princeton University Press, pp.1–20.
Chatterjee, Piya, and Sunaina Maira. 2014. *The Imperial University*. Minneapolis: University of Minnesota Press.
Cole, R.M., and W.F. Heinecke. 2020. "Higher Education after Neoliberalism: Student Activism as a Guiding Light." *Policy Futures in Education* 18(1), 90–116. doi:10.1177/1478210318767459
Cosgrove, Serena. 2010. *Leadership from the Margins: Women and Civil Society Organizations in Argentina, Chile, and El Salvador*. New Brunswick NJ: Rutgers University Press.
Cosgrove, Serena, José Idiáquez, Leonard Joseph Bent, and Andrew Gorvetzian. 2021. *Surviving the Americas: Garifuna Persistence from Nicaragua to New York City*. Cincinnati: University of Cincinnati Press.

Ellacuría, Ignacio. 1999. *Escritos Universitarios*. San Salvador: UCA Editores.
Ergül, Hakan, and Simten Coşar. 2017. *Universities in the Neoliberal Era: Academic Cultures and Critical Perspectives*. London, UK: Palgrave Macmillan.
Feldman, Jonathan. 1989. *Universities in the Business of Repression: The Academic-Military-Industrial Complex and Central America*. Boston, MA: South End Press
Gusterson, Hugh. 2017. "Homework: Toward a Critical Ethnography of the University." *American Ethnologist* 44(3), 435–450.
Hyatt, Susan B., Boone W. Shear, and Susan Wright, eds. 2015. *Learning under Neoliberalism: Ethnographies of Governance in Higher Education*. New York, NY: Berghahn Books, Incorporated.
Levy, D.C. 1991. "The Decline of Latin American Student Activism." *High Education* 22, 145–155. doi: 10.1007/BF00137473
Lima, Valesca, and Sue A. S. Iamamoto. 2020. "'Culture War' against Brazilian Universities: How Budget Cuts and Changes in Tertiary Education Policies Are Affecting the Academic Community." *Alternautas* 7(2), 8–19.
Livingston, Julie. 2019. *Self- Devouring Growth: A Planetary Parable Told from Southern Africa*. Durham, NC: Duke University Press.
Mendoza, Pilar, and Dorner Lisa. 2020. "The Neoliberal Discourse in Latin American Higher Education: A Call for National Development and Tighter Government Control." *Education Policy Analysis Archives* 28, 176. doi: 10.14507/epaa.28.5610
Muir, Sarah. 2021. *Routine Crisis: An Ethnography of Disillusion*. Chicago, IL: University of Chicago press.
OED. 2021. "preparation, n." *OED Online*. Oxford University Press, March 2022. Web. 8 May 2022.
Rosenberg, Brian. 2021. "Administrators Are Not the Enemy: Faculty Contempt for Nonfaculty Employees is Unjustified and Destructive." *The Chronicle of Higher Education*. October 27, 2021. https://www.chronicle.com/article/administrators-are-not-the-enemy?cid2=gen_login_refresh&cid=gen_sign_in
Silber, Irina Carlota. 2022. *After Stories: Transnational Intimacies of Postwar El Salvador*. Stanford, CA: Stanford University Press.
Scheper-Hughes, Nancy, and Carolyn Sargent. 1998. *Small Wars: The Cultural Politics of Childhood*. Berkeley: University of California Press.
Vrana, Heather, ed. 2017. *Anti-Colonial Texts from Central American Student Movements, 1929–1983*. Edinburgh: Edinburgh UP.
Williams, Bianca C., Dian D. Squire, and Frank A. Tuitt. 2021. *Plantation Politics and Campus Rebellions: Power, Diversity, and the Emancipatory Struggle in Higher Education*. New York: State University of New York Press.

PART 4
Coda

9
A BRIEF HISTORY OF VIOLENCE IN NICARAGUA

James Quesada

Introduction

My flight landed in Nicaragua on May 22, 2018, almost a week before the Mothers' Day March that was so brutally repressed by police and paramilitary youth. As a Nicaraguan-American anthropologist who's worked in Nicaragua for decades, I was so happy to see old friends who came to pick me up at the airport. However, Nicaragua amid an uprising presented many challenges; it took hours to reach the mountainous city of Matagalpa to the north of Managua due to all the barricades or "tranques" that the youth of the country had erected protesting the government. I think what really struck me in that drive to Matagalpa was that the people at the blockades appeared to totally distrust the dialogues and were not about to back down, and each day there were deaths here and deaths there because of street skirmishes by the Sandinista Juventud, the 19th of April movement, disaffected youth, peasants and recontra contingents who would rather try and resolve things through force. The blockades are ubiquitous and remain in place in cities, towns, and main roadways, as well as spontaneous constructions of barricades that may be up hours or days. Being in Matagalpa feels a little like being in a garrison city from which the interior of the town feels sort of safe and yet is protected by the blockades on the periphery that fend off encroachment of forces loyal to the government. I think there is a dawning awareness that there is no going back in time, meaning the future is uncertain, daily life sporadically upended, social life constrained and permeated by suspicion of friends and neighbors alike. It is a harsh turn of events, and for someone like me who strongly identified with the original Sandinista revolutionary project, to see it come to this is very disappointing. A legacy of the revolution visible today is the heightened political consciousness ordinary people uphold ... but political consciousness of what? Therein lies the messiness, disorganization, and confusion of how as a people, a collective, an imagined national community, the country can establish a semblance of stability and consistency in everyday life. This short-lived doldrums has come to a sudden profane end. Over this last weekend (July 7–8), the Ortega-Murillo government unleashed coordinated attacks in cities and towns throughout the country where protests have been the strongest and the barricades the longest standing. What happened, and continues to happen, is full-scale government-ordered attacks by paramilitary youth, against a largely unarmed or under-armed people, mainly young people in their twenties who rose up initially in solidarity with their elders who had been made scapegoats to corrupt and arbitrarily imposed austerity measures, which ballooned into a mass rejection of government corruption, cronyism, and neglect. It was common to hear from various individuals that the police and paramilitary attacks on the barricades were un-Nicaraguan. Upon reflection, I too had become comforted by a relatively peaceful state the country had enjoyed over the last ten years, but the level of conflict that I was witnessing made me rethink just how calm the country has been over time. It is as if the recent history of relative stability and security was imaginatively projected to be a status quo in which Nicaragua was not beset by internal random states of criminal violence like the northern triangle countries of Honduras, El Salvador, and Guatemala. Indeed, Nicaraguans reveled in the early 2000s as being more like Costa Rica, as a destination tourist spot, and unencumbered by the narco-trafficking and rampant gang violence that has beset their neighbors to the north. The paramilitary attacks on the barricades were immediately condemned by government spokespeople, yet the immunized perpetrators were protected as a public secret and sanctioned by the authoritarian turn the Ortega-Murillo administration had taken. The use of paramilitary or unconventional, irregular armed forces is not new to Nicaragua, although the relative calm before 2018 lulled many Nicaraguans into a belief that violence and the insecurity it inspires were behind them. Now back home in San Francisco after spending over six weeks in Nicaragua, I am left with more questions than answers. One thing is certain: I want to understand the history of Nicaragua better so I can trace this legacy of state and paramilitary violence, something that the current government is using against its own people, even as it proclaims its Christian and socialist values.

Many may wonder how the current Nicaraguan government with its revolutionary roots has become an authoritarian state, similar in many ways to the Somoza dynasty it overthrew in 1979. Using the historical record, I argue that a history of weak governance and paramilitary violence simultaneously facilitates state and paramilitary repression against protestors and other institutions. I will trace the history of violence—particularly *caudillista* or strong-arm violence—and I will describe how it has been used to subdue resistance, protest, and uprisings by those excluded from power, including disenfranchised groups as well as college students in the twentieth and twenty-first centuries. This chapter traces the imprint of the legacy of present-day violence through a historical survey of the use of violent means to secure power beginning with Spanish colonialism, and from there the post-colonial independence period that saw the intense rivalry between Liberal and Conservative forces that impeded consolidation into a nation-state, leading to U.S. intervention. A period of relative stability followed, which led to a Liberal administration that culminated in being overthrown by a renewed intervention of U.S. Marines that dominated Nicaragua the first quarter of the twentieth century and incurred the anti-imperialist resistance of Augusto César Sandino. The United States established the first national armed forces, the National Guard of Nicaragua, under the tutelage of Anastasio Somoza Garcia who assassinated Sandino and usurped the Presidency of the country, ushering in a 43-year dictatorial dynasty before the Sandinista insurrection of 1979. Since then, the Sandinistas in their political rivalry with neoliberal parties have echoed the past in their use of state and paramilitary force against protesters.

Colonial Period

The early years of Spanish colonialism led to a dramatic demographic destruction of the Indigenous population because of battles and European diseases. While estimations of the Indigenous population vary, it is generally thought that it numbered over 800,000 (Newson 1987) at the time of contact. A little over 150 years later, the Nicaragua Indigenous population is estimated to have been reduced by over 90% (Newson 1987: 338–340) due mainly to enslavement, the introduction of European diseases, and human slaughter. Thirty years after Columbus arrived to the Americas in 1492, Nicaragua was visited again by Spanish explorers in 1522, and two years later settlement and colonization commenced.

Early Spanish colonialism in Nicaragua involved establishing towns and cities where Indigenous communities were located and could be exploited for labor, with colonialists engaged in "entrada y saca" (enter and take) methods of forced labor recruitment (MacLeod 2008: 300), by intruding into Indigenous towns and pressganging people into service while stealing local resources. Purportedly during early colonization, Indigenous resistance toward the Spaniards was sporadic and unsuccessful, with community members opting to evade the Spaniards by moving into the mountains and remote eastern regions (Newson 1987: 92–93). Yet almost from the beginning of colonial rule, numerous competing Conquistadores (soldier-explorers) were in conflict with each other for territorial rule, leading to what has been referred to as the "War of the Captains" (Duncan 1995). These early contestations set the pattern for perennial conflict between local powerholders.

Nicaragua had markedly distinct geographic regions and a mix of Indigenous, Afro-Indigenous, and Afro-descendent groups that the Spaniards were not able to consolidate under their control, with their dominion mainly unfolding in the coastal Pacific lowlands and a good portion of the central highlands. The highlands dipping to the Caribbean lowlands were left largely untouched and uncolonized. In the vacuum of Spanish rule, the British took advantage of occupying the Caribbean coast until the 1850s. Where the Spanish did dominate, they supplanted Indigenous elites while still relying "on traditional village rulers to collect and deliver tribute. In return, the Indian leaders, or caciques, not only received a share of what was collected … and [among other rewards] were given special privileges like using swords and guns" (Patch 2013: 93). During the colonial period, Spanish armies remained small and colonial administrators had to rely on local militias, who were themselves often commanded by self-styled military commanders creating personal armies (Kruijt 2017: 8–9). The reliance on local political elites to enforce colonial rule came about through coercion in getting the local population to comply with the demands of Spanish overseers (Gabbert 2012: 263). Under colonization, Indigenous people and mixed-race mestizos, also called ladinos, served local colonial administrators, the Church, Spanish and Spanish-descendant or creole landowners, and merchants by being mobilized to shore up local militias and private armies.

In the absence of a strong centralized military institution that operated at a national level, local armies were based on "personalism and strongly localized kinship ties combined with traditional loyalty and 'patria chica' hardening patron-client alliances [which] creat[ed] a nefarious dynamic of destruction" (Holden 2004: 80). Colonial administrators had to rely on local militias and were in turn contested by self-styled local-born military commanders who forged local and regional militias. Indigenous people could evade having to pay tribute by enlisting in regular militias under the jurisdictional military (Newson 1987). Spanish colonial rule in Nicaragua went through several phases that involved local people seeking means to avoid, limit, or survive contact with *penisulares* (Spanish born residents in Latin America), *creoles* (New World born Spanish residents in Latin America), whereas penisulares, creoles, and mestizos persistently sought means to acquire or enlarge productive land and scarce labor. When unable to evade the colonialists, another Indigenous survival strategy was to enter into alliances with one faction of Spanish colonialists (e.g. large landholding hacendados or religious orders) over others. By the nineteenth century, mestizos came to outnumber Indigenous people and came to occupy all economic positions from that of the most menial day laborer to owners of large estates.

Independence

Geographically Nicaragua is the largest Central American country and for its vastness, the demographic transition Nicaragua experienced during the colonial period resulted in a sparse dispersed population numbered at 186,000 in 1821 at the moment of independence from Spain (Roniger 2013: 210). By this time, the multiple factions in the Nicaraguan body politic splintered even further. Practically stateless during its first 40 years of nationhood, Nicaragua degenerated into little more than constant civil war (Holden 2004: 80). The incapacity to establish intra-regional national identity and a functioning state mainly related to how "Nicaraguans became entangled in logics of mutual distrust and disbelief in themselves which reinforced time and again vicious cycles of internal divisiveness, civil war, and mutual annihilation" (Roniger 2013: 46). In the scramble for political and economic control during this tumultuous period, conservative and liberal elites deployed various means and tactics to consolidate power throughout the Central America region. In Nicaragua, this polarization was literally located in two principal cities, León and Granada, city-states that competed for power and prestige with the Liberals in León and the Conservatives in Granada. Following independence from Spain, the Central American countries that had been subjects of the Spanish colonial viceroyalty of New Spain (Mexico), decided not to join newly formed Mexico and decided to form their own federal republic, called the United Provinces of Central America, in 1823. Resistance to incorporation into the Mexican Empire was mainly led by Central American Liberals, who instead supported the establishment of the United Provinces of Central America that lasted till 1838. However, because of a vast array of competing interests and ideological differences across the region, the United Provinces of Central America fragmented.

In Nicaragua, León and Granada mobilized armed groups to defend their economic interests, ideological positions, and political goals.

> In Nicaragua, liberal León was primarily involved in exporting animal products such as leather and tallow and soon became the center for free-trading liberalism. The conservative elite in Granada, however, had made their fortunes under the old protectionist system and resisted change.
>
> *(Holden 2004: 80)*

In time, the hatred and violence between the two cities and their two factions became institutionalized, even after the original ideological differences had been forgotten. With Spain eliminated as a referee, the violent rivalry between liberals and conservatives was one of the most important and destructive aspects of Nicaraguan history, a characteristic that would last well into the twentieth century and continues to inform the country's politics to this day. Politicians frequently chose party loyalty over national interests, and, particularly in the 1800s, the nation was often the loser in interparty strife. It is important to note that features of early post-independence state formations in Central America, whether as a government or state institutions, had an improvisational character whereby numerous local and regional socio-political collaborations had to be configured. Each change was being reconfigured according to an assemblage that offset the political and social claims these collaborators made on the state and to each other. These collaborators were hacendados, merchants, regional caudillos and their followers, municipal-level authorities and strongmen, and later, the armed forces themselves and more or less autonomous vigilante groups (Holden 2004: 25). Each of these collaborators led their own little armies, militias, or gangs to realize their goals, which, in turn, catalyzed resistance.

> These elite conflicts fueled the rise of peasant movements that posed grave challenges to the existing social order. The strength of such movements was especially evident in the rural revolts that rocked Nicaragua in

the late 1840s ... Centered in the Pacific zone, the popular revolts drove Nicaragua's warring elites to join forces for the very first time. Thanks to this unprecedented alliance, elites were able to crush what they deemed "communist" movements. Shortly thereafter, however, elites resumed their internecine war.

(Gobat 2005: 25–26)

Bradford Burn begins his historical account of Nicaragua following independence from Spain as emerging: "... from the violence—always endemic and often erupting among the patriarchs of the dominant families, the folk communities, and the foreigner ..." (1991: Introduction). Independence from Spain intensified the rivalry of Conservatives and Liberals, that broke out in open warfare in 1823, with 79 men killed (Millet 1977: 16). A period of anarchy prevailed that has been variously described by Nicaraguan observers and intellectuals as "the Period of Anarchy". Moreover,

...the wars of the post-independence period [were due] to the confrontation between 'aristocrats' who wanted to preserve their noble privileges, and 'republicans' who defended the idea that all men are equal by nature. This resultant contradiction led to the violence as a result of the militaristic tradition incubated in the three centuries of colonial rule.

(Arancibia in Tijerno 1997: 180)

This nineteenth-century division between liberals and conservatives common throughout the whole of Central America in variant forms, signified different postcolonial paths toward economic and societal development that have influenced social and political dynamics to this day.

While both Liberals and Conservatives welcomed independence from Spain, their respective visions for remaking society although distinct were perhaps not so dissimilar as evinced in their shared pursuit of establishing local and regional patrimonial regimes[1] and embracing to various degrees a classic liberal economic model. The divergence between Conservatives and Liberals was based on apportioning their loyalties to maintaining (Conservatives) or altering (Liberals) old status hierarchies from their colonial past, to either enthusiastically or warily embracing liberal capitalist practices and the resultant post-independence status hierarchies associated with these practices. The Conservative Party and Liberal Party were established by landholding and bureaucratic elites that differed in their approaches to developing the country (Woodward 1984), yet their respective fidelity to a core of distinct ideological principles was diluted or discarded in the expediency of shifting power alliances and affiliations to enhance and secure local or regional political power and economic interests. The competing political orientations and alliances that emerged following independence were based on sectoral economic interests (Holden 2004: 80) that impeded Nicaragua from consolidating into a nation-state, which came late in contrast to the other post-colonial Central American nation-states. Indeed, the idea of a Nation-State hardly applied to Nicaragua in the early to mid-nineteenth century as competing city-states, conservative Granada and liberal León, were in constant and violent competition for the seat of power. Moreover, this left other regions to establish their own modes of governance and since there was no functioning central state to guarantee order and "where the threat of violence was especially great because of ethnic and racial conflicts, people had to help themselves and take the execution of law into their own hands" (Keil & Riekenburg 2001: 48). These elite conflicts fueled the rise of peasant movements that posed grave challenges to the existing social order.

Between 1824 and 1842, 17 major battles with significant loss of life took place while 18 individuals exercised "executive authority" (Millet 1977: 16), between Liberals and Conservatives. In 1845, the Conservatives with the help of troops from Honduras and El Salvador drove out the Liberals; with the Liberals mounting persistent efforts to overturn Conservative rule. One such Liberal self-ordained military leader was Bernabé Somoza who was considered brutal and was popularly regarded as a "bandit" whose familial descendants became the twentieth-century dynasty that ruled over Nicaragua for 43 years (Millet 1977: 16). He mounted multiple attacks in 1847–1849, in Chinandega, Managua, Rivas, and León against local elite landowners. The escapades of Bernabé Somoza symbolize the plethora of local caudillo revolts occurring across the country, in which the rivalry between Conservatives and Liberals was manipulated by elites to consolidate their power.

State Building and U.S. Intervention from Walker to Sandino

The United States played an outsized role in the formation of Nicaragua as a nation-state: from the incursion by William Walker that drew the feuding city-states of León and Granada together in unity, to occupation by U.S. Marines in the early twentieth century that spawned a national military force, the National Guard that became the private army of the Somoza dictatorship. In 1851, warfare between Liberals and the ruling Conservatives intensified into a rolling civil war. By mid-1850s, the Liberals, hard-pressed in their efforts to overtake the Conservatives, turned to hiring the infamous filibuster William Walker. Walker, a North American lawyer-journalist from Tennessee who had waged war against Mexico's Conservative government in 1853–1854, was admired by Nicaraguan Liberals. William Walker led the first U.S. incursion into Nicaragua that lasted beyond him into the early twentieth century and shaped the country. Walker planned to turn Nicaragua into a settler colony of the United States and establish a transoceanic canal. In 1855, William Walker took control of the country, initially in support of Liberal efforts to oust the Conservatives. He was able to do so in part because of the weakness of Nicaraguan troops who "were recruited by compulsory dragooning, [with] those who sought to escape being simply shot down" (Millet 1977: 18) and were fielded with "no training, no uniforms, no adequate weapons ... armed with antiquated Muskets or simply machetes ..." (Millet 1977: 19). Walker was aided by local native caudillos who had led popular uprisings—Mariano Méndez of León, Máximo Espinoza of Rivas, Francisco Bravo of Masaya, Ubaldo Herrera of Granada, and José María Valle of León—who all assisted Walker's rise to power (Gobat 2005: 33).

Walker proclaimed himself President, decreed English as the official language, and legalized slavery. This disgraceful outcome discredited the Liberals. The Nicaraguan civil war of 1854–1857 involved the Nicaraguan conservatives along with international forces (Costa Rica, Guatemala, El Salvador, Honduras, the Mosquitia of the Atlantic coast) fighting Liberals who had invited William Walker and his mercenaries and ultimately led to the defeat of Walker and the Liberals. It also marks the first time Conservatives and Liberals entered into a pact to bury their differences and pull their military forces together against Walker. The *Pacto Providencial* (1856)[2] established a precedent of competing political parties entering power-sharing agreements, an approach not unlike the Ortega-Aleman Pact in 1999 that eventually led to Daniel Ortega becoming President in 2007 with only 35% of the popular vote.[3] The outcome of this first pact between the Conservatives and Liberals not only contributed to ousting Walker, but created the conditions for a reconciliation pact between the former enemies and inaugurated a 30-year period of relative calm in contrast to the anarchy and disorder that had marked Nicaraguan history since independence.

The era of Conservative rule has been cast as an era of relative peace (Cruz 2016). Conservatism lasted until 1893, longer in Nicaragua than any other Central American country (Dunkerley 1988: 17–18), resulting in a power-sharing arrangement forming a bipartisan government including liberal and conservative elites, with the Presidency ceded to the Conservatives along with Liberals nominated to key government ministries (Gobat 2005: 49). While the Conservatives dominated politics and power, the intense competition and occasional public violence did not altogether subside. Occasional coup attempts and Indigenous resistance exemplified the political, class, and ethnic tensions and enmities that remained close to the surface. The Conservative regimes implemented "the usual policies of mobilizing workers through the alienation of communal lands, vagrancy laws, debt peonage, and other coercive devices" (Weaver 1994: 89). This in part led to the last significant Indigenous uprising in 1881 in Matagalpa. This uprising was catalyzed by land grabs by mestizos (Tellez 1999: 137–141), as well the "compulsory and underpaid labor for building the telegraph from Managua, roads, and the cabildos ... [and] other grievances: census taking for tax and military purposes and a prohibition against making chicha" (Gould 1998: 33). Although 36 years of Conservative rule is often cast as a period of relative stability, the local economic elites were divided between the established cattle raisers and small growers and the new coffee-producers sector.

Following the 36 years of Conservative rule and civil war, the Liberal President Zelaya came to power and ruled for 16 turbulent years. In order to consolidate perpetual rule, Zelaya began a serious effort to establish and modernize a national armed force. Among various initiatives to construct an army, he tasked his officers, who were widely distributed across regions, in local communities and settlements throughout the Pacific area of Nicaragua, with conscripting and raising "a body of armed local partisans" as rank and file soldiers, and forcibly rounding "up members of the lower classes, tying them together, and shipping them off to the nearest army camp" (Millet 1977: 21–22). There were a series of conservative revolts that were unsuccessful in 1896, 1899, 1903, yet Conservatives finally came to power again in 1909 with the military support of the United States. Zelaya had incurred the wrath of the United States by establishing a Central American confederation and being an obstacle to U.S. hegemony in the region. In 1909, with the backing of U.S. troops, a Conservative coup took place. Conservative rule was weak and the United States, interested in protecting its investment in maintaining conservative rule, sent troops that remained in Nicaragua till 1925.

> The U.S. ran Nicaraguan affairs through a series of Conservative presidents … The relationship was symbiotic. The U.S. needed the Conservatives, and the Conservatives—who had neither military strength nor the popular backing to maintain themselves in power—needed the Unites States.
> *(Walker 1991: 19)*

While ostensibly the tensions were between Conservatives and Liberals, actual political violence played out at local levels of competing interests between large landowners, municipal magistrates, and small communities often besieged and attacked by marauding bands of armed men. The United States continued to support conservative regimes with the backing of U.S. Marines. The United States withdrew the marines in 1925, when mobs were used by conservatives in support of Emiliano Chamorro. Emiliano Chamorro was the Nicaraguan who led more revolutions than any other leader and is considered the archetype of a caudillo leading uprisings against the Liberal President José Santos Zelaya and established himself as the leader of the Conservative Party. The coalition government did not work out, and again civil war broke out, which, in turn, led to the return of the U.S. Marines in 1927. The United States justified the return of the Marines because

> the long-continued disorder and violence had also produced a general disintegration in the social fabric of the country; semi-independent bands of marauders were taking advantage of the situation to plunder even settled districts … and a general condition of anarchy ….
> *(Stimson 1927: 41)*

The United States brokered presidential elections and a peace settlement between liberals and conservatives that was refuted by the only Liberal general, Augusto Cesar Sandino, who rejected the U.S.-imposed peace treaty.

In 1927, after the rest of the Liberals had agreed to the U.S.-sponsored peace settlement, Sandino chose to continue the battle against the puppet governments. Variously regarded either as a heroic anti-imperialist nationalist or a ruthless, blood lust bandit, Sandino was lumped together with marauding armed bands that were at the behest of local political caudillos or big landowners (Schroder 2005; Baylen 1951). However, one chooses to interpret his actions, Sandino was the Liberal anti-imperialist who waged guerilla warfare that led to the withdrawal of the marines. From 1927 to 1933, though maligned by Nicaraguan leaders, Sandino was viewed internationally as a capable anti-U.S. imperialist who forced the United States to withdraw their military and secure the sovereignty of Nicaragua. Extant documents make abundantly clear that the U.S. drive to create the Nicaraguan National Guard (Guardia Nacional, GN), combined with the war against Sandino, led to the rapid consolidation of an enduring national military at once powered by U.S. technology and resources and that profoundly shaped local actors and local political culture (Brooks & Schroder 2018: 9).

The early years of the National Guard included "the upward displacement of violence making from local and regional caudillos to the national state …" (Brooks & Schroder 2018: 4). Local caudillos "whose politico-military powers were predicated on personal as opposed to institutional loyalties, and who combined control of political office and autonomous violence-making capacities through private armies or gangs mobilized through webs of patronage and clientage" (Brooks & Schroder 2018: 8) became consolidated. Upon their withdrawal in 1925, the U.S.

> Marines left behind the National Guard, a robust new institution that rapidly displaced all competitors (Holden 2004: 89). The biggest difference with caudillismo of old was that now all such militias were legally subordinated to the central state, and the law was enforced. Standardized forms were developed for previous hybrid practices, all of which made unequivocal the Guard's ultimate authority.
>
> *(Brooks & Schroder 2018: 11)*

By 1933, the whole national territory had just two organizations capable of sustained violence making: Sandino's Army of Nicaragua Sovereignty and Somoza's National Guard (Brooks & Schroder 2018: 25). Somoza's style of leadership represents a throwback to earlier Nicaraguan practices, tossing out the notion of nonpartisan military as initially inculcated by the U.S. Marines, in favor of a graft-financed national organization that owed its allegiance to a supreme leader (Brooks & Schroder 2018: 31).

The first comandante, *jefe director*, of the newly U.S. installed National Guard was Anastasio Somoza, who shortly after the withdrawal of the U.S. Marines masterminded the assassination of Augusto Sandino in 1934 and began his ascendancy to the presidency. As President, he retained the role of the Jefe Director of the Guardia Nacional in effect making him the maximum caudillo with his own private army.

> While the Guardia provided Somoza with a potent force for the advancement of his ambitions, it did have certain limitations, it was less than an ideal force. To supplement the Guardia, Somoza began to support a native fascist organization, the *Camisas Azules* (Blue Shirts). A gang of thugs evidently modeled on Hitler's brown shirts, who were trained by the Guardia and supplied with government money and identity cards.
>
> (Holden 2004: 93)

This rather ragged group was made up of about 100 young reactionaries who hoped to set up a fascist government in Nicaragua. The use of the Blue Shirts, and the Liga Militar Liberal Nicaraguense, exemplified the resort to unofficial militias to exercise coercive power to maintain official power.

Somoza Paramilitary Rule and Student Protests

The predominance of the Somoza period was not exercised solely by authoritarian rule but was aided by non-official agents or paramilitary groups. It is important to remember how authoritarian states use unofficial thugs and militia to consolidate their rule. Somoza was able to remain in power and founded an authoritarian dynasty fueled by U.S. funds, which passed from father to son, to brother over the ensuing 43 years. During this period, the National Guard was able to quell local insurgencies through its monopolization of violent means. Certainly, labor unrest and local skirmishes occurred but they were largely put down and controlled by the Somoza political machine and the National Guard. However, a veneer of democracy still compelled even Somoza to run for office to forestall charges of outright political maneuvering (Walter 1993). He did rely on other extreme measures to ensure political monopolization of the ballot box by mobilizing non-state actors to coerce people to abide by Somoza rule. Somoza deployed the Blue Shirts, the fascistic, death squad secret police force that helped oust President Sacasa and rig the 1936 elections. Somoza also could rely on Nicolasa Sevilla, a Somocista mob leader, directing groups to suppress strikes, teacher protests, and opposition political acts. Nicolasa founded the Somocista Popular Front, a paramilitary organization that acted in conjunction with other ex-military and government employees in mob actions.

Simultaneously, there were actions being taken in the National University that refuted the social and political proceedings occurring at the time. The National

Autonomous University of Nicaragua had been founded in 1812 in León yet did not become an autonomous institution until 1957 at which time a portion of the university community adopted an oppositional stance to the Somoza dictatorship. University students have always been part of the resistance to totalitarian states, whether under the Somoza regime or the current Ortega-Murillo administration. Throughout the mid to late 1940s, university and secondary students played a significant role in the opposition against Somoza. Students led a major protest against the dictatorship in June of 1944 and supported the short-lived reforming government of Leonardo Arguello in 1947, even offering to defend it through armed resistance against the National Guard should the need arise (Barbosa 2005: 191–192). Heightened state repression also spurred the growth of student political movements and student participation in armed resistance against the state increased. After the 1956 assassination of Anastasio Somoza Garcia and subsequent rise to power of his son Luis, the regime began to use a pattern of brute force to subjugate its political enemies, which more frequently involved repressing student movements. While, the passing of the Law of Educational Autonomy in 1957 bolstered student politics and engagement with national issues by reducing government intervention and oversight, by 1959, Nicaragua was becoming a police state under the watchful eye of the National Guard, headed by Anastasio Somoza Debayle. To note is that by the end of the decade, many university students were involved in some form of oppositional political activity (ibid).

Specifically, the students of León were heirs to a long history of political activity, much of which had centered upon the desire for university autonomy from the state (Galeano 1990). On July 23, 1959, students from the Universidad Nacional Autónoma de Nicaragua (National Autonomous University of Nicaragua or UNAN) requested permission to conduct a first-year student hazing ceremony in contravention to the state of siege currently in place. Instead, a solemn protest took place. A month earlier, the National Guard forces in collaboration with the Honduran army had ambushed a band of guerillas in the mountainous region of El Chaparral, Honduras near the border of Nicaragua. Carlos Fonseca Amador was wounded and captured in the ambush. Several other young revolutionaries (some former university students) were killed. The students of León were outraged and organized several vigils and protests for the slain students. The National Guard halted attempts for vigils for the victims and so the Consejo Universitario de la Universidad Nacional (University Council of the National University or CUUN) asked permission for a parade. The parade turned into a demonstration against the National Guard who reacted by firing on the students, killing four university students on July 23, 1959. In the aftermath, the four dead were put on public display. Throughout this public wake, people from the city of León of all ages and social classes formed long lines to view the bodies in their caskets, holding vigil with the families of the deceased. The speeches at the procession provided powerful symbolism of violent death in a narrative of a beleaguered and powerless people, at the hand of a cruel illegitimate state (Barbosa 2005: 202).

The "Generation of 59" is significant to the establishment of the modern National Sandinista Liberation Front (FSLN) based on radical student politics with the Federation of Revolutionary Students (FER) becoming an important conduit for insurgent recruiting. Indeed, July 23, 1959 was a foundational moment in the new Nicaraguan movement in the early 1960s and is tied to the anniversary of the FSLN founding in July 1961. Sergio Ramirez, the former Vice President of Nicaragua from 1979 to 1990 stated that July 23 changed his life and shaped his political and cultural identity. Besides joining the guerilla movement, student political organizations such as the CUUN, the Nicaraguan Democratic Youth, and the Nicaraguan Patriotic Youth built opposition to the dictatorship within Nicaraguan universities. In the 1960s and 1970s, many National Autonomous University of Nicaragua (UNAN) students participated in the revolutionary guerilla movement of the FSLN. University autonomous actions and student activism that were decidedly pro-revolutionary were met with increased state violence.

Sandinismo from Insurrection to State Building

The 1972 Managua earthquake and the 1978 assassination of Pedro Joaquin Chamorro bookended the 1970s, during which time the Somoza dictatorship floundered and the FSLN gained traction and took over the government in 1979. The Sandinistas have a long and effective history of training and promoting youth mobilization and resistance. This was a crucial part of the resistance mounted against the Somoza dictatorship in the 1960s and 1970s, and it continued during the country's defense against the Contras in the 1980s (Philips 2018). The *turbas divinas* (the divine mobs), which were Sandinista-affiliated youth, often armed with everything from iron pipes to rifles were often mobilized even during the revolutionary period. In 1980, state-controlled mobs attacked a rally organized by Nicaragua Democratic Movement leader Alfonso Robelo. In a speech, Ortega threatened to unleash the turbas divinas on any opponent. Mobs attacked the homes and businesses of Sandinista opponents, often beating the victims as well. During March 1981, mobs painted insults on the house of Violeta Chamorro, widow of the editor Pedro Chamorro and former member of the Sandinista junta following the triumph of the revolution (Ciment 2007: 367). In 1981, the Sandinistas had established "militias" consisting of factory workers, bureaucrats, and other Sandinista supporters. The divine mobs were unleashed on La Prensa and religious demonstrators by extremist members of the CDS (Sandinista Defense Committees) and the Sandinista Youth. In the 1984 presidential elections,

> pro-Sandinista crowds-critics called them turbas (mobs)-disrupted opposition political rallies ... [however] the internationally hyped disruptions of

opposition meetings by Sandinista turbas actually occurred in only five instances out of some 250 rallies during the campaign period; that is, [they] did not constitute a pattern of activity but [were] rather the exception.

(Walker 1991: 137)

Regardless, of the economic resort to use mobs, an open option was established to use para-institutional modes of public violence.[4]

After the electoral defeat in 1990, the FSLN opted for a "rule from below" strategy which involved mobilizing its unions and popular civil society organizations to influence government policies and actions. Recourse to use agitators to destabilize the succeeding governments from 1990 to 2006 commenced. Victor Cienfuegoas, a Danielista[5] enforcer participated in the seizure of UNO's (National Opposition Union) house in 1993, to the assault of Radio Ya in 1999.[6] And although universities as institutions of critical higher learning were often at odds with the government, many, like the UCA, mounted an autonomy campaign to secure 6% of the national budget that it gained in 1992 with the understanding that the university has a significant and meritorious role to play in Nicaraguan society. Daniel Ortega seized the issue of the 6% allocation of the national budget toward the university to fight the neoliberal austerity measures of the successive Chamorro, Aleman, and Bolaños administrations. However, the struggle to retain the 6% allocation by Ortega was distinct from the struggle by university administration and students whose interests were in achieving academic excellence. Ultimately, Ortega manipulated the 6% issue to wrest control of the university and undermine the autonomy of the university administration and student organizations, which he continued to do upon winning the presidency in 2006.[7] Following the resumption of the Ortega administration in 2007, Councils of Citizen Power (CDCs) were established that moved beyond the political manipulation of university budget allocations to the physical repression of young people exercising their citizenship rights. Youth groups began speaking out against the government of Daniel Ortega and were met with increasing recrimination as evidenced at the Ruben Dario roundabout in 2008 and the actual slapping of strikers who protested in front of the Supreme Electoral Council in 2012.

Where does this brief accounting of a history of violence in Nicaragua lead us? What seeming paradox does it beckon us to unmask? We must ask these questions because there has appeared to be a dual trajectory in recent Nicaraguan history, when during the early 2000s Nicaragua appeared to have enjoyed a social and economic revival of a burgeoning real estate and tourist market, that compared to its northern neighbors beset by narco-trafficking and rampant public and gang violence, lulled many into believing that Nicaragua was turning around. However, another reality was being played out, from the Ortega betrayal of Indigenous and Afro-Descendant people legally recognized communal lands by greenlighting colonization of Atlantic lands by mestizo settlers, to the Anti-Canal Campesino Movement that has demanded the cancellation of the law authorizing the Interoceanic Grand Canal which threatened to deprive thousands of Nicaraguans of their land and in their five years of resistance, the movement has been victim to repression, threats, and persecution. This latter project was an agreement the Ortega administration entered into with a Chinese private infrastructure development firm Hong Kong Nicaraguan Canal Development Investment group (HKND) in 2013, and in spite of falling through, the Ortega administration indicated it would go ahead with the dry land expropriation under the Canal Law 840. The Anti-Canal Campesino Movement militated against the law and was persecuted. A coalition of environmentalists, human rights organizations, and campesinos protested the passage of Law 840 by filing 38 suits, the largest number of cases to be brought against a single law in the nation. The Juventud Sandinista (JS) and the Consejos de Poder Ciudadano (Citizen's Power Councils, CPC) engaged in intelligence work, identifying people who attended marches, and who they were in contact with. On the night of June 21, 2013, a combination of police and masked gang members assaulted protesters on the grounds of the Instituto Nicaragüense de Seguridad Social, leaving several wounded. Victims of the assault claimed that JS members participated in the attacks and kidnapped individual protesters. One protester recalled the JS "had license to do anything. They could rob, beat, destroy, assault … under the protection of police agents" (Jillson 2020). She noted the next day that the JS marched for non-violence, a demonstration she called, "cynical … they show[ed] up the next day in the roundabout after they had destroyed the camp, with their songs, 'choose love over hate'" (Jillson 2020).

The legacy or contestation of this hollow political rhetoric can be seen in the events of April 3, 2018, when a wildfire in the Indio Maiz Biological Reserve in south-east Nicaragua prompted hundreds of university students to organize a peaceful demonstration for the government to act quickly to save the reserve. Their initial demand was for a more effective government response to wildfires burning out of control in the country's most precious repository of biodiversity. Soon, a social wildfire took hold in Managua and then spread across the country. Thousands of Nicaraguans added a second demand to the first: for President Daniel Ortega to revoke his recent changes to the country's social security law, which had simultaneously raised social security taxes (upsetting private enterprise) and cut benefits to seniors (angering many ordinary people). In the ensuing clashes, close to 300 Nicaraguans died, hundreds have been arrested, and thousands injured, almost all at the hands of anti-riot police, unidentified snipers, or gangs of pro-government thugs on motorcycles (Jillson 2020). Their protests were repressed by the police and para-militia groups days before the fateful April 19 social uprising. This was just the precursor to the public violence unleashed by para-militias that has since April 19, 2018, transformed Nicaragua into a brutal dictatorship and disputes the bucolic image of a resurgent Nicaragua.

Conclusion

University students took the lead in refuting the excesses of the Ortega-Murillo administration. The image of an untroubled country restored from the darker days of conflict and violence has been broken since the April 19, 2018 demonstrations. Since then, civil society organizations have found themselves subjected to investigations, funding restrictions, forced closures, and, when they have organized protests, attacked by gangs of FSLN supporters and increasingly, the police. Government critics have suffered break-ins at their offices, lost their academic posts, and at times been physically attacked (Thaler 2017: 163–164). The country is at the crossroads, and it remains to be seen how a sense of stability and safety will be reestablished. The polarization that has marked Nicaraguan history still lies beneath the surface of everyday life and yet it need not be the defining characteristic of Nicaraguan society if a genuine democracy prevails. The challenge is how Nicaragua relinquishes its history of intense political competition that has often devolved into violent conflicts and establishes a social order that is just and fair. Unfortunately, under Ortega and Murillo, the FSLN has become a hegemonic ruling party from left-wing revolutionary populist to right-leaning neo-patrimonial dictator in the older Latin American style of caudillismo (Thaler 2017: 157).

> All of this brings a certain feeling of déjà vu when it comes to the entire history of Nicaragua ... The abuses of power and the way power gathers- and the structures themselves-always repeat themselves. It's a kind of circular constant in Nicaragua's history throughout the whole twentieth century to the present day.
>
> *(Sergio Ramírez in Jones 2021)*

It remains to be seen whether Nicaragua will be able to overcome this turn away from democratic processes and non-authoritarian rule.

Notes

1 Patrimonialism (patron-client politics) refers to relationships between political, administrative systems and formally constructed on rational-legal terms, in which two ideal-type status hierarchies, one oriented toward individual achievement and organized along bureaucratic and legal rational lines, and the other ascriptive, particularistic, and personalistic.
2 The Pacto Providencial was a power sharing agreement to form a bipartisan government between Conservatives and Liberals that included regional elites. The Liberals ceded the presidency to the Conservatives, in exchange for Liberals being nominated to key government ministries (Gobat 2005).
3 *El Pacto*, was brokered between the two leaders, Arnoldo Alemán and Daniel Ortega. This undemocratic arrangement, negotiated by self-serving political elites to the detriment of the electorate, is characterized by being blatantly corrupt and represents a telling blow to free electoral process and legitimate governance. The pact made in

1999 gave the two leaders a strong control over around 90% of the legilslature: the agreement united their two parties in the National Assembly and gave Ortega and Alemán control over nearly 90 percent of the legislature—granting the unified duo near dictatorial powers over the nation. The leaders used their majority control for the cynical assertion of conclusive influence over many facets of Nicaraguan public life, including the Supreme Court and the Supreme Electoral Council (CSE). http://www.coha.org/2006/08/10/the-upcoming-nicaraguan-elections/.

4 Para-institutional violence

> is committed by groups that are loosely—and usually covertly—affiliated with organs of the state, that may depend on them for support, and that may even have been created or licensed by the state itself to collaborate in the elimination or intimidation of its enemies.
>
> *(Holden 2004: 14)*

5 The term refers to a loyal or unquestioning supporter of Daniel Ortega rather than the FSLN.
6 See coverage by *Envio* on the attack of this media. https://www.envio.org.ni/articulo/1402.
7 See chapters by Bellanger and Lara this volume.

References

Barbosa, Francisco. 2005. July 23, 1959: Student Protest and State Violence as Myth and Memory in León, Nicaragua. *Hispanic American Historical Review* 55:2: 187–221.
Baylen, Joseph O. 1951. Sandino: Patriot or Bandit. *Hispanic American Historical Review* 31: 394–419.
Brooks, David & Michael Schroder. 2018. Caudillismo Masked and Modernized: The Remaking of the Nicaraguan State via the National Guard, 1925-1936. *Middle Atlantic Review of Latin American Studies* 2:2: 1–32.
Bradford, Burns. 1991. *Patriarch aand Folk: The Emergence of Nicaragua, 1798–1858*. Boston, MA: Harvard University Press.
Ciment, James. 2007. *Encyclopedia of Conflicts since World War II*. New York, NY: Routledge.
Cruz, Arturo. 2016. *Nicaragua's Conservative Republic, 1858-93*. Berlin, Germany: Springer.
Duncan, David. 1995. *Hernando de Soto: A Savage Quest in the Americas*. New York, NY: Crown Publishers.
Dunkerley, James. 1988. *Power in the Isthmus: A Political History of Modern Central America*. London: Verso.
Gabbert, Wolfgang. 2012. The Longue Duree of Colonial Violence in Latin America. *Historical Social Research* 37:3: 254–275.
Galeano, Marcia Trana. 1990. Algunas Notas sobre el Movimineto Estudiantil Nicaraguense en la primera mitad del Siglo XX. *Revista de Historia* 1: 97–109.
Gobat, Michel. 2005. *Confronting the American Dream: Nicaragua under U.S. Imperial Rule*. Durham, NC: Duke University Press.
Gould, Jeffrey. 1998. *To Die in This Way: Nicaraguan Indians and the Myth of Mestizaje 1880–1965*. Durham, NC: Duke University Press.
Holden, Robert. 2004. *Armies without Nations: Public Violence and State Formation in Central America, 1821–1960*. New York, NY: Oxford University Press.
Jillson, Chris. 2020. "The Anti-Sandinista Youth of Nicaragua." NACLA: https://nacla.org/news/2020/02/05/anti-sandinista-youth-nicaragua

Jones, Sam. 2021. Nicaragua, "A feeling of déjà vu": author Sergio Ramirez on ex-comrade Ortega and Nicaraguan history repeating. *The Guardian*, September 18, 2021: https://www.theguardian.com/world/2021/sep/18/sergio-ramirez-interview-nicaragua-ortega-novel

Keil, Hartmut & Michael Riekenburg. 2001. Violence in the United States and Latin America in the 19th Century: A Comparative Approach1. *Iberoamericana* 4: 45–67.

Kruijt, Dirk. 2017. *Guerillas: War and Peace in Central America*. New York, NY: Zed Books.

MacLeod, Murdo. 2008. *Spanish Central America*. Austin, TX: University of Texas Press.

Millet, Richard. 1977. *Guardians of the Dynasty: A History of the U.S. Created Guardia Nacional de Nicaragua and the Somoza Family*. Maryknoll, NY: Orbis Books.

Newson, Linda. 1987. *Indian Survival in Colonial Nicaragua*. Norman, OK: University of Oklahoma Press.

Patch, Robert. 2013. *Indians and the Political Economy of Colonial Central America, 1670–1810*. Norman, OK: University of Oklahoma Press.

Philips, James. 2018. "Complicating the Narrative on Nicaragua." *NACLA*: https://nacla.org/news/2018/09/24/complicating-narrative-nicaragua

Roniger, Luis. 2013. *Transnational Politics in Central America*. Gainesville, FL: University of Florida Press.

Schroder, Michael. 2005. Bandits and Blanket Thieves, Communists and Terrorists: The Politics of Naming Sandinistas in Nicaragua, 1927–36 and 1979–90. *Third World Quarterly* 26:1: 67–86.

Stimson, Henry. 1927. *American Policy in Nicaragua*. New York, NY: Charles Schribner's Sons.

Tellez, Dora Maria. 1999. *Muera la Gobierna! Colonializacion en Matagalpa and Jinotega*. Managua, Nicaragua: Universidad de las Regiones Automas de la Costa Caribe Nicaraguense (URACCAN).

Thaler, Kai. 2017. Nicaragua: A Return to Caudillismo. *Journal of Democracy* 28:2: 157–171.

Tijerno, Frances Kinloch. 1997. El Periodo de la Anarqia: Imaginarios y Valores en Transition Nicaragua, 1821-1857. In, *Historia y Violencia en Nicaragua*, NOS-OTROS. Managua: Nicaragua: Imprimatur Artes Graficas.

Walker, Thomas. 1991. *Nicaragua: The Land of Sandino*. Boulder, CO: Westview Press.

Walter, Knut. 1993. *The Regime of Anastasio Somoza, 1936–1956*. Chapel Hill, NC: University of North Carolina Press.

Weaver, Frederick. 1994. *Inside the Volcano: The History and Political Economy of Central America*. Boulder, CO: Westview Press.

Woodward, R. Lee. 1984. The Rise and Decline of Liberalism in Central America. *Journal of Interamerican Studies and World Affairs* 26: 291–312.

INDEX

Pages followed by n refer to notes.

Aburto, Lludely 71
academic capitalism theory 7–8, 40–41, 46, 53, 55n20, 141
academic solidarity 137–139; Solidarity 3.0 147–152, 164–165; with UCA 34, 36, 109, 125, 137–138, 149–152, 165
access to university education 43, 94
Acción Universitaria 43–44
accompaniment to student struggles 63–79, 145, 163–166; holistic accompaniment 66–70; holistic accompaniment *vs.* political indoctrination 72–76
accreditation process: laws introducing xxi, 50–51; at UCA 45, 48–50
acompañamiento 145
activist anthropology 9–10
Agudelo, Irene 128–130
Ahmed, Sara 120–121, 129, 133n3
Alegría, Claribel 108–109
Alemán, Arnoldo 178, 186n3
Alemán, Lesther 74–75
ALFA Tuning Latin America Project xx, 55n19
Amnesty International 29–30, 32
April 2018 uprising xxi, 3–4, 21–22, 28–31, 93, 95, 139–140; antecedents 25–28, 96, 122–124; and atmosphere of fear xii, 32, 80, 140; attacks on barricades 30, 171–172; as *autoconvocado* 25, 29, 95; claims of a coup attempt 30–32; cyborg solidarity 125, 127–130; deaths and injuries 3, 29, 31; fleeing Nicaragua 3, 30–31, 95, 139; government concessions after 29–30; the "horror in your hand" 127–130; imprisonment of protestors 3, 31–32, 139–140; international response 30–33; legacy in 2021 31–33, 186; national dialogue 30; nonviolence, commitment to 35, 98–99; organizing of protests 96, 98–99, 101, 128–129; power of social media 99, 125, 128–130; professors' support for students struggle 72–76; rhizomatic solidarity 99; slogans 101, 109; terminology 6; UCA students' routes to involvement in 94–95, 99–101, 103–105; UNEN collaboration with government 44; unique aspects 101; violent state repression 29–30, 80–83, 140; watching from Seattle 120–121, 125, 127–130
Arab Spring 127–128
audit culture 7, 41, 46; and weakening of university autonomy 39–42, 45–51, 54
autoconvocados 5–6
autonomy of universities, *see* university autonomy

Baltodano, Ricardo 69, 71, 75–76
Barragán Fernández, Ana Karen 162, 167n8
Barrera, Ernesto 68
barricades, attacks on 30, 171–172
Battle of Seattle 126–128
Bellanger, Wendi 6–7, 47
Biehl, João 165
Binford, Leigh 144–145, 152
Black Lives Matter protests 149
Blue Shirts, also *Camisas Azules* 181
Bolivia 140
Brackley, Dean 144, 147
Brooks, David 180
Burns, Bradford 176

Camisas Azules, also Blue Shirts 181
Canal Law 840 185
Cantwell, B. 55n20
Caracas, Madelaine 74
caudillismo 101, 180–181
caudillista 172
censorship, media 31, 85–86, 90
Central America: corporatization and audit culture in higher education 46–47; funding for universities 54n10; Jesuit universities 39, 67, 94, 101–102; Northern Triangle surge in migration to U.S. 159; public and private universities 45; solidarity movement 139, 142, 146, 150–152; state-sponsored violence against higher education 141; university autonomy 40–42, 53; violence and postwar era 8–9
Central America Initiative, Seattle University 150–151
Central American Superior Council on Universities (CSUCA) xviii, 40–42
Centro Universitario de la Universidad Nacional (CUUN) student massacre xix, 68–69, 78n7, 182–183
Chamorro, Emiliano 179
Chamorro, Pedro 90, 183
Chamorro, Violeta 8, 70, 126, 183
Chatterjee, Piya 158, 166n1
civil war 1854–1857 178
CNEA (National Council for Evaluation and Accreditation) 50–51, 56n31
CNES (National Council of Higher Education) xix, 70
CNU (National Council of Universities) xx–xxi, 41, 43, 45, 50, 54n13, 56n31

colonial period 173–174
colors 6
compañerismo 144–145
Confidencial 31, 85, 90, 98
Conrado, Álvaro 36
Conservative elite, nineteenth-century 174–180
Constitution of Nicaragua xix, 4, 31, 42, 63
consumers, students as 47–49
contras 139, 143–144, 183
corporatization of higher education 39–40, 45–50, 53, 141
corruption 26–27, 30, 96, 172
Cosgrove, Serena 35, 149, 159
Costa Rica 3, 30–31, 139–140, 172, 178
Cruz, J. Martínez 128–130
cyborg solidarity 120–122; in April 2018 uprising 125, 127–130; digitalization of world and 125–127; in an entangled, yet unequal world 130–132; of "horror in your hand" 127–130

dedazo form of politics 100
Deleuze, Gilles 94, 112n37
dialogue at UCA, need for intergenerational, multisectoral 107–108
digitalization of world 125–127
divine mobs 183

economic crisis 32
education 97–98
Ellacuría, Ignacio: analysis of Law of the University of El Salvador 44; drawing on legacy of 23–25; on international relationships 137; murder 24, 125, 141; on role of university 4–5, 21–22, 24–25, 34, 46, 65, 67, 80–81, 94; on university autonomy 44, 53
El Salvador 8–9, 25, 51, 145, 159; "José Simeón Cañas" UCA 4, 23–25, 39, 141
Escobar, A. 126
ethnography 9–10, 165–166
exiled Nicaraguans 3, 30–31, 109, 139–140

Facebook 86, 127, 129, 149
Fanon, Frantz 133n2
fear, atmosphere of 32, 80, 140, 152–153
Fiallos Gil, Mariano 42, 67; Núñez on 67–68; Ramírez on 68–69

Finzer, Erin S. 142–143
flags 6
Follow-up Mechanism for Nicaragua (MESENI) 30
FSLN, *see* Sandinista National Liberation Front
"fugitive anthropology" 10
funding for universities: 6% campaign xix–xx, 42–43, 70–72, 162, 184; in Central America 54n10; cuts to UCA funding xxii, 50, 105, 140

Gabriel 94–95, 102, 104–107
"garage universities" 43, 45, 51, 98
GIEI (Interdisciplinary Group of Independent Experts) 30, 35
Gobat, Michael 175–176, 178
Godrej, Farah 159, 166n3
Gómez Praslin, Eddy Antonio 32
Granada, city-state 175, 177
Guatemala 8–9, 25, 39, 145, 172
Guattari, Félix 94, 112n37

Holden, Robert 174–176, 180–181, 187n4
holistic accompaniment: current challenges 76–77; defining 64–65; *vs.* political indoctrination 72–76; and university autonomy 66–70
Honduras 9, 25–26, 143, 159, 182
Hooker, Juliet 3, 6, 120, 123, 129, 147–148, 152
Huete, Jorge 26–27
humanities education, UCA 96–98, 102

Idiáquez, José (Chepe) 125, 127, 140, 150; manifesto 15, 21–37, 160–163
independence from Spain 174–177
Indigenous people: in colonial period 173–174; dispossession of 26, 122–124, 149; Matagalpa uprising, 1881 178; population 173
Indio Maíz Biological Reserve forest fire 21, 28, 63, 93, 96, 119, 121, 185
insurrections 6
Inter-American Commission on Human Rights (IACHR) 30–31
Interdisciplinary Group of Independent Experts (GIEI) 30, 35
international academic relations 35–36, 149, 165; importance of institutional partnerships 147; solidarity with UCA 34, 36, 109, 125, 149; UCA-Seattle University partnership 137–138, 150–152, 165
International Association of Jesuit Universities 125
International Association of Universities (IAU) 41, 54n5
International Monetary Fund 146, 148
international pressure 30–33
interoceanic canal 26–27, 185

Jesuit universities 162, 167n8; of Central America 39, 67, 94, 101–102; global network of 53, 123, 149; International Association of Jesuit Universities 125; interuniversity solidarity 137–138, 150–152, 165; "José Simeón Cañas" UCA 4, 23–25, 39, 141; of U.S. and solidarity with UCA 125; *see also* Universidad Centroamericana (UCA), Nicaragua
Jesuits 5
Jones, Sam 186
"José Simeón Cañas" UCA 4, 23–25, 39, 141
Josué 94, 100–102
journalism students: interrupted class 80–83, 163–164; online learning 87–89; seeking information for an assignment 89–92; worries and challenges for 83–87
journalists: catacomb 86; future 91; killings around the world 90; pressures and attacks on 83, 85–86, 90; working in exile 86
July 23 1959 student massacre xix, 68–69, 78n7, 182–183
Juventud Sandinista (Sandinista Youth), *see* Sandinista Youth (Juventud Sandinista)

knowledge society 7, 39–40

laws: to allow government "review" of social media 96; Canal Law, Law 840 185; General Education Law, Law 582 xxi, 50; introduced in 2020 4, 31; Law for the Autonomy of Higher Education Institutions, Law 89 xx, 42–43, 70; Law of Access to Public Information, Law 621 xxi; National University Law xviii–xix, 42; quality assurance and accreditation xxi, 50–51
Left-Right political analysis 148–149
Leon, city-state 175, 177

Leslie, L. 7, 40, 53
LGBTQ rights 100, 102
Liberal Constitutional Party (PLC) xx, 72
Liberal elite, nineteenth-century 174–180
Lidia, Maria 124
Lila 94, 97, 100, 102–103, 106–109
López, Amando 24

Magnitsky Act 30, 37n2
"Magnitsky Nica Act" 30, 37n2
manifesto, university 15, 21–37; mobilizing 160–161; need for 161–163
map vi
Mbembe, Achille 120, 129
media: censorship of 31, 85–86, 90; online 86
Medina, Ernesto 43–44
mental health issues 34
methods, research 10
Mexico 9, 162, 175
migration 3, 30–31, 109, 139–140; from "Northern Triangle" 159
Millet, Richard 176–179
Miskitu people 122–123
Morales, Evo 140
Mora, Miguel 31, 90
Mother's Day march 2018 xxi, 22–23, 29, 36, 127
Muir, Sarah 164
Murillo, Rosario 26–27, 29, 31, 127; see also Ortega-Murillo regime

National Autonomous University of Nicaragua (UNAN), see UNAN (National Autonomous University of Nicaragua) [formerly Universidad Nacional de Nicaragua
National Council for Evaluation and Accreditation (CNEA) 50–51, 56n31
National Council of Higher Education (CNES) xix, 70
National Council of Universities (CNU) xx–xxi, 41, 43, 45, 50, 54n13, 56n31
national dialogue 30
National Guard 68, 80, 143, 173, 177, 180–182
National University Law xviii–xix, 42
nation-state, consolidation into 177–181
neoliberalism 126, 141, 146, 148; and impact on higher education 7–8, 39–41, 141, 159; and universities in U.S. xiii–xiv, 159–160, 166n1, 166n3

Nicaraguan Academy of Sciences 27
Nicaraguan Open Online University (UALN) 43
Núñez, Vilma 67–68, 72

Office of the U.N. High Commissioner for Human Rights (OACNUDH) 30
online teaching and learning 43, 87–89
Organization of American States (OAS) 30, 32
Ortega-Aleman Pact 178, 186n3
Ortega, Daniel xi–xii; amassing and consolidating of power 26–28; presidential election 2007 178; presidential election 2021 4; 6% funding allocation for universities 184
Ortega-Murillo regime: closing of news media outlets 31, 85–86, 90; describing April uprising as a failed coup 30–32; dismantling of university autonomy xxi, 43–44, 50–54, 184; physical repression of young protestors 172, 184, 186; political analysis of 148–149; public education under 97–98; social security reforms 28–30, 134n9, 185; Solidarity 3.0 to support opposition to 147–152; state repression and fear xii, 3–4, 24, 29–33, 80, 139–140; state repression and university resistance 80–83, 184; student struggles against political indoctrination of 72–76; U.S. sanctions against individuals 30–31, 37n2, 148

Pacto Providencial 178, 186n2
pedagogy of accompaniment 65, 73–76, 163
Perales, I. 126
Petryna, Adriana 165
Philipps-Universität Marburg 47, 55n23
Pineda Ubau, Lucía 31, 90
Piura, Joaquin Solís 66–67
PLC (Liberal Constitutional Party) xx, 72
police patrols 38, 77, 85, 87, 140
political clientelism 43–44, 52–53, 162
political culture, new 35, 149
political indoctrination, holistic accompaniment vs. 72–76
"postwar" studies 8–9
precarity, condition of 120–122, 129–130, 132
private universities 43, 45, 51, 98

professors: academic freedom of 77–78; accompaniment to student struggles 63–79; in early years of university autonomy 66–69; hiring and firing dependent on FSLN 72–73, 75, 97; as managed personnel 39, 47–49, 52; repression in public universities 72–73, 75–77; self-censorship 75; support for 6% campaign 70–72; support for students since April 2018 uprising 72–76

proyección social 5, 22, 24, 94, 103

public universities 45; expulsion of students from 38, 41, 96–97, 139; hiring and firing of professors 72–73, 97; loss of academic freedom 26, 41, 43–44, 51–52, 69, 72–73, 75–77; political clientelism 43–44, 52; student enrollments 45

quality assurance 7–8; laws introducing xxii, 50–51; and weakening of university autonomy 39–42, 45–51, 54
questionnaires, evaluation 47–48

Ramírez, Sergio 68–69, 183, 186
Randall, Margaret 123–124, 138
Reagan, Ronald 143, 146
recession 32
relations of care 120, 133n2
research methods 10
rhizomatic solidarity 94, 99, 105–108
Rhoades, G. 7, 40, 53
Roniger, Luis 174

sanctions 30–31, 37n2, 148
Sandinista National Liberation Front (FSLN): control of UNEN 26, 43–44; dismantling of university autonomy 43–44, 72, 75–76; "Generation of 59" and establishment of 183; from insurrection to state building 183–185; legacies of 1980s women 123–124; after 1990 electoral defeat 70–71, 125–126, 144, 184; opposition to U.S. misrepresentation of revolution 138–139; under Ortega and Murillo 186; overthrowing of Somoza dictatorship 143, 183; PLC cedes quotas of power to xx, 72; political indoctrination in universities after 2007 xxi, 72, 75–76; Reagan supports *contras* against 138–139, 143; "rule from below" 184; start of decline of university autonomy in 1980s under 69–70; terminology 6; training and promoting youth mobilization and resistance 183–184; *see also* Ortega-Murillo regime

Sandinista Youth (Juventud Sandinista) 15n1, 139, 154n8, 183–184; persecution of people opposed to Canal Law 840 185; shock troops for attacking of protestors 26, 28, 125

Sandino, Augusto: assassination 173, 181; fight against U.S. marines 123, 142–143, 180; legacy of women who fought alongside 124; U.S. activists standing in solidarity with 142–143

Schroder, Michael 180
Seattle University 153n2; Central America Initiative 150–151; partnership with UCA 137–138, 150–152, 165
Seattle WTO Protests 126–128
self-censorship 75–76
Sevilla, Nicolasa 181
sexual abuse xi, 103
Silber, Irina Carlota 6, 145, 149, 164
six percent campaign xix–xx, 42–43, 70–72, 162, 184
Slaughter, S. 7, 40, 53, 55n20
social change, educating for 95, 98, 101–105, 107
social justice, struggle for 96, 101, 105, 123, 167n8
social media: April 2018 uprising and power of 99, 125, 128–130; facilitating solidarity today 149–150; intergenerational political activism debate 98; law to allow government "review" of 96; transmitting news reports on 86
social movements: broad, youth-led 149, 160; formation of interest-based 125–126; social media and communication needs of 149–150; unarmed 99; women's 122–124
social security reforms 28–30, 134n9, 185
Society of Jesus 5
solidarity: achievements and limitations 144; defining 144–146; dissipation of long-term efforts 146–147; movements unprepared for consequences of neoliberalism 146; rhizomatic solidarity 94, 99, 105–108; social media facilitating 149–150; Solidarity 1.0 142–144; Solidarity 2.0 143–144;

Solidarity 3.0 147–152, 164–165; see also cyborg solidarity
Solís-Cortez, C. 64
Somocista Popular Front 181
Somoza, Anastasio 80, 143, 181–182; assassination of Sandino 173, 181; catacomb journalism during dictatorship of 86; closure of universities xviii, 66; holistic accompaniment and struggle for university autonomy under 66–70; style of leadership 180; U.S. backing for 181
Somoza, Bernabé 177
Somoza Debayle, Anastasio 143, 182
Somoza dynasty 143, 181; overthrowing of 6, 143, 183; paramilitary rule 181–183; reviving "ghost" of 27–28
Somoza, Luis 68, 86, 143, 182
Stimson, Henry 179
Stokes, S.C. 43
student massacre of July 23, 1959 xix, 68–69, 78n7, 182–183
students: accompaniment to struggles 63–79, 145, 163–166; April 2018 uprising and "criminalization" of 3–4, 140; challenges and responses in classroom 83–87; classroom resistance to state repression 80–83, 163–164; commitment to nonviolence 35, 98–99; as consumers 47–49; enrollments 45; expulsions from public universities 38, 41, 96–97, 139; killing and injuring of youth activists and 3, 29, 139; online learning 87–89; organizing of 2018 protests 96, 98–99, 101, 128–129; protests and Somoza paramilitary rule 181–183; routes to involvement in April 2018 uprising 94–95, 99–101, 103–105; seeking information for an assignment 89–92; struggles against political indoctrination of Ortega-Murillo regime 72–76
students' union (UNEN) 44, 71; FSLN control of 26, 43–44
Stuelke, Patricia 132, 145–147, 152

"talk of quality" 7, 41, 47, 52–53
terminology 5–6
Thomas, Deborah 130, 152
Tijerno, Frances Kinloch 176
timeline for university autonomy xviii–xxii
transitional justice 8, 35

Trump, Donald 131, 134n16
Tsing, Anna 120–121, 130–131
Tünnermann Bernheim, Carlos 41–42, 50, 66–67, 70–71, 73

UNAN (National Autonomous University of Nicaragua) [formerly Universidad Nacional de Nicaragua (UNN)] 41–42, 66–67, 183; Léon 42–43, 69, 75, 181–182; Managua 72, 75
UNEN (students' union) 44, 71; FSLN control of 26, 43–44
UNESCO 41, 53
United States (U.S.): activism to stop support for *contras* 139, 143–144; Black Lives Matter protests 149; comparing political turmoil in Nicaragua and 131–132, 134n16; intervention in state building in Nicaragua 177–181; Jesuit universities and solidarity with UCA 125; resistance to sending U.S. marines into Nicaragua in 1926 123–124, 142–144; sanctions 30–31, 37n2, 148; solidarity movements with Central America 139, 142, 146, 150–152; universities in xiii–xiv, 159–160, 166n1, 166n3; see also Seattle University
Universidad Católica del Trópico Seco (UCATSE) 73
Universidad Centroamericana (UCA), Nicaragua: accreditation process 45, 48–50; autonomy xix–xx, 53, 73–77, 140–141; challenges and responses in classroom 83–87; comparative study with Marburg university 47, 55n23; developing a rhizomatic solidarity 105–108; differing perspectives on what to do 33–34, 38–39; educating for social change 98, 101–105, 107; founding of xix, 45; funding reduction xxii, 50, 105, 140; humanities education 96–98, 102; Idiáquez's manifesto 15, 21–37, 160–163; impact of repression on 23, 33–36, 38, 80–83, 163–164; inclusion in CNU 54n13; Indio Maíz conference 28; interrupted class 80–83, 163–164; island for critical thought and dialogue 105, 123, 140, 151–152; Jesuit universities and solidarity with 125; loss of students xxii, 33; Mother's Day march 2018 xxi,

22–23, 127; need for intergenerational, multisectoral dialogue 107–108; Nicaraguan Academy of Sciences forums 27; police patrols around 38, 77, 85, 87, 140; preparing to lead 23–25; *proyección social* 103; raising visibility internationally 151; removal of School of Engineering xx, 54n13; research experience at 104–105; Seattle University partnership with 137–138, 150–152, 165; similarities with UCA of El Salvador 24–25; solidarity with other universities 34, 36, 109, 125, 137–138, 149–152, 165; struggle for social justice 96, 101, 105, 123, 153; student movements at 106–107; timeline for autonomy xix–xxii; Virtual Learning Environment (EVA) 87–89
Universidad Nacional de Nicaragua (UNN) 66–67
university autonomy: asphyxiation of 51–54; in Central America 40–42, 53; corporatization, audit culture and weakening of 39–42, 45–51, 54; Ellacuría on 44, 53; FSLN and dismantling of xxi, 43–44, 50–54, 72, 75–76, 184; funding and xix–xx, 42–43, 70–72, 162, 184; guaranteed in Nicaraguan Constitution xix, 42; holistic accompaniment and 66–70; Law for the Autonomy of Higher Education Institutions, Law 89 xx, 42–43, 70; a lost opportunity for 70–72; 1980s and decline in 69–70; in public universities 26, 41, 43–44, 51–52, 69, 72–73, 75–77; struggle in Nicaragua 41–45; timeline xviii–xxii; at UCA xix–xx, 53, 73–77, 140–141

university partnerships 35–36, 149, 165; importance of institutional partnerships 147; solidarity with UCA 34, 36, 109, 125, 149; UCA-Seattle University 137–138, 150–152, 165

Valle, Ernesto 98–99
values, holistic accompaniment and teaching of 73
Venezuela 26–27, 162
violence, history of 171–187; colonial period 173–174; independence 174–177; Indio Maíz Biological Reserve forest fire protests 21, 28, 63, 93, 96, 119, 121, 185; interoceanic canal protests 26–27, 185; Sandinistas from insurrection to state building 183–185; since April 2018 uprising 171–172, 186; Somoza and student protests 181–183; state building and U.S. intervention 177–181
Violeta Barrios Chamorro Foundation 90
Virtual Learning Environment (EVA) 87–89

Walker, Thomas 143, 179, 183–184
Walker, William 177–178
WhatsApp 38, 84, 86, 125, 127, 129
"Witnessing 2.0" 152
women: social movements of resistance 122–124; violence against 103
Workers' Party of America 142
World Bank 46, 53, 146, 148
World Trade Organization (WTO) 46, 53; Seattle protests 126–128

Zapatistas 126
Zelaya, Jose Santos 179

Printed in the United States
by Baker & Taylor Publisher Services